The Mountbattens are one of the world's most famous families. But how much do we really know about this distinguished "clan" whose members are heirs to the thrones of Spain, Greece, and Great Britain?

In this accessible history Antony Lambton lifts the veil surrounding the Mountbatten lineage and gives a vivid account of the lives and careers of some of its most famous - and controversial - figures. Special attention is paid to the early years of perhaps the family's best-known member, Earl Mountbatten of Burma.

"Before this book, Lord Mountbatten stands bemedalled and magnificent at the top of a handsome tree, whose branches contain Russians, Bulgarians . . . numerous swashbuckling warriors and glamorous Barbara Cartland heroines. By the end of it, Lord Lambton has Lord Mountbatten dangling uncomfortably from one of the branches and, as if not happy with that, he then wields the spade to undermine the tree's roots." - *The Times (London)*

"A spirited polemic . . . there is much that is fascinating and Lambton must be commended for his determination to strip away the lies . . . " - *The Daily Telegraph (London)*

ALSO BY ANTONY LAMBTON

Snow and other stories (1983)
Elizabeth and Alexander (1985)
The Abbey in the Wood (1986)
Pig and other stories (1990)

EDITED BY ANTONY LAMBTON

Bad Company and other stories (1986)

ANTONY LAMBTON

The Mountbattens

The Battenbergs and young Mountbatten

M&S

An M&S Paperback from
McClelland & Stewart Inc.
The Canadian Publishers

To my dear stepmother Hermione who has with kindness and generosity
put up with my vagaries for nearly sixty years.

An M&S Paperback from McClelland & Stewart Inc.

First printing July 1990
Cloth edition printed 1989

Canadian Cataloguing in Publication Data

Lambton, Antony.
The Mountbattens

(M&S paperback)
Includes bibliographical references.
ISBN 0-7710-4617-0

1. Mountbatten family. 2. Battenberg family. 3. Mountbatten of Burma,
Louis Mountbatten, Earl, 1900-1979. 4. Great Britain. Royal Navy -
Biography. 5 Admirals - Great Britain - Biography. I. Title.

DA89.1.M59L35 1990 941.0820'92 C89-090752-8

Cover design by Kong Njo

Printed and bound in Canada

Originally published in Great Britain by
Constable and Company Limited

McClelland & Stewart Inc.
The Canadian Publishers
481 University Avenue
Toronto, Ontario
M5G 2E9

Contents

ILLUSTRATIONS

Emperor Franz Joseph of Austria *(by permission of the Hulton Picture Company)*

Prince Louis V of Hesse *(by permission of the Hulton Picture Company)*

Prince Henry of Battenberg and Princess Beatrice *(by permission of the Hulton Picture Company)*

Admiral Lord Charles Beresford *(by permission of the Hulton Picture Company)*

Admiral Lord Fisher *(by permission of the Mansell Collection)*

Crown Prince William of Prussia as a boy *(by courtesy of John Fabb)*

The young Mountbatten *(by permission of the Hulton Picture Company)*

Lord Mountbatten in old age *(by permission of the Hulton Picture Company)*

ACKNOWLEDGEMENTS

I would like to express my thanks to Her Majesty the Queen for allowing me to see the files at Windsor, and to the librarian, Mr Oliver Everett, for his kindness and help.

I am also grateful to the late Sir John Colville, for writing for me last year an account of his extraordinary interview with Queen Mary which led to Queen Elizabeth's Declaration that the name of the ruling House of England was Windsor.

To Lady Celestria Noel for her voluminous information on the effects of syphilis on the brain. To Lady Mosley who read my uncorrected manuscript and made many suggestions. To Mrs Giles Lascelles, a Bradman of proof-readers. To Monsieur and Madame Marcel Wurlod for giving me invaluable photographs of the Château de Grancy and detailed information about the de Grancy family, the probable ancestors of Prince Alexander and the Battenbergs.

To Mr Richard Hough, for a number of years closely connected with Lord Mountbatten who fulsomely praised him. His books *Louis and Victoria* and *Mountbatten: Hero of our Time*, are larders of information. It is not an exaggeration to say I could not have written this book without the information which the late Lord Mountbatten dictated to him.

To the dead Count Egon Corti, the family historian of the House of Hesse, who before he was muzzled by respectability, gave many glimpses of the contents of the then 'Erbach', now Darmstadt and Hesse papers. To Mr Jasper Guinness for his translations from the German.

To my secretary Miss Vicky Gillespie who has with unfailing good nature endlessly typed the following pages. To Professor Franz for his polite letters explaining he was forbidden to show me anything in the Darmstadt Archives.

To Lord Brabourne who courteously answered my letters making it plain I was not to see any of the Battenberg Archives. This in itself was as interesting as Sherlock Holmes's dog, who did not bark in the night. It made me draw the conclusion that every author who was not prepared to accept the Mountbatten myth would be starved of information. In the past the favoured few were fed with carefully selected passages. The main bulk of the files have been carefully hidden. This burial of skeletons has robbed the historian of the fascinating diaries and correspondence of Prince Alexander of Hesse, the brother-in-law of Tsar Alexander II of Russia, and grandfather of Lord Mountbatten.

During the middle of the last century Prince Alexander was in close touch with the ruling courts of Europe. The concealment not only of his many volumes of letters and diaries but those of his childhood tutor, General Frey, who daily recorded his and the future Empress Marie's childhood, is a tragedy; they must give a unique glimpse of life in Darmstadt at the beginning of the nineteenth century. I hope these manuscripts are still in existence: Mountbatten's aunt, Countess, later Princess, Erbach, deliberately destroyed the papers describing the pre-marital love life of her father Prince Alexander of Hesse and her mother Countess Julia Hauke. Today the concealment of these papers by the Hesse—Brabourne axis is a folly. They hide two romantic love stories which would appeal to the present generation, and anyhow it is no use trying to close the stable door when the horse has gone.

To Madame Elfgard Wintersteller for her long and valuable investigations in the Vienna Archives. I would also like to thank Sir John Junor, Lord Hailsham, the late Mr Charles Douglas-Home, Mr Alastair Forbes, Lord Hutchinson, Mr W. E. Mosse, Vice-Admiral Sir Geoffrey Robson, Mr Orlando Fraser, Professor Dr Krause-Vilmar, Commander P. R. Compton-Hall, Captain David Brown, Captain David Husband, R. N., Miss Susan Moore, Count Alexis Teissier, Mr James Money, Mr P. Beaven (Ministry of Defence, Army Historical Branch), M. Genequand (State Archives, Geneva), Dr G. Hirschfeld (German Historical Institute), Lady Reid, M. Jean Etienne, the Hon. David Macmillan and many others who do not wish to be named.

I am grateful to the authors named at the end of this book who have allowed me to quote extracts from their works.

In conclusion, I would like to express my gratitude to Count Adam Zamoyski, a member of a noble Polish family and an authority on the

House of Hauke, and especially to Princess Louis of Hesse and her champion, Princess Tatiana Metternich who stimulated me into relevant investigations into the history of the Houses of Hesse which I might otherwise have neglected.

PREFACE

PHILIP ZIEGLER dealt in such detail with the life of the late Lord Mountbatten (in *Mountbatten*, Collins 1985) that readers might question what I am writing about. My answer is simple, that his biography devoted only a few paragraphs to its subject's ancestors. This was, with respect to an admirable writer, a mistake as I hope this book, the first of two volumes, will show. They had a profound influence on his life and explained many characteristics for which he has been mocked and blamed. I may be criticised for dragging up long hidden truths about the status of his family, but the efforts Mountbatten made since 1938 to obliterate unpalatable historical facts and replace them by figments of his imagination were distasteful. Nothing I have rediscovered is blameworthy by present day standards. If at an early age he had admitted the truth about his antecedents he would probably have been less troubled about the status of his family and had less pretensions of grandeur which made him, even to his closest friends, a figure of fun.[1]

In a second volume I plan to write a series of essays on aspects of his public life which Ziegler mentioned but then skirted around. His position as an official biographer was difficult, his skill and bravery were commendable but the family looked over his shoulder: he could mention, but not elaborate.

Lord Mountbatten courted publicity more than any of his contemporaries in the three services. His ghost, freed from worldliness, should not resent an unbiased reassessment in this volume of his family's history and in the next a dissection of his fantasies which, when intertwined with a complaisant memory, made nonsense of the truth.

Note The reader may observe that from time to time I interrupt the text to compare the actions of dead members of the Battenberg family with the character of the late Lord Mountbatten. I make no apologies for this; this work is primarily a study of his character. His ancestors influenced him to an unusual degree.

NOTES
1. See Appendix 1, The Family Game.

INTRODUCTION

O N 28 or 29 October 1914 a fourteen-year-old cadet of pure
German blood, Prince Louis of Battenberg,[1] could have been
seen, with tears running down his cheeks, saluting the
flagpole on the parade ground at Osborne Naval College. His grief was
caused by the news that his father and namesake, the First Sea Lord,
had resigned.[2] The historian Richard Hough,[3] who taped many of
Lord Mountbatten's memories, asked him if this story, considered
apocryphal by doubters, was true. The answer was, 'Absolutely true.'[4]
True or not, Mountbatten had every reason to be sad. His father had
been publicly and privately criticised for months on account of his
German origins and the outcry had been taken up with merciless
brutality by the boy's contemporaries at Osborne. He had borne this
persecution bravely, but now the unimaginable had happened; his
father, another Prince Louis, whom he had seen all his life advancing
on the deck of great ships towards his goal of First Sea Lord, had been
publicly humiliated, his career brutally ended. The effect on his son
was profound and made him dedicate his life to success, believing his
achievements could alone right a great wrong. It is no exaggeration to
say from this period he was dedicated to the pursuit of his own holy
grail.

The quest became an obsession, dominating his life, justifying every
action which advanced his career and added to the grandeur of his
family. No mistake could be admitted, every failure should be con-
cealed, and if events of the past conflicted with the tablets of his belief,
it was his business to contradict or destroy the evidence. During the
last twenty-five years many books have been written about Mountbatten's life but I have never read an analysis of his feelings when his
father was dismissed, or an investigation into the status of his family
among the courts of pre-1914 Europe. Authors assumed – with
encouragement from Mountbatten – that while the shock of 1914

15

stimulated his ambition, he was born in the purple, an equal, cousin, and friend of the royal families of Europe. To understand whether these assumptions were true it is necessary to examine first his background before he stood by the flagpole, and secondly the adoration of his ancestors which guided his life.

His early years were uninteresting except to his family, but he seems to have been a perfectly happy, ordinary, not particularly bright little boy, unfashionably educated by his mother Victoria, daughter of the Grand Duke of Hesse and Alice of England. She was a garrulous, serious, clever woman, considered a tremendous bore by her detractors and loquacious by her friends, who at an early age had been faced with the responsibility of bringing up a large family after her mother's death. Later she treated her husband with a coldness which caused her grandmother Queen Victoria to remonstrate,[5] and although her letters to her son are loving, rational and kind, they lack devotion and suggest her life was governed more by logic than emotions. Mountbatten's parents were comparatively old, forty-five and thirty-seven, when he was born and they unconsciously raised their little son in the high Victorian tradition. Late children are often spoiled by formerly strict parents, and Mountbatten, years younger than his brother and sister, was brought up as a single child and more indulged than they had been. He was tremendously proud of his father, who in 1905 was given the command of a squadron of six armoured cruisers and flew his flag in HMS *Drake*. Christmas that year was spent at Gibraltar, where the excitement of running about a huge ship committed the little boy for ever to the British Navy.

Prince Louis's career prospered. In 1907 he was promoted to Acting Vice-Admiral and Second-in-Command of the Mediterranean Fleet, and later held the same position in the Atlantic Fleet, flying his flag in the *Prince of Wales*. During this period the son saw his father wearing a halo; nothing could have been more stimulating to a boy in love with the sea. However, one unusual aspect of his early life cannot be ignored: his father never had a country house in England, escaping whenever he could to his old home, Heiligenberg, near Jugenheim, a few miles south of Darmstadt in Hesse. Here Prince Louis was more highly regarded than the sovereign, the Grand Duke of Hesse, a kind, weak, precious *fin de siècle* 'apostle in the high aesthetic band', despised by his first wife who deserted him for the Grand Duke Cyril of Russia, and overwhelmed by his pedestrian second choice who

16

crushed his elfin spirit by her Teutonic dullness and respectability. During Mountbatten's youth the Grand Duke collected colonelcies, glamorous uniforms and medals, and was regarded with the good-natured amusement his antics merited. He was once seen flying up the steps of his house, Wolfsgarten, screaming with fear, with one of his first wife's stallions close behind him intent on biting a lump out of his behind. On another occasion, during imperial army manoeuvres he was given a leg up onto his horse and shot clean over the other side. The Kaiser, taking after his grandmother, was not amused; the army was. When war broke out in 1914, the Grand Duke's passion for military accoutrements and war games waned; declaring himself a pacifist he ran a hospital train.

Another close relation was Mountbatten's uncle by marriage, Prince Henry of Prussia, younger brother of the Kaiser and the Grand Admiral of the German Navy. Mountbatten spent happy holidays with these German relations, including his aunt Alix, his mother's younger sister, and wife of Tsar Nicholas II, whose marriage had maintained the pure German blood in the Holstein-Gottorb-Romanov cousins he visited in St Petersburg in 1912. Not surprisingly, his early life made him believe he belonged to the great German clan of rulers of the kingdoms of Europe.

When the time came for him to go to his preparatory school he had been flattered by circumstances, if not spoilt by affection, and seen sights which most boys of his age had only dreamt about. It is also doubtful if his German background made it easy for him to get on with his British, landed gentry, contemporaries. He was nearly ten when he arrived at Lockers Park, which can't have helped, as most boys of his age had been there for a year or two forming friendships and joining cliques. As a result he was bullied and teased. However, he settled down and the next three years of his life are uninteresting to any but the most rabid investigator.

In May 1913 Mountbatten entered Osborne Training College. Again his family did not help him, for his sea chest was inscribed: 'His Serene Highness The Prince Louis of Battenberg'. This caused a certain amount of hilarity and antagonism as his father was already a contentious celebrity, whose appointment as First Sea Lord at the end of 1912 had been unpopular in many old-fashioned naval families, who considered him an untrustworthy German. As war grew closer some of Mountbatten's friends, influenced by their fathers' anti-

German prejudices, grew increasingly unpleasant. This was partly due to his father's tactlessness as although Louis was a man of integrity and honour, much loved by those who served under him, he had few friends except in royal circles. His self-satisfaction, efficiency and success made him both feared and an object of jealousy. Lord Fisher[6] once wrote Louis only had three friends, including 'Winston and myself'.[7] This was an exaggeration, but he certainly had enemies, among them Admiral Lord Charles Beresford, the leader of the old-fashioned aristocratic clique who resented and distrusted his nationality and tried to block his progress. When, despite their efforts, he succeeded, they joined in a whispering campaign concerning the dangers of having a German First Sea Lord.

Lord Charles had many powerful supporters, and while Mountbatten and his mythmaker historians portray him as a malignant idiot, Admiral of the Fleet Lord Wester Wemyss, who succeeded Jellicoe as First Sea Lord, described him as '. . . an old family friend whose genial and delightful personality, added to his brilliant abilities as a seaman, made him an ideal commander to serve under'.[8] Certainly Beresford was popular, British and a conservative with sentimental roots going back into the supposedly romantic past of the British Navy. His views filtered down into Osborne, where many of the cadets came from junior branches of the peerage and landed gentry with their traditional distrust of foreigners, and especially of a full-blooded German who blatantly spent his leaves in Germany, and exchanged visits not only with his brother-in-law Prince Henry of Prussia, but also with the Kaiser. To add weight to their criticism Louis had never been able to rid himself of a thick Hessian accent, which accentuated his foreignness. Mountbatten admitted years later his father was unwise to ignore his critics and insist on living in Germany, but he would never admit his garrulous mother added to the general distrust of the family. Hough quotes a friendly witness, the late Princess Alice, Countess of Athlone, who described Victoria Battenberg's failings:

> She did talk a very great deal, and not always tactfully. She could not have been more absolutely English and patriotic, but she talked too much. She had a very strong influence over Prince Louis's professional life, and it was partly because of her that he lost his position. She knew so much because she was sister-in-law to Prince Henry. She was very valuable to Prince Louis because she would get

so much information about the German Navy, about their ships and so on, from him. And because she also told everybody else who cared to listen to her, people wondered what she would be saying about the British Navy when she went to Germany. All the family knew this and they all regretted it.[9]

This opinion from such a reliable source illustrates the damage the couple's retention of their German loyalties and Princess Louis's indiscretions did to his popularity, and as war approached Victoria became more of a liability to her husband and strengthened the Beresford clique's argument that the Battenbergs were compromising British security. Prince Louis obstinately ignored what he considered narrow-minded, unfair criticism, and never appeared to realise what was bearable to him as the First Sea Lord was unbearable to his sons. Mountbatten's misery at this difficult time may be estimated by a letter he wrote to his mother: 'I have only one real chum left now, Graham Stopford, who got so ragged about being chums with me that he has chucked it.'[10]

Too much attention has been paid to Prince Louis's own trials and too little to his young son's months of torture at Osborne and the effect his sufferings had on his character. His position was unpleasant: boys like to conform. How could Mountbatten conform when he had only enemy blood in his veins? The male reader has only to imagine himself at school in Germany at war with England, to realise his loneliness when bullies mocked, shunned and sent him to Coventry. Such treatment was harder to bear than physical bullying, which he could have answered with his fists. How could he deny the unpleasant truth that his father and mother were both Germans? The position was made worse by his parents' incomprehension of the intensity of his sufferings: both of them appeared to dwell on their own trials without thinking of the little 'Germ hun',[11] isolated at Osborne with no refuge except his memories, showing remarkable courage as he forced himself to concentrate on work and pass his exams.

Mountbatten's resolution can be understood only if it is realised that when war broke out in 1914 patriotism in England became a passionate national religion. None worshipped with more zest than those who due to age or health were unable to join up. They nearly exploded with frustration; often their sense of uselessness at being confined to their homes instead of serving and dying for their country, drove them to vent their repressions on innocent and peaceful German tradesmen who had flourished in England, in the case of one family for a hundred years. Even dachshunds were chased and kicked, and expressions of vitriolic hatred appeared daily in the newspapers, reviling the barbarity of the Hun and proclaiming the necessity of cleansing the country of traitorous scum. Beresford, grasping the chance of revenge with both hands, proclaimed in his club: 'All Germans, including highly placed ones, ought to leave the country as they are in close touch with Germans abroad,'[12] and added, 'He [Battenberg] is a German and as such should not be occupying his present position. He keeps German servants and has property in Germany.' Unfortunately this was true. Later Mountbatten hated Beresford and his friends for influencing public opinion. He was wrong. They only swam with the tide.

The prejudice against Germany was increased by often fanciful and exaggerated accounts of German atrocities in Belgium which encouraged decent men and women to believe hate was a national virtue. This is not surprising; wilful self-deception soon turns lies into truths, and for generations Englishmen had looked down with insular superiority on foreigners of all kinds.

A more influential anti-German was Horatio Bottomley, an old enemy of the Battenbergs, who labelled Prince Louis a 'dachshund' in December 1911, on his appointment as Second Sea Lord. This scurrilous critic spasmodically continued his attacks until war was declared, when his antagonism blossomed into venomous flowers.

From Osborne came a brave letter to Mountbatten's mother.

What d'you think the latest rumour that got in here from outside is? That Papa has turned out to be a German spy & has been discreetly marched off to the tower . . . by Beefeaters . . . I got rather a rotten time of it for about three days as the little fools . . . insisted on calling me a German Spy . . .[13]

It did not help that the war was going badly at sea; it was easier to blame Battenberg than Churchill.

Mountbatten was later accused of snobbery, of avoiding the upper classes, and only bothering with members of the royal family. Why should he have liked a class which, when he was fourteen, persecuted his beloved father who had lived for and loved the Navy, while at the same time its younger generation was mercilessly bullying him, leaving him no alternative but to retreat into himself to remember happier times? This led him to romanticise the past and determine to erase, by his own actions, the insults to his father. Naturally his wounded imagination inflated his family's importance; how otherwise could he have endured those insufferable days? Events gave him no alternative to twisting the truth in order to put out of his mind the daily accusations in the papers.

Even after his father's resignation his misery did not end. Conceive of a son's feelings at seeing his father, the late First Sea Lord of the greatest navy on earth, whom he had known, magnificent, on the decks of his flagship, sitting in Kent House in the Isle of Wight, broken, silent, uncomplainingly cataloguing naval medals. How can Mountbatten be blamed for a lifelong dislike of a class which he believed had destroyed his father?

His days of hidden torment formed characteristics for which he was afterwards blamed but without which he could not at the time have survived. If this is realised, many of his actions and romanticisms, criticised in his later life, become explicable. A German saying illustrates the consequence of his trials: *Was uns nicht umbringt macht uns stark.* (What does not kill or destroy makes us strong.)

Certainly Mountbatten never admitted until old age he had been tormented in his youth, and insisted until his death that the Battenbergs had been equal members of the great German royal family. The Mountbatten myth, which he laboriously created in a series of books whose sources were controlled by him, constantly repeats he was brought up with a silver spoon in his mouth, which began to heat up in 1913, and for six months in 1914 was made so unendurably hot by his upper-class contemporaries and the newspapers, that unhappiness made him replace truth by fable. At the height of his suffering he must have looked back nostalgically to his holidays at Heiligenberg, magnified in his mind into a large romantic *schloss*: it was and is two bald houses opposing each other across a court, joined up by an ugly ballroom and other uninteresting buildings. One of his biographers pointed out it resembled less a hereditary castle than a *nouveau riche*'s suburban villa. This is correct. But it had been a part of his happy youth before the war, and his grandiose recollections were typical delusions adults often manufacture about their old homes. But whereas most of us in old age recognise our childish exaggerations, his, due to the sorrows of 1914, could not be rationally discarded and became sacred memories, upheld in defiance of the evidence of his own eyes.

Mountbatten's fantasies increased as he grew older, and this trait, combined with his habit of convincing himself that what he wished was the truth, made his colleagues consider him a tricky Machiavellian, without realising the seeds of his faults had been sown in 1914. In the same year persecution pushed him into safe royal circles where he felt secure. Who can blame him for sheltering for the rest of his life among those he believed had helped his family in their time of troubles? Luckily he was unaware of the compliant role King George V played in his father's dismissal after receiving many letters criticising Louis and 'the German connection'.[14]

His childish sufferings made him worship, with Chinese enthusiasm, his ancestors and his relations, whom he compared favourably with his contemporaries who loudly applauded the hanging of his mother's first cousin in effigy. How could he believe kindly uncles had turned into devilish Huns who should, like the Kaiser, be shot? To him these so-called devils were loved friends and relations whom he had known leading happy, carefree lives; while the only cruelty he had suffered was at the hands of those he had thought were his English 'chums', who showed him, by unkindness and ostracism, that he belonged to a detested alien species.

His confusion was extreme. His father and duty bound him to England, but his happiest memories lay in the enemy camp peopled by relations and friends. This complicated division of loyalties survived two wars, and Mountbatten visited Germany with pleasure up to the end of his life. I saw last year a memorial to him in the garden at Heiligenberg, lying neglected, stained, on top of his grandfather's unkempt grave. I wonder if anywhere in England there is a memorial to a German who spent ten years fighting for Germany against this country.

It is impossible to guess what sort of man Mountbatten would have become without the war. Certainly he would not, at an impressionable age, have become blindly dedicated to a fixed intention which demanded the obedience of his intellect and froze his intellectual growth, leaving him with perpetual adolescent conceptions and beliefs. Fortunately these did not impair his practical and inventive abilities and extraordinary powers of leadership. Towards the end of his life he became aware how oddly his intellectual aridity contrasted with his

22

worldly success. This belated discovery caused him such obvious concern that Lord Butler remembered '. . . he felt he had missed something important in life, that it had been one-sided, that whatever else he had achieved, he had missed the academic and intellectual side. He felt he had been left out of that world, and he resented it.'[15] On the other hand as his concentration on the practical as opposed to the intellectual showed, it could have been advantageous to him to have missed civilising activities, which would have interfered with the working experiences and concentration on technical problems, out of which grew his genius for innovation. His lack of culture was only disadvantageous after his retirement, when he could not fall back on the usual consolations of an educated man and had to fill his time with odd engagements, discussions about his past, and continual playing of the television series devoted to his life, which he enjoyed night after night with the enthusiasm of a conceited schoolboy.

It has been argued he was a cold man. This is true and untrue; I wrote earlier that his early experiences had made him profoundly distrustful of the English upper classes with whom he never appeared to be at ease, but he took an intense interest in his many relations to whom he was kind and thoughtful. They were his family and he remembered the old and neglected, and brightened, by his thoughtfulness and generosity, their old age. To the younger generation he was sympathetic, encouraging, uncritical, always ready to help with advice, remembering how much he had lacked sympathy when he was young.

His passionate wish to belong to the royal circle was a common characteristic of semi-royalties, who are often more concerned with 'position' and the importance of 'blood' than the heads of their families. Mountbatten's morganatic and uncertain ancestry made him desperately desire to be a trusted part of an inner circle which, when he was a young man, had reigned on the thrones of Europe east of the Rhine. Defending his birthright he collected, and then ignored and hid away, papers in his own archives, and created myths flattering to his vanity by romantically rewriting his family history. To his critics his obsession was and is ridiculous, but it should be balanced against his fearlessness and the greatest of all qualities in a leader, the ability to inspire those under his command.

Mountbatten insisted his mythmakers should show him to be an immaculate cardboard figure, always right and never wrong. Obediently they did what they were told and by avoiding the past missed the secrets of his ancestry, which he covered up with tomes of fairy stories. Their obedience caused them to ignore the insults suffered by his grandfather, father and two uncles, which altered his character and persuaded him it was his duty to pervert history. They also treated him unjustly by failing to discuss his own errors, which left him open to attack by posterity, no respecter of pretence. It is a rule of history that great men have great faults; his pretended perfection illustrated his biographers' reluctance to judge their hero impartially.

Philip Ziegler began his official biography with the words:

Admiral of the Fleet, the Earl Mountbatten of Burma, was a man who, for his own amusement, rarely took up any book unless it were one of genealogy, most especially one relating to his own forebears. During the reaches of the night in the Viceroy's House in Delhi, when his predecessors might have diverted themselves with the verses of Macaulay or the latest detective story by Mrs Christie, Mountbatten would relax over the tapestry of his ancestry, enumerating the generations that divided him from the Emperor Charlemagne and marvelling at the intricate web of cousinship which bound him many times over to the Wittelsbachs and the Romanoffs, the Habsburgs and the Hohenzollerns.[16]

Well, well, well! Surely at that time in India Mountbatten was the only man thinking every night of Charlemagne. But doubtless his labours refreshed and comforted, enabling him to work like a giant the following day. Nevertheless, his obsession was interesting and makes it necessary, if he is to be understood, to examine the background of his family as well as the conventions and rules of nineteenth-century royal conduct, which could only be flouted at the cost of social ruin. I also probe the 'verboten subjects' surrounding the legitimacy of his grandfather, his relationship to the Hesses, and the way his family were spurned or esteemed by the emperors of Russia, Austria, Germany and the Queen of England. Without knowledge of these matters it is impossible to understand why his ancestry was a primary source of the social insecurity which lay behind his arrogance.

NOTES

1. Lord Mountbatten was in turn called Prince Louis of Battenberg, Lord Louis Mountbatten, Viscount Mountbatten, Earl Mountbatten. His

father and numerous relations were also called Louis. To avoid confusion I will refer to him as Mountbatten.

2. The elder Louis of Battenberg, who was naturalised in order to join the British Navy.

3. Richard Hough, authority on Mountbatten, author of *Mountbatten*, *Edwina* and *Louis and Victoria*.

4. Richard Hough, *Louis and Victoria*, Weidenfeld and Nicolson, 2nd ed., 1984, ch. 14, p. 311.

5. Ibid., ch. 5, p. 134.

6. Admiral of the Fleet Lord Fisher of Kilverstone, First Sea Lord, 1904–10, 1914–15.

7. Richard Hough, *Mountbatten: Hero of our Time*, Weidenfeld and Nicolson, 1980, ch. 1, p. 13.

8. Lady Wester Wemyss (ed.), *Life and Letters of Lord Wester Wemyss*, Eyre and Spottiswoode, 1935, ch. 2, p. 37. The Beresford-Fisher controversy is dealt with in greater detail in ch. 17.

9. Hough, *Louis and Victoria*, ch. 14, pp. 313–14.

10. Hough, *Mountbatten*, ch. 1, p. 27.

11. A phrase coined and first used by Horatio Bottomley in his magazine *John Bull* in December 1911.

12. Hough, *Louis and Victoria*, ch. 13, p. 303.

13. Hough, *Mountbatten*, ch. 1, p. 30.

14. H. H. Asquith, *Letters to Venetia Stanley*, Oxford University Press, 1982, p. 287, letter 191.

15. Hough, *Mountbatten*, ch. 10, p. 245.

16. Philip Ziegler, *Mountbatten*, Collins, ch. 1, p. 21. See also Appendix 1.

1

THE lives of Mountbatten's ancestors cannot be understood without knowledge of German history. Napoleon, not Bismarck or Frederick the Great, created modern Germany. After his conquest of Austria he decided to kill off the aged, ghostly, disintegrating Holy Roman Empire, a federation of independencies, free cities, fiefdoms, individual church properties, bans of noblemen, etc., relics of the rule of Charlemagne. The majority of these remnants were insignificant anachronisms, less than fifty could be described as states, and of these, many were divided into scattered plots of land whose unimportance was illustrated by the reply of a tutor to a question from a young Prince of Hesse about his country's history: 'You must learn your country has no history.'

Apart from Austria the only other power in this loose federation was Prussia, where in 1701, the Hohenzollern Count Frederick III of Brandenburg was allowed by the Habsburgs to call himself King in Prussia (*König in Preussen*), not King of Prussia, instead of King of Brandenburg, as he wished.

The Habsburgs, despite this concession, remained splendid, isolated in their grandeur, regarding the Landgraves, Margraves, and Electors (the Electors or *Kurfürsten* had a special significance – they were princes by birth allowed to sit in the German *diet*) with goodnatured contempt, until Napoleon appeared and shattered their unsubstantial dream. They reluctantly realised the myth of Charlemagne was at last buried, and, not wishing to lose their imperial title (they had taken over the once elective title of Emperor of the Holy Roman Empire) created for themselves the title of Emperor of Austria in 1804. This was wise, as on 6 August 1806, after the French victory at Austerlitz, Napoleon's commissioner announced in Vienna the death of the imaginary Empire and the absorption of the irrelevances into neighbouring and more viable states.

The German princelings, who had at first looked down with scorn on Napoleon, came cringing around their new overlord arousing the scorn of Goethe, begging for styles and titles long denied by the Habsburgs. The French Emperor had been willing to sell such conceits but asked in payment thousands of the buyers' faithful subjects. The princelings paid up. In Saxony the Elector pledged 20,000 men to Napoleon, and in return was allowed to style himself King and absorb a number of his poorer neighbours into his new realm. In Württemberg, the Duke, whose wretched subjects threw themselves into ditches at the sight of his carriage, was allowed to call himself King in 1806 of a territory enlarged by former Austrian lands in Swabia. Later he was allowed to call himself Emperor of the Swabians as long as he provided a satisfactory flow of recruits. He did. As a reward, between 1806 and 1809 he was granted lands with 270,000 inhabitants.

Napoleon varied his tactics and created a new kingdom of Westphalia out of Hesse Cassel and its surrounding states for his brother Jerome.

The new king's reign was one long party, paid for by human exports. Not surprisingly he was soon loathed. But he did not care and continued to lead a life of luxurious uselessness until the Battle of Leipzig in 1813 brought his house down.

The situation in Bavaria was different. The country had been reluctantly forced by its proximity to fight with Austria against France in 1799. After their joint defeat at Hohenlinden in 1800 they freed themselves from the losing side, joined the French, increased their territory and contributed soldiers to Napoleon. As a reward in 1806 the Elector became King of Bavaria, but as in Württemberg, had to give Napoleon a daughter, Princess Augusta, who married the French Emperor's stepson, Eugène de Beauharnais. The proposal was put to the Wittelsbachs in plain words: 'Either donate the bride or a regiment will come and fetch her.' The sad climax came in 1812 when it is estimated the German states sent 125,000 to 140,000 men to fight in the Russian campaign.

The *nouveau riche* dynasties were not allowed to forget that they owed their elevation to Napoleon. Their inbred obedience made them accept an ignominious role. It is not a pretty story. Today, few German princes will admit their country was created by Napoleon, whose work was completed by Bismarck.

After 1806 the Holy Roman Empire was dead but belief in the

shibboleths of blood remained untouched, and the social traditions of the Habsburgs survived and continued to impose penalties on presumptuous morganatic families. Although the sovereignty of the new states created by Napoleon was confirmed in Vienna in 1814, the problem of the princes and counts whose independencies had been swallowed up in the new kingdoms and grand duchies remained. These deprived wanderers claimed a sacred, ancient privilege granted to their ancestors by the Holy Roman Emperors, the right to marry into the Habsburg family, the aim of every German princeling. As far as Napoleon was concerned they had ceased to exist; he lumped the lot into his new kingdoms and forgot them. But once he was defeated, the disinherited caused endless trouble and embarrassment, which increased when Metternich created a German Federation of states based on Napoleon's divisions, guided by Austria with a federal parliament or *diet* in Frankfurt. The deprived were determined not to lose their sacred right of *Ebenbürtigkeit*, or equality of birth. To quieten them Metternich allowed the *diet* to find a solution, and in 1825, after ten years of deliberation, it decided that certain princely families could be mediatised (the Oxford Dictionary defines to 'mediatise' as to 'reduce (a state) to dependence without depriving its ruler of his titular position'). This enabled them to call themselves *Durchlaucht* or Serene Highness. After three more years of bitter discussion a select number of counts were also mediatised, and allowed the qualification *Erlaucht*, and to call themselves His or Her Illustrious Highness. These newly mediatised families were allowed into the second section of the *Almanach de Gotha*,[1] while the unmediatised withered in the third. The Bonapartes, despite their overthrow, were placed in the second section of this royal Bible. How could they not be? Napoleon had married a member of the Habsburg family who looked down on the new royalties with the infinite disdain of those who had worn the crown of the Holy Roman Empire since the fifteenth century, and had in all that time only allowed an occasional king within the bounds of their historic if imaginary realm. As for poor old Britain, she was not thought worthy of consideration – not one of our Dukes was placed in the sacred second section of the *Almanach*. The omission was unnoticed as with insular superiority the English aristocracy regarded the Germanic fascination with blood as comic, stupid and productive of inbreeding and madness. To them the sensible thing was to marry for property, love or money and, if possible, for all three.

The German obsession with blood was illustrated in Arthur Benson's diary, written at the turn of the last century at Claremont during a visit to the Duchess of Albany, formerly a princess of Waldeck and Pyrmont and at the time a widowed daughter-in-law of Queen Victoria:

> The Duchess entertained me with very humorous stories of small German courts, especially the Count of Erbach, living in a filthy and ruinous house, no money, but always driving four-in-hand and refusing to see any but the nobility. 'Blood-royal' is the one thought, and to keep the blood pure. 'There is no such snobbishness in the world,' she said, 'as at small German courts.' She told me how the Prince of Saxe-Weimar would not take in Princess Marie of Baden to dinner because she was married to the Duke of Hamilton. 'I can't go in with an English Duchess,' he said pathetically. Later in the evening he offered the Duchess of Albany his arm. 'I thought you said you could not go in with an English Duchess,' she said. He was very angry.
>
> At 8.00 we assembled for dinner. One of the few things that makes me absolutely furious is the way in which all these Royalties who are poor and poky, but yet feel that they may marry sovereigns. 'Royal blood is the only thing that matters,' she said. 'It makes them different from all the world, with a line around them.' But I expect that the Duchess suffers too from the disease, and none the less because she thinks that she has got rid of it all. What else would excuse being taken in by your son-in-law night after night, or sending your son and daughter arm-in-arm into dinner *first*. A boy and girl of 20 and 21!'[2]

The extract is of interest in illustrating that German princes up to the twentieth century still considered English dukes 'untouchable', while Benson's opinions (he was a son of an Archbishop of Canterbury) reflected the upper-middle-class English distaste of continental snobbery.

Apart from mediatisation the question of morganatic marriages continued to cause headaches to the imperial and royal houses. I don't wish to go into the origins of the word 'morganatic' as it involves entering bottomless bogs of heraldry; it is enough to state that the word came in the nineteenth century to mean a marriage in which the wife could not take the name and title of her husband's family, while the children had to give up any claim of succeeding to the family titles. England took up a careless, isolated position on the question and Queen Victoria allowed her daughter Beatrice to marry a Battenberg, shocking imperial Russia, Austria and Prussia who rigorously upheld the sanctity of pure blood.

In the nineteenth century a King of Württemberg insisted that a son who married a morganatic wife should call himself Teck. The morganatic daughter of this marriage was Queen Mary who, an old relation of the family recalls, was so resentful of the way Alexandra of Hesse-Darmstadt (the last Empress of Russia), treated her as a girl, that in 1917 she influenced King George V to overrule his ministers and prevent the escape of the Tsar and his family from Russia in an English warship.

The grand duchy of Hesse-Darmstadt, scornfully referred to by Stein as a 'stud farm', was brim full of morganatic marriages. Louis III and his brothers all had morganatic wives. Among them was Prince Alexander of Hesse, (grandfather of Mountbatten), whose life I later describe. Even Louis IV, the son-in-law of Queen Victoria, after his wife's death secretly married a divorced woman,[3] upsetting the Queen who had the marriage annulled. Her conduct on this occasion did not reflect her views on morganatic marriages, merely her disapproval of her son-in-law's choice of a divorced woman who she judged belonged to the demi-monde. Surprisingly, she was not critical of illegitimacy and considered it of value in bringing new blood into the overbred and often mad European royal families. Fortunately her liberal opinions were shared by King Edward VII, who allowed his son to marry the morganatic Princess Mary of Teck, King George V whose son married Lady Elizabeth Bowes-Lyon, and King George VI whose daughter, our Queen, married Prince Philip of Sonderberg-Glucksberg-Schleswig-Holstein, whose mother was morganatic. These three marriages were conspicuous successes, but had our kings and queens been forced to marry into mediatised families, England would probably by now have been ruled by a lunatic. As it is the tradition has been continued by Prince Charles who has also made a morganatic marriage which has enchanted the English public.[4]

NOTES

1. An annual publication from the eighteenth century until 1939, which graded the grandest European families into three groups, the first reigning

sovereigns, the second those who could marry into imperial families, the third those who could not.

2. A. G. Benson, *Edwardian Excursions*, ch. 12, pp. 177–9, Introduction by David Newsome, John Murray, 1981.

3. Hough, *Louis and Victoria*, ch. 5, p. 117. Varying accounts are given by numerous historians of this surprising wedding. This marriage is also dealt with on pp. 176–7.

4. I am indebted in this and the next two chapters to three books: Lord Bryce's *The Holy Roman Empire*, which has never been out of print since its publication in 1864; *The Secrets of the Gotha* by Ghislain de Diesbach, translated into English by Margaret Crosland for Chapman and Hall in 1964, a brilliant book which should be reprinted; and lastly A. J. P. Taylor's *The Course of German History*, published by Hamish Hamilton in 1945.

2

'You must remember your country has no history'
Tutor to a young Prince of Hesse

MOUNTBATTEN often referred to the Grand Duke of Hesse-Darmstadt as 'the head of the House of Hesse, the oldest reigning Protestant dynasty in Europe'. The only thing wrong with this statement was that he did not belong to the eldest branch of the Hesse family and it had not been a reigning house since 1918. The precedence of the family is clearly stated in editions of the *Almanach de Gotha*: in 1567 the Landgrave of Hesse divided his property among four sons, and to underline his supremacy the eldest, the Landgrave of Hesse-Cassel, was left half the property, and the remainder was divided among the three younger sons, of whom the Landgrave of Hesse-Darmstadt was the youngest.[1]

Let me deal first with the senior branch of the family, the Hesse-Cassels, seldom mentioned in the Battenberg-Mountbatten myth. They were by 1790 famous for the wealth of their ruler. This they owed to the ingenuity of the Landgrave Charles (1670–1730) ('Slave Trader I') who excelled in the common German method of raising money by hiring out his peasants as mercenaries or selling them abroad. This profitable trade reached its apex under the Landgrave Frederick II (1760–1785) ('Slave Trader II') who, in one advantageous deal, hired 22,000 troops to England for £3,191,000[2] and packed them off to fight against the American rebels (many of their descendants are American citizens today). He also sold 5,000 luckier men to the Austrians to keep order in Venetia. They only had to climb over the Alps.[3]

The royal 'Slave Trader III', Landgrave William IX, couldn't wait to get into the same business and when he succeeded, sold his favourite Hanau regiment. He was considered exceptionally devious, even by eighteenth-century standards; after fighting with Austria and her allies against the French in 1792, he made peace with the victor Napoleon and accepted territorial gains at his neighbour's expense. In 1803 the

33

French Emperor allowed him the title of 'Elector'. Three years later his wealth and double-dealing made Napoleon expel him from Cassel and search desperately for his immense treasure. Fortunately William had placed his finances in the hands of Jewish bankers, among them the Rothschilds. While he scuttled away to safety they, by cunning and bravery, managed to retain a large part of his fortune. As for his unfortunate subjects, they spent the next seven years fighting for France against Spaniards, Russians, Austrians and Germans.

It is interesting to note the respect a large section of the German nation has always given to those who lead them to their death – Frederick the Great, Napoleon, Bismarck, the Kaiser and Hitler are examples. In his account of the retreat from Moscow, Sergeant Bourgogne gave an illustration of the selfless devotion of simple Hessian soldiers:

> Prince Emile of Hesse-Cassel was with us, and his contingent, composed of several regiments of cavalry and infantry. Like us, he bivouacked on the left side of the road, with the remainder of his unfortunate men, now reduced to five or six hundred. About a hundred and fifty dragoons were left; but these were almost all on foot, their horses being dead and eaten. These brave men, almost frozen with the cold, sacrificed themselves in this awful night to save their young Prince, not more than twenty years of age. They stood round him the whole night wrapped in their great white cloaks, pressed tightly one against the other, protecting him from the wind and cold. The next morning three-quarters of them were dead and buried beneath the snow, along with ten thousand others from different corps.[4]

How noble to sacrifice your life for one whose family had sold your ancestors like bales of cotton for a hundred years! But it must be remembered the German rulers bred soldiers like chickens to be sold when they reached maturity. Without this trade they could not have maintained their courts.

So much for the Hessians who became, after the Elector had fled, Westphalian subjects of Napoleon's brother Jerome, but what of the Napoleonic Elector? Wisely he remained safely abroad until the French defeat at Leipzig in 1813. He then returned in triumph to claim his lands and put the clock back to the year of his departure, 1806, by insisting officers and officials returned to the rank they had held at the time of his expulsion. This was unsettling; in the Napoleonic wars promotion had been rapid, and generals found themselves demoted to majors or captains while private soldiers, to their dismay, were forced again to grow pigtails and powder their hair in eighteenth-century style.

William was succeeded by his coarse and avaricious son Frederick William II, who morganatically married a woman called Falkenstein. Such a marriage caused puzzling complications. His descendants were allowed to call themselves 'Princes or Princesses of Hanau', but only on condition they married countesses or ladies of superior rank. If not, they had to call themselves 'Count' or 'Countess' Schaumburg. Most of his surviving descendants are known by this name.

Unrest in 1830 forced the Elector to summon the estates and grant a liberal constitution. This drove him into such a rage he momentarily retired from public life.

He lost his nerve again in 1848, tried to destroy the *diet* he had created and chose as his chief minister Hans Friedrich Hassenpflug, who was loathed even more than his master. Sacked, he was recalled to suppress the liberals and enabled the Elector to enjoy himself, make vast sums of money, curb industrial growth, limit education to the teaching of his own views, and forbid railways to come through his territory to link Prussia with its Rhineland possessions. He infuriated the young Bismarck, who decided Hesse-Cassel should one day be incorporated into a German empire.

Hassenpflug's policy forced the Elector to support Austria against Prussia. Hesse-Cassel was at once overrun by Bismarck's new army and absorbed into the growing German empire. Admiration for arbitrary rule reappeared in the family in this century, and several nephews of the late Kaiser and great-grandsons of Queen Victoria ardently supported the Nazi regime. The eldest, Prince Philip, was referred to by William Shirer in his *Rise and Fall of the Third Reich* as 'the former messenger boy of the Führer to Mussolini who had been hanging about headquarters'. True to family traditions, he changed sides when he saw the war was lost but too early, and paid the price of losing his wife (Mafalda of Savoy) in a German prison camp. Prince Philip was detained for months by the Americans and reluctantly released; certainly he was not such a fanatical Nazi as his younger brother Christopher, a brutal associate of Himmler who bombed

London. It was later claimed by Mountbatten that Hitler, distrustful of his loyalty, had him killed by a bomb planted in his aeroplane which crashed in Italy. Perhaps he had genuinely changed sides but I have never seen evidence to support this charitable view, and would a valuable aeroplane have been wasted on an unimportant Nazi traitor? A bullet would have been as effective and infinitely cheaper.

The Hesse-Cassels should not be judged too harshly. The distinguished historian A. J. P. Taylor aptly described their Achilles heel.

> German royal houses ran easily to eccentrics and lunatics. Ceaseless inbreeding, power territorially circumscribed but within these limits limitless, produced mad princes as a normal event. The mad King of Bavaria, the mad Duke of Brunswick, the mad Elector of Hesse, the imbecile Emperor – these phrases are the commonplace of German history; and of the utterly petty princes hardly one was sane.[5]

Queen Victoria agreed, and justified her daughter marrying a Battenberg with the words:

> . . . if one enquired into the history of all the royal and princely families I feared many black spots would be found – and finally, that if no fresh blood was infused occasionally the races would degenerate finally – physically and morally – for that almost all the Protestant Royal Families were related to each other and so were the Catholic ones![6]

NOTES

1. For an account of the splintered family of Hesse-Homburg see Appendix 1.
2. 'Hesse-Cassel', *Encyclopaedia Britannica*, 1926 edition. This estimation may be an exaggeration or misprint. Other authorities suggest the Hessians only sold 12,000 peasants.
3. Thackeray, *Four Georges*, Smith Elder, 1869, ch. 3, p. 84.
4. Memoirs of Sergeant Bourgogne, *Retreat from Moscow*, translated by J. W. Fortescue, Folio Society, 1985, ch. 5, p. 65 (original ms. Municipal Library, Valenciennes).
5. Taylor, *The Course of German History*, ch. 4, p. 65.
6. Roger Fulford (ed.), *Beloved Mama*, Private correspondence of Queen Victoria and the Crown Princess of Germany, 1885, Evans Bros, 1981, p. 180. Letter dated 17 January 1885. Quoting Royal archives.

3

I turn without regret from a short history of the heads of the half crazy House of Hesse-Cassel to their kinsmen, the Hesse-Darmstadts, from whom the Battenberg family are descended. The younger branch was provincial, undistinguished and acquisitive. The most notable figure in the family's history was the wife of Louis IX (1719–1790), the Margravine Caroline the Great. Examples of her fascination are rare and authorities usually consider it enough to say: 'She was a friend of Goethe' or was 'admired by Frederick the Great' and made Darmstadt 'a centre of culture and learning'. The description suggests an advertisement for a pretentious girls' school. In the Napoleonic era her son behaved in the usual weather-cock Hesse way, originally fighting against France, then accepting from the enemy his former German allies' land in Westphalia, Mainz and Worms. From 1805–1813, encouraged by Napoleon, he styled himself Grand Duke of Hesse, and out of gratitude sent his peasant-soldiers to die for France against Austria, Prussia and Russia. Of course he quickly abandoned the sinking French ship after the Battle of Leipzig, and at the Congress of Vienna was allowed to retain his Napoleonic grand dukedom, thanks to his family's connection with the Tsar.[1]

Unlike his kinsman in Cassel he allowed his people a constitution in 1820, and was an uninteresting and, for Germany, liberal ruler. He was succeeded by his son, the innocuous, simple-minded Louis II, who was dethroned because of his mental deficiencies in 1848, leaving *his* son Louis III, the elder brother of A (I shall refer to Prince Alexander as 'A' to avoid confusion between uncles, first cousin and son, who all had the same Christian name), to face one of the many European revolutions of that year. Terrified, he made concessions which he withdrew as quickly as possible, and for over twenty years the country was ruled by his reactionary minister, Karl Friedrich Reinhard von Dalwigk.

Louis III was variously and accurately described, with his great-nephew Mountbatten's approval, as 'dull and eccentric',[2] 'slothful',[3] '. . . gross, eccentric and alarming, a figure fit only for a Hans Sachs farce',[4] 'that old bogey of a Grand Duke.'[5] He also had an original habit: when he wished to blow his nose he would ring a bell for a lackey to bring him a handkerchief on a silver salver. His poor servants must have had a busy time when he had a cold.

His laziness and inability to rule were in the end disastrous, for Dalwigk forced his master to make the same mistake as his Cassel kinsman and take the side of Austria against Prussia in 1866. The consequence was a large fine and a loss of territory which would have been far more severe if his sister had not married Alexander II. For the second time in sixty years the Romanov connection saved the fortunes of the rulers of Hesse-Darmstadt.

The reprieve was brief. After the defeat of France in 1871 and the birth of the German Empire the small, powerless Hesse became a satellite of Prussia. Louis IV, who married Queen Victoria's daughter Alice, and their son, later the Grand Duke Ernst, retained local powers until 1918. Louis IV was described by his uncle as wearing short breeches and multi-coloured garters. 'He is very fond of sherry and horses, reads as little as possible and never writes at all',[6] and is chiefly remembered for his amazing stupidity in marrying a woman of ill repute on the same day as his daughter Victoria married Prince Louis of Battenberg.[7]

The last Grand Duke Ernst was a kind, artistic, ineffective man, despised and finally left by his first, dissatisfied wife 'Ducky', a daughter of the Duke of Edinburgh. Perhaps the most shameful action of his undistinguished career was his refusal to see Anastasia after she announced she had met him in Russia during the First World War. Summers and Mangold in *File on the Tsar*[8] put forward the argument that Ernst believed if his peace-making journey to Russia became public knowledge it could have affected a possible restoration. That is supposition, but if he refused to see his claimant-niece for this reason (and no other has ever been given) he behaved in a cowardly and brutal manner; his 'peace' visit to Russia was commendable and could have won the war for Germany.

His younger son and eventual heir Louis behaved equally badly to the wretched wanderer. He was allowed to morganatically marry a middle-class English girl, Margaret Geddes; 'granddaughter of the builder (in India) of Jumna bridge and many railways'.[9] They had no children. It is a pity, as having a similar background to Julia Hauke Princess Louis might have produced an heir comparable in talents to the Battenbergs. It is interesting that from the creation of the grand dukedom by Napoleon until the death of Prince Louis of Hesse-Darmstadt in 1968, the family produced remarkable, if sometimes mad women, but only mediocre men. Lower-middle-class blood might have revived the inbred line.

Louis met his future wife in England before the war when he was serving in the German Embassy under Ribbentrop; Hitler was already persecuting the Jews, and Dachau was in use. He certainly lacked the heroic qualities of his Battenberg cousins, once refusing a dinner invitation on Ribbentrop's orders. He succeeded to the Grand Duchy when his elder brother with his wife and children were (with one exception, who died shortly after) killed in an aeroplane crash, coming over to his wedding, fulfilling, Mountbatten thought, a family curse. He was popular in Hesse where his widow has efficiently maintained the family properties, and is admired and respected as 'our beloved housekeeper princess'.[10]

After this précis of family history I return to the past and the life of Mountbatten's grandfather, Prince Alexander of Hesse-Darmstadt (1823–1888) who was the husband of the first holder of the Battenberg title. Undoubtedly the most reliable authority on A[11] is his diary, which forms the basis of Count Corti's partial biography.[12] In its preface the author discusses the material available to him.

The Empress Marie of Russia, the wife of the Emperor Alexander II, left instructions in her will that all her papers, and especially the letters of her brother, Prince Alexander of Hesse, should be sent to him after her death. These papers, which have been most generously placed at my disposal by Prince Alexander Erbach-Schönberg, comprise the fourteen volumes of the diary of Prince Alexander of Hesse as well as thousands of notes and letters exchanged between him and his sister the Empress Marie. Prince Alexander kept his diary with great regularity from his eighteenth year until a week of his death. In addition to the diary and correspondence I have also made use of the diplomatic correspondence preserved in the State archives of Vienna.

Prince Alexander's career took him first to one and then to

another of the great European empires. His diary affords us glimpses of what was passing behind the scenes on the European stage. It is in the nature of memoirs not to include the whole of history, and therefore to give the reader only a cross-section of events. In the case of Prince Alexander's diary this cross-sectional view of European politics is rendered wider by the personal relationship between the writer and the rulers of Europe. The purpose of this book is to give its readers a picture of the lives of these rulers that will also reveal their emotions and thoughts. It is intended to show how love, gratitude, and wisdom, or again folly, envy, and jealousy determined actions, entangled the threads of high politics, and sought to unravel them again. Passing moods and outbursts of feeling throw a revealing light upon the individual temperament. I have not hesitated, therefore, to quote at times spiteful sayings, bitter words, etc. exactly as they are recorded in the correspondence and diary, although I am very well aware that they were frequently not seriously meant and were simply due to a momentary impulse. Hasty words and impulsive actions, nevertheless, often have fateful results both for private lives and national destinies. In the interests of truth the historian cannot therefore pass them over in silence.

I have sought to avoid any personal bias in the narration of events. It has been my endeavour throughout to arrive at the truth.

These words were written in approximately 1930, when Corti had not yet shown the desire to please his patrons, which flawed his last work, *The German Empress*. It's true he had little choice, as the book was published by permission of Prince Philip of Hesse-Cassel, who despite his Nazi record wrote a self-satisfied introduction. But his two books *The Downfall of Three Dynasties* and *Alexander von Battenberg*, written before he had become the unofficial Hesse historian, quote freely from letters and manuscripts now carefully hidden away. For many years A's indiscreet, frank papers, now owned by Princess Louis of Hesse-Darmstadt and the Mountbatten Trust in Darmstadt, have been unavailable to historians, and even in 1930 Corti wrote that they had already been tampered with by his wife and daughter.[13]

A's life was full; he was brother-in-law to the Tsar, a general in the Austrian army, an intermediary between the Emperors of Austria, France and Russia, and a frequent visitor to Queen Victoria's court. The concealment of his papers is a minor historical tragedy. I wrote to

Princess Louis of Hesse asking permission to see them; I received no reply, but later, to my surprise, I was told they now belonged to the Mountbatten Archives, which Lord Brabourne informed me politely were being reorganised and consequently out of bounds. Considering the late Mountbatten's passion for his ancestors and the spate of books which have appeared in the last forty years glorifying himself, his father and his ancestors, I was at first amazed that this fascinating secret river of history should not be available to historians. My surprise was increased when I read Corti's *Alexander von Battenberg* and discovered the existence of another pile of unexamined documents, the Hartenau Archives, of equal interest, also now hidden away in Darmstadt. These two collections relate the unvarnished daily lives of Mountbatten's grandfather and uncle, who both inspired his youth. Why, I wondered, had they only been published in selected driblets, when their publication, with a foreword by Mountbatten, would have been a major literary event? After a second reading I understood, as even Corti's discreet accounts reveal, two secrets relating to A and his wife which would have destroyed Mountbatten's recreation of his family history, and ruined his ancestral game by turning his kings and queens into pawns. The first was the illegitimacy of Prince Alexander of Hesse and his sister Marie, later Empress of Russia. This secret has been frequently mentioned by many diverse authors: Maurice Paléologue,[14] French Ambassador to Russia in the First World War, the German Chancellor von Bülow[15] in his three-thousand-page autobiography, Queen Victoria[16] who had no delusions about the Battenberg's history and Count Corti[17] with all the now hidden family secrets, papers, letters and diaries before him. Unpalatable facts and embarrassing truths never daunted Mountbatten. They could be denied or destroyed, as the books in which the disclosures appeared were only read by a small circle, and English interest in the Hesse family has always been very lukewarm. He hid (some say destroyed) the compromising family papers in his book prisons, hoping, like an ostrich, they would be forgotten. His desire for secrecy was comprehensible – he was born in the Victorian era. But now there is no harm in examining the reasons behind his fantasies, and describing the tribulations of his grandfather, who was forced to leave Russia (Mountbatten's second secret) because he wished to marry an unmediatised, six months' pregnant girl.

A was born in Darmstadt, capital of the Napoleonic grand dukedom of Hesse, in 1823, officially the third living grandson of the recently elevated Grand Duke Ludwig, self- or Napoleon-created, you can take your choice. His mother was Wilhelmina, a Princess of Baden, and he was brought up, with his younger sister Marie, in unusual circumstances, the two living together in a little house on the edge of a forest[18] on their mother's country estate, Heiligenberg, near Jugenheim.

The Princess – her father-in-law was still alive – had bought the property in 1820, to enable her to live with her chamberlain Baron Augustus Senarclens von Grancy.[19]

In the next five years three children were born (the eldest died). When A was ten the Grand Duke Louis II, although privately lamenting his wife's behaviour, accepted with reluctance paternity of his two youngest children, and made the boy a second-lieutenant in the first company of the Hesse-Darmstadt Life Guards. His belated recognition was probably caused by the intercession of his wife's brother and sisters, the Grand Duke of Baden, the Empress of Russia, the Queens of Bavaria and Sweden and the Duchess of Brunswick, a formidable quintet. But despite his reluctant acceptance of the two children, they did not live with him, although they appeared together on certain public occasions, but were educated from the ages of five and six in their country cottage by a Captain (later General) Frey, who wrote a detailed diary[20] covering these years. This daily account of the two children's lives, which I was refused permission to see, is owned by the Mountbatten family and is housed, according to the Director, in the Darmstadt State Archives. The last sighting of a selected photographed section of the work was by E. H. Cookridge in 1955. He was incorrectly informed the rest of the diary had been destroyed in the war. It is to be hoped this unique record has not, like A's diary, been mutilated. It is difficult to think of a reason why it is shut away except for its frank account of the two little embarrassments' upbringing by the forest.

Their mother, the grand duchess, died in 1836. In 1838 the Tsarevitch Alexander, on a tour of Europe to find a wife, visited Darmstadt and fell in love with the 'Cinderella' Marie, aged fourteen. Despite the doubts of his father Nicholas I, who resisted his son's passionate wishes for a year, they became engaged in 1839. A letter from the Austrian ambassador to St Petersburg shows scant imperial enthusiasm, but suggests the Tsar was anxious to distance his future daughter-in-law from her homeland as quickly as possible.

To Prince Metternich
St Petersburg, 1 April/20 March 1839

My Prince,
The Emperor has told me, that Princess Marie had so impressed his son, he had asked permission to pass by Darmstadt on his return from England and spend some days there. The Emperor thought it likely she would become his daughter-in-law. Therefore it might be possible he is going to ask the parents to let her come here to await the age to be married and to have her prepared here for her new position.

Grant me the honour, My Prince, to express my profoundest respect,

le D. de Ficquelmont[21]

The Tsar made the best of things when his friend Count Orlov mentioned the concern of the Russian court at Marie's illegitimacy, by laughing and giving the sibylline reply:

Goodness me, who are you and who am I? Who on earth can ever prove such a thing? And I should not advise anyone to suggest that the heir to the Russian throne is marrying a bastard.[22]

There was good reason for the Tsar's 'Who are you and who am I?' as his grandmother the Empress Catherine suggested in her auto-biography her son Paul was the illegitimate son of Soltykov.[23] The Tsarevitch's own qualms had been quickly settled the year before when the Russian Ambassador in Darmstadt, Count Oubril, had told him 'everybody in Darmstadt' knew the real father. He asked 'Is Princess Marie in the Almanach de Gotha?' When the Ambassador answered 'yes' he replied impatiently, '*Alors de quoi vous mêlez-vous, imbécile?*'[24]

Mountbatten and the late Prince Louis of Hesse made a pact to deny the illegitimacy. E. M. Almedingen gave a typical example of the myth-writers' methods of concealing unwelcome truths:

On finding the Hesse story repeated in a short life of Alexander II recently printed in England (*Alexander II and the Modernization of Russia* in the Teach Yourself History Series by W. E. Mosse, the

English Universities Press, 1958, p. 34) I asked Prince Ludwig of Hesse and the Rhine, the present head of the family, if he knew when the story came to be invented. He thought that it must have been later than 1839 . . . Even a breath of an imagined illegitimacy would have been enough to wreck the betrothal.[25]

That the story was not invented after 1839 and that even a breath of an imagined illegitimacy did not wreck the betrothal is shown by the Austrian Ambassador's dispatch to Prince Metternich:

St Petersburg, 26/14 April 1839

My Prince,

The last time the Emperor honoured me by discussing the likelihood of his son's marriage to Princess Marie of Darmstadt, he told me that he is well aware of what is said about the irregularity of her birth but that, as the Grand Duke of Darmstadt chooses to ignore it, he finds it presents no obstacle. His son, despite only spending one day at Darmstadt, found his attention drawn to the Princess because she was not very well treated, and the Emperor quite understands how this would heighten the interest his son already felt for her; that he would feel the same way in his son's place.

So it would seem very probable that this marriage will take place, and that it will not go down well either here in Russia or abroad; above all in Germany where nobody is unaware of the circumstances surrounding and subsequent to the Princess Marie's birth. In short, the Emperor cannot be too happy about his children's marriages . . .

Ficquelmont[26]

The bride was collected and taken to Russia by the Tsar and Tsarina in June 1840. She was joined by her brother, by now a captain of the Imperial Chevalier Gardes on 7 September of the same year. The next day the future bride made her official, oriental entry into Moscow, to be welcomed by countless thousands who had come to see the shy, sickly girl. Marie was overwhelmed and looked for her brother as if to say, 'You are the one piece of home here to give me a little help amidst all this splendour and strangeness.' Shortly afterwards A was given a Russian general as a tutor. The Grand Duke's unhidden desire to turn his unwanted son into a Russian was explicable; it rid Hesse of the second of the two embarrassing afterthoughts the Grand Duchess had left behind her. Marie was also pleased; she was lonely and overwhelmed by the savage grandeur of the Russian court, and was delighted to have her brother as a companion until her marriage on 16 April 1841.[27]

The following extracts support the view that until the Mountbatten campaign, the illegitimacy of Prince Alexander and his sister was uncontradicted.

Maurice Paléologue, French Ambassador to Russia, 1912–1917:

About the spring of 1823 the little Court of Darmstadt was astounded to learn that the Grand Duchess was pregnant. On the 15th July she gave birth to a third son, Prince Alexander, who was later to found the Battenberg family. For the honour of his crown and family, Louis II assumed paternity of the child. But everyone knew the real father; he was so insignificant no one dared to name him. The following year, on the 8th August 1824, the Grand Duchess was delivered of another child, of the same origin, Princess Marie.[28]

Prince von Bülow, Chancellor of Germany, 1900–1909:

In the Russian royal family the descent of the future Tsarina Maria Alexandrovna and Prince Alexander of Hesse from the handsome Master of the Horse was well-known. When I was attached to the Embassy of St Petersburg in 1865 or 1866, I drove with the Grand Duke and Grand Duchess Vladimir from Tsarskoie Selo to St Petersburg, the Grand Duke, who had gone to bed late, fell asleep on the way, and his wife called my attention to his fine, almost classical features. One could see, she said, that her husband was not the grandson of Louis II of Hesse, renowned for his ugliness, but of the handsome Grancy. As a matter of fact, the Senarclens von Grancy were a good family and came from the Canton Vaud, not far from Lausanne, where the ancestral castle stands.[29]

Bülow was well-qualified to give an opinion. His great uncle had been Ambassador to England from 1827–1840. His father, a contemporary of A's, after a lifetime of diplomacy in the German states, became Foreign Minister of Prussia. It is also interesting to read in

Corti that in 1866 the Empress Marie, during her visit to Darmstadt, 'drove out to Heiligenberg to visit the grave of an old friend of her childhood, Baroness Marianne von Grancy, who had just died, and to whom she put up a splendid memorial'.[30] Would the Frey papers show Marianne shared the cottage in the wood? It would have been odd of the Tsarina to 'put up a splendid memorial' to a childhood friend, but a natural way to express affection for a half sister! I could not find the monument at Heiligenberg!

The close relationship of the future Tsarina to the De Grancys was emphasised after Marie's marriage:

Count Ficquelmont to Prince Metternich, St Petersburg, 4 May/ 22 April 1841
Madame de Grancy, a lady of the court of Darmstadt, formerly connected to the Grandduchess Alexandrovna, will now receive a pension of 1000 ducats per annum for life.[31]

To return to A, as a reward for his relationship he was made a colonel at the age of eighteen, given the Order of St Andrew and a pension of 12,000 silver roubles a year as long as he lived in Russia.[32] However, perhaps because he had outgrown his strength, his military career was not an immediate success, and on one occasion when unable to control his horse he was, to his intense humiliation, publicly rebuked by the Tsar: 'See to it that you get a horse that will carry you properly, understand? You are no ornament to your regiment! You simply throw it into confusion.'[33] This severity may have been caused by A's flirtation with the Grand Duchess Olga, the Tsar's daughter. As a punishment A, to his dismay, was packed off to Darmstadt. Ghislain de Diesbach, after writing A had followed his sister to Russia, explains the Tsar's decision tersely:

'. . . le prince Alexandre de Hesse l'accompagna dans le louable désir de se faire une position à la cour de Saint-Pétersbourg. Une excellente opportunité s'offrit à lui sous les traits de la grande-duchesse Olga dont il s'éprit aussitôt, mais l'empereur, déjà peu satisfait du mariage du tsarévitch avec une princesse de naissance douteuse ne voulut pas entendre parler de donner sa fille à un jeune prince qui, malgre sa bonne mine, n'était qu'un mince personnage, passant pour le fils d'un baron suisse; . . .'[34]

When this marriage did not come off she was offered unsuccessfully to the Habsburgs as the Tsar could not understand that the grandest of all the imperial families considered the Russians savages, and would never consider marrying into the Russian orthodox church.

During the next four years A led the life of any carefree young man, and enjoyed many amorous successes while continuing to flirt with the beautiful, unmarried Olga. When in 1843 his sister gave birth to an heir, A was raised to the rank of a major general and was attached to the First Guards Division.[35] The promotion was not a reward for prowess but, as Corti politely put it: 'in honouring the brother of the Tsar, Nicholas I was really honouring the mother of his grandson'[36], a correct interpretation as A was banished abroad again a month after his promotion.

He returned to continue his gay life until in 1845, to his surprise, Olga suddenly said, 'Tell me, have you heard about the new campaign in the Caucasus,'[37] a plain hint he should go and fight. Lavishly equipped he went to war, fought bravely and, after a dangerous campaign in which he narrowly escaped death, was awarded the Cross of St George. He returned to Moscow a minor hero, to continue his philanderings.

As he was attractive, good looking and possessed of extraordinary charm, a characteristic he was to pass on to his descendants, he had many successes which resulted in further banishments. His romantic – his critics called it dissipated – life continued undisturbed by 'the year of revolutions', 1848, which terrified the monarchies of Europe and even reached little Hesse, where A's official, by now simple, father was toppled and replaced by his reluctant elder son, who accepted his elevation with the melancholy words: 'There, that's how a grand duke abdicates.' A did not return to Darmstadt to help his official brother or console his official father.

The Tsar observed the disturbances with dismay and willingly answered an appeal for help from the Emperor Franz Joseph of Austria, after Prince Metternich had fled by train from Vienna. Russian troops quickly and brutally subdued the Hungarian rebels. A merely devoted himself to Countess Sophie Shuvalov[38] – who used as her go-between a lady-in-waiting to the Tsarina, the twenty-three-year-old Countess Julia Hauke,[39] the daughter of a soldier of mixed ancestry, son of a one-time private who had settled in Poland and fought first for Napoleon and later for the Tsar, who made him a general, and in 1829 the minister for war. In 1830 he was killed in the streets of Warsaw during a typical Polish insurrection.[40] Shortly afterwards his wife died; out of pity for the orphaned family Nicholas I educated the younger girls. Julia became, when she grew up, a lady-in-waiting to the Tsarina. As she was neither pretty, well born nor an heiress, her life was difficult, but she retained A's interest after Sophie's father, realising the brother-in-law of the future Tsar would not be allowed to marry his daughter, withdrew her from the court.

A was forced to promise he would not see her again and the Tsar pointedly suggested he settled down and married his niece, the Grand Duchess Katherine,[41] daughter of the Grand Duke Michael. He ignored the offer, but pretended sadness for his love Sophie, confined in her father's country house. At the end of the year he wrote in his diary, 'Julia Hauke is looking lovely'. Shortly afterwards the lovers were caught by the Tsar in her bedroom,[42] adding to his gallant reputation and hardly affecting hers; the maze of the Winter Palace encouraged love affairs. That A should marry Julia never entered anybody's head – why should he throw himself away on a penniless, low-bred, by no means beautiful orphan?

In 1850 it was the Tsarina's turn to advise A to marry the Grand Duchess Katherine, but he still had no wish to tie himself down, and also had a love affair with another of the Tsar's daughters, Marie Duchess of Leuchtenberg.[43] This again annoyed her father who, as usual when he was angry, sent A away to Hesse, Paris and London. In England he showed how completely he had given up pretensions to German birth by saying to the caretaker at Warwick Castle: 'Your unicorn is just as true to life as our Russian eagle.' On his return A continued his love affair with Julia until one day in 1851 she said she was pregnant.[44] The news must have been an unpleasant surprise, as while he knew love affairs were regarded with closed eyes, illegitimate babies were not. The first to point out the poor girl's condition was the Master of the Horse, who made a coarse equine comparison.[45] Her condition may have been obvious to trained eyes, but the Tsar and Tsarina were surprised and horrified when A announced he would marry Julia rather than allow her to be fobbed off in marriage with an impecunious baron, who would send her to rusticate in a remote country estate. We can only guess at the love-struck girl's relief when he belatedly proposed. This decision infuriated the whole imperial family, who considered A was lowering both himself and them by marrying a disgraced common girl. The word 'Pole' was frequently flung at Julia as if to belong to such a race was a calamity. Actually she had very little Polish blood in her veins and was a lower-middle-class, German - Dutch - French - Swiss - Hungarian - Polish - Jewish[46] goulash, which was, in the eyes of the Romanovs, an impossible combination.

A was given a final warning that if he married he would have to leave Russia. He remained firm, and could not have behaved more honourably and bravely in the face of united opposition and threats to have his income and rank of general revoked. He knew he was making a gigantic sacrifice and could, if he gave up Julia, marry the Tsar's niece with a huge dowry and country estates – a temptation to a penniless man! When the Tsar understood A's inflexibility, he demoted him to sergeant and banished him from Russia. A few days afterwards A left St Petersburg, his home for ten years, and twenty-four days later, on 28 October, morganatically married the six months' pregnant Julia, in Breslau.

These bald facts should be compared with Mountbatten's mythland fairy story, which he insisted on foisting for the rest of his life on his mythmakers, despite contradictions in his own archives:

Steadily the opposition to the match increased. Under pressure from the Tsar, the slothful Grand Duke of Hesse was driven to writing a letter of warning to his young brother. But the pressure of gallant duty was more powerful still. Alexander had promised himself to Julie, and Julie – in her joy and pride and excitement – had let this promise be known about the gossip-loving court. Both honour, and the deepest love he had ever known, were therefore at stake, and were driving him towards the inevitable confrontation with the Tsar. There was no escape from this meeting, for legal as well as protocol reasons, because Alexander had to make a request for the hand of His Majesty's charge.

For many uncomfortable and miserable weeks, the Tsar kept Alexander on tenterhooks. When he at last granted a formal audience and Alexander made his request, the consequence was all that he had feared it would be. The Emperor did not spare his protégé. After all that he, and the Russian court, had done for him, promoting him at the age of 20 to the rank of Major General, granting him countless privileges! No, it was impossible. Alexander bravely pressed his case. The Tsar responded by threatening to strip him of his military ranks and Russian decorations, and of course banishing him for ever from the Russian court. And what would he do then, a penurious soldier of fortune? No royal army in Europe would engage him after this . . .

Alexander bowed himself out of the Tsar's presence. It was the end. He could do no more. There were no good-byes. Silently and separately and secretly, the 28-year-old Prince and his 26-year-old fiancée left the Winter Palace at St Petersburg and headed west.

Some reports say that they did not meet again until they reached Warsaw and continued their elopement together from that city. Others say that Alexander acquired a droshky outside the palace, and that they travelled together, wrapped in furs, across the snow-covered steppes, beneath a new moon. Whichever happens to be true, the romance and the daring of the occasion make the disparity unimportant, although in fact the moon was almost new on the night of 4 October when the couple made their escape. Perhaps the more romantic story is true.

No doubt the Tsar did not trouble to send his cavalry in pursuit, nor issue orders to hold the eloping couple at the frontier. No doubt in his anger he reasoned that they would pay the price, and that was an end to the matter.

It is 700 miles to Warsaw. But they scarcely paused there. By 27 October they were in Breslau, another 200 miles on, and there – without ceremony, without the presence or even the knowledge of their closest relatives – this tall, soldierly Prince of Hesse was married to the clever, determined passionate 'poor little Polish orphan girl', as she was so often called behind her back at the Russian court.[47]

Mountbatten's version of his grandfather's banishment is a series of inventions, but even the cynic will be touched by his magical trans-formation of the blatantly pregnant Julia, subject of coarse jests, into a Barbara Cartland débutante: 'Alexander had promised himself to Julie, and Julie – in her joy and pride and excitement – had let this promise be known about the gossip-loving court.' Another sentence: 'No doubt the Tsar did not trouble to hold the eloping couple at the frontier,' is also comic as having just banished the pair it was highly unlikely he would have sent cavalry to bring them back! An even funnier suggestion is that having 'silently and separately and secretly' left the Winter Palace, they should then have 'hired a droshky' in the street, cried 'Warsaw' and set off on a seven-hundred mile trip to the Polish capital. And why did they drive over the Steppes, which lie in the opposite direction? Their seven-hundred-mile moonlit journey would have been long and cold enough as it was!

To return to reality: when A arrived with his bride in Hesse he was met with a cold reception from his official brother who, prompted by the Tsar, had angrily written forbidding the marriage. Reluctantly the Grand Duke made Julia, Countess of Battenberg, reviving a title connected with a ruined castle no longer in Hesse-Darmstadt, and hustled the unwanted couple out of the way, officially to Switzerland but actually to Strasbourg, where she gave birth to a baby girl, Marie, on 15 February 1852, who years later in her memoirs created the myth she was born on 15 July (her father's birthday), on the shores of Lake Geneva:

> My advent into the world was not hailed by the thunder of cannon, nor by any of the usual demonstrations of the joy of loyal subjects; indeed, I believe that apart from my parents no one was greatly overjoyed by the birth of the little girl who first opened her eyes in beautiful Switzerland. For my father, however, on whose birthday I was for the first time laid in his arms, I was a gift from God. He has told me since how he rushed out to the blue lake repeating to himself, 'I have a daughter, given me as a birthday present.'[48]

The inaccuracy of her memoirs has been confirmed by the Director of the Hesse State Archives who informed me:

> L'Allemagne dynastique by M. Huberty et al. (vol. I, 1976, with addenda vol. II, 1979) has published the entry in the Strasbourg parish registers which proves that Princess Mary (later Erbach-Schönberg) was born 15 February, not 15 July 1852, the date which has been given (in) Gotha.[49]

Considering Victorian respectability, Marie's pretence was understandable; but undoubtedly she knew the truth, as she had read and censored A's diary.[50]

For decency's sake, after spending a few months in Switzerland, the young parents returned to Hesse with their, fortunately, small baby. A asked for and was refused the command of the grand ducal army, a high-sounding title for a paltry collection of 'drill soldiers', ghosts of Napoleon's Hessians. Appeals to Austria and Queen Victoria also failed, probably more from distaste at the reason for his sudden marriage than because of Julia's lowly birth. The future looked grim. A had to face the bleak truth. His wife was not acceptable to his family or the courts of Europe. Luckily his sister and brother-in-law the Tsarevitch continued to help with money and influence and eventually[51] in July 1853, twenty months after his marriage, Franz Joseph was reluctantly persuaded to allow him to join the Austrian army, with the reduced rank of brigade colonel. The Austrian command did not welcome strangers, especially if their wives had Julia's background. To make the point, A was sent to the country garrison of Graz to keep company with the Archduke John of Austria, whose morganatic wife was a postmaster's daughter. After the exciting life A and Julia had led in St Petersburg, this backwater must have been intolerably dull. Their only excitement was table-turning.[52]

NOTES

1. The new Grand Duke's aunt was the stepmother of the Tsars Nicholas I and Alexander I.
2. Hough, *Louis and Victoria*, ch. 1, p. 7.
3. Ibid., ch. 1, p. 8.
4. Ibid., ch. 1, p. 21.
5. Ibid., ch. 1, p. 26.
6. Count Egon Corti, *The Downfall of Three Dynasties*, Methuen, 1934, p. 145, quoting letter of Prince Alexander of Hesse.
7. Ibid., pp. 294–6. Elaborated in this book pp. 174–6.
8. Anthony Summers and Tom Mangold, *File on the Tsar*, Fontana Books, 1981, ch. 18, pp. 218–21; ch. 22, p. 273; Notes, p. 340.
9. *Burke's Peerage*, entry for 'Geddes'.
10. Comment by a taxi driver in Darmstadt.
11. I shall refer to Prince Alexander as 'A' to avoid confusion between uncles, first cousin and son, who all had the same Christian name.
12. Corti, *Three Dynasties*, Preface, pp. v and vi.
13. Ibid., note 51, p. 381. 'In this part and only here, numerous erasures have been made in the diary, and occasionally whole pages have been cut out. The changes have been made in the handwriting of the Princess Marie

Erbach – the eldest daughter of Prince Alexander and of the Countess Julia Hauke, later his wife.'

14. Maurice Paléologue, *Tragic Romance of Alexander II*, translated by Arthur Chambers, Hutchinson, 1920s (undated), ch. 2, pp. 49–52.

15. Prince von Bülow (Chancellor of Germany), *Memoirs 1849–1897*, translated by Geoffrey Dunlop and F. A. Voight, Putnam, 1932 (Germany 1931), vol. 4, ch. 27, pp. 384–5.

16. Fulford, (ed.), *Beloved Mama*, p. 180.

17. Corti, *Three Dynasties*, p. 8. See also Appendix 3.

18. Ibid., ch. 1, p. 8.

19. Ibid., ch. 1, p. 1. Von Bülow, *Memoirs*, vol. 4, ch. 63, pp. 603–4.

20. E. H. Cookridge, *From Battenberg to Mountbatten*, Arthur Barker, 1966, Preface, Corti, *Three Dynasties*, pp. 2, 3, 5, 6.

21. To His Highness the Prince of Metternich by English courier from Berlin. In code – numbers – and decoded. Vienna Archives.

22. Corti, *Three Dynasties*, ch. 1, p. 8.

23. See *Memoirs of Catherine the Great*, Trubner and Co., 1859, ed. Alexander Hertzen, ch. 8.

24. Von Bülow, *Memoirs*, vol. 4, ch. 27, pp. 384–5.

25. E. M. Almedingen, *The Emperor Alexander II*, Bodley Head, 1962, p. 60.

26. Count Ficquelmont to Prince Metternich, Vienna Archives, 26/14 April 1839.

27. Corti, *Three Dynasties*, ch. 1, p. 9.

28. Paléologue, *Tragic Romance of Alexander II*.

29. Von Bülow, *Memoirs*, vol. 4, ch. 27, pp. 384–5.

30. Corti, *Three Dynasties*, p. 153.

31. Vienna Archives.

32. Ficquelmont to Prince Metternich, 4 May/22 April 1841, Vienna Archives.

33. Ibid.

34. Ghislain de Diesbach, *Les Secrets du Gotha*, René Julliard, Paris, 1964.

35. Corti, *Three Dynasties*, ch. 3, p. 22.

36. Ibid.

37. Ibid.

38. Ibid., ch. 4, p. 52.

39. For a history of the Hauke family, see Appendix 3.

40. The myth relates he was killed in front of his wife and children defending the palace of the Governor the Grand Duke Constantine. In fact he was killed at night in the street. See Appendix 3.

41. Corti, *Three Dynasties*, ch. 4, p. 57.

42. Ibid., ch. 4, p. 64; Hough, *Louis and Victoria*, ch. 1, p. 6.

43. Corti, *Three Dynasties*, ch. 4, p. 65.
44. Ibid., ch. 4, p. 66.
45. Von Bülow, *Memoirs*, vol. 4, ch. 62, pp. 603–4. Confirmation of pregnancy in Corti, *Three Dynasties*, ch. 5, p. 74.
46. Conversation with the late Prince A. Clary. For details of her ancestors' occupations see Princess Marie of Battenberg, *Reminiscences*, George Allen Unwin, 1925, Preface, p. 3. See Appendix 3.
47. Hough, *Louis and Victoria*, pp. 8–9.
48. Marie of Battenberg, *Reminiscences*, ch. 1, p. 4.
49. Correspondence with Director of Darmstadt State Archives.
50. Corti, *Three Dynasties*, note 51, p. 381.
51. Ibid., ch. 4, p. 68.
52. Ibid., ch. 5, pp. 74–5.

4

I N 1854 tension increased between Russia and Turkey, while
Austria, fearful of the Tsar's intentions in Europe, remained
quiescent. A wrote in April an indiscreet letter to his uncle, Prince
Emil of Hesse, opened by the secret police, which, while expressing
sympathy for Russia, included the phrase 'I shall never draw my sword
against our erstwhile brother in arms',[1] a rash comment if he wished
for promotion, and certainly fatal had not the Austrians found it useful
to know the inner thoughts of the Tsarevitch to whom A wrote
frequently.[2] When the Crimean War broke out the Tsar bitterly
resented Austria not declaring war against Turkey, England and
France; pointing out neutrality was a poor repayment for Russia's
armed intervention in Hungary which had saved Franz Joseph's
Empire in 1848. On 11 October A went too far and wrote to his
brother-in-law: 'The deep respect that I bear to His Majesty and my
love for Russia (which I still regard as my true home) must have of
course made me look at things from exactly the same standpoint as
you do. My feelings are being subjected to severe ordeals. I am
condemned to life in a hostile camp and forced to display a half-
hearted sympathy.'[3] Such words would have destroyed any but a
privileged mercenary. As A's loyalty was now doubtful and war
with Russia a possibility (Austria had signed a treaty with
England and France),[4] a decision was made to send him to Verona,
then an outpost of the Empire, where his disloyalty would be
harmless.

On 18 February 1855 A's prospects changed dramatically. Nicholas I
died, the new Tsar at once asked Franz Joseph to send his brother-in-
law on a mission to Russia, encouraging him to believe the bleakest
part of his life was over and he would be asked to return to live there
with his family; after all, his sister was now the Tsarina. He was
disappointed. No word was spoken, but he still optimistically believed

that his family would one day be allowed to live in his adopted homeland.

The Empress Elizabeth increased his depression in Vienna by cutting him 'with infinite grace' in a public garden.[5] She looked, he wrote in his diary, 'as pretty as a picture, leading her daughter by the hand as she walked silently past'. Corti describes A's further humiliation when the imperial couple visited Verona in January 1857:

> . . . The Emperor and Empress treated [A's] wife badly. They did indeed invite her to dinner with her husband, but did not admit her to their private apartments. At dinner the Empress addressed only a few curt phrases to her, the Emperor merely inquired: 'Were you at the review this morning?' Afterwards the Emperor passed by the Countess Julia, who stood at the head of the ladies-in-waiting to speak to him, without saying a word, and began to talk to a lady-in-waiting standing next to her, the Countess Orti. 'Such rudeness', wrote Alexander indignantly in his diary, 'naturally mortified poor Julia terribly, especially since she was accustomed to the friendly gallantry with which the Tsar treated ladies.'[6]

The Emperor's visit was a vain attempt to placate his Italian subjects. Austria's position in Italy was becoming untenable due to the growth of emotional nationalism in northern Italy, stoked up by Cavour and Napoleon III,[7] working together to start a war to begin the unification of Italy. During his summer leave A, whose Heiligenberg house was conveniently situated, became his brother-in-law's intermediary and arranged a meeting between the Tsar and Napoleon III. These talks made Franz Joseph nervous and he said he would like a reconciliation with Russia. 'Evidently,' A wrote with some satisfaction to the Tsar in 1857, 'I am designed by all the emperors, your august colleagues, to act the flattering part of the Genius of Reconciliation. Here I am once again with an olive branch in my hand, and this time I am speaking in the name of the Emperor of Austria, who also requests a personal interview with you.'[8]

The change in A's status was remarkable. Two years before he had been an unwanted outcast; now he was employed by three emperors. Their choice was wise; at this stage of his life he was reliable and trustworthy if insensitive, with the ability to influence those who disagreed with him. He was of course helped by the family interests and the Austrian Emperor's desire to dispel the belief he had 'abominably and ungratefully' betrayed Russian in the Crimean War.

A's success can be judged by contemporary comments and his rewards. At Stuttgart Napoleon said, 'Adieu, my prince, and many thanks, for you brought about this meeting.'[9] After the Russian and Austrian emperors had met at Weimar, the Tsar allowed A to wear his 'Russian general' uniform again, and Franz Joseph presented him with the Grand Cross of the Order of St Leopold. But A was disappointed when he learned Napoleon had persuaded his brother-in-law to give an assurance he would keep Russian troops on the Austrian border, to ensure the retention of Franz Joseph's forces in the East which otherwise could have been used against Piedmont and France in Italy.

The Russian promise to help France horrified him; he saw Napoleon as an enemy of autocracy and a revolutionary whom it was unwise to encourage. His correspondence with the Tsar, as usual opened by the Austrian Secret Service, pleased Franz Joseph; it showed A had changed sides and was now strongly critical of the Tsar's foreign policy. The Grand Duke of Hesse also changed his opinion of A, when he learned he had the Tsar's ear, and had become a diplomatic success. To show his approval, he made Julia and her children Princes and Princesses of Battenberg in 1859.

In Italy Cavour had cemented France's support for the Piedmontese by the sacrifice of the innocent little fifteen-year-old Princess Clothilde of Sardinia, to the debauched old roué, Prince Jerome Bonaparte. The die was now cast, and A wisely sent both his valuable possessions and his family over the Alps to Darmstadt. Austria, knowing Napoleon and Cavour were only waiting for a pretext to begin a war, should have taken the initiative and attacked the French and Piedmontese before their armies joined. Instead Franz Joseph, as usual, took a long time to do the wrong thing, and sent an ultimatum to Piedmont giving Napoleon and Cavour the opportunity of arguing Austria was the aggressor. He then compounded his mistake by ensuring his commanding officer General Gyulai did nothing.

This unfortunate old soldier has been criticised by historians for his inertia, but as Franz Joseph wouldn't allow him to move, he had no alternative to sitting still. At last, after two wasted weeks, the General was allowed to send a proportion of his army forward, giving A the chance to show his bravery in a minor skirmish at Montebello. He led his men skilfully, and was made a general and given command of a division. The Tsar stood aloof and the Tsarina wrote smugly to A, his heart 'beats as always for the Austrian army'.[10] To Austria the state of Alexander's heart was irrelevant, but Franz Joseph resented the Russian troops on his eastern frontier which forced him to keep them there instead of sending them to Italy, where the French continued to advance.

A was again approached by Franz Joseph and asked to try and make the Tsar realise that if he encouraged revolution in Italy the spirit of insurrection would spread to Russia. He was doubtful about the request as he knew his brother-in-law was still resentful of Austria's behaviour in the Crimean War and would not change his mind until Franz Joseph was humiliated.[11] This did not take long as Franz Joseph dillied and dallied, ensuring Gyulai, through forced inactivity, lost his nerve and the control of his army at the defeat of Magenta. He was dismissed but it was too late; the Austrian army was defeated again at Solferino where A distinguished himself. For some unknown reason the Napoleonic victory was not as decisive as it could have been, as the routed Austrians were allowed to escape in helpless confusion over the river Minicio, the French declining to destroy them on a blocked bridge. The explanation of this odd lapse may have been a nervous telegram to Napoleon from his wife Eugénie, saying she had heard if he crossed the river, Germany would march on France. This false alarm may have made Napoleon III temporarily lose his nerve. In any case, he lost the opportunity to win a decisive victory, but his volatile mind soon regained its confidence and he continued to advance. It was a war of amateurs.

By 4 July the Tsar's pleasure at Austria's defeat was reduced by the enthusiasm with which it was – as A had warned him – greeted in liberal Russian circles. Alarmed, he sent a message to the French suggesting peace. Napoleon accepted gratefully, his army was sick and hungry, his supply lines extended and vulnerable to a German attack. He also wished to please Russia. Without a qualm he broke his solemn promises to his Italian allies and sent a letter to Franz Joseph proposing a truce. Austria finally agreed to give up Lombardy, but insisted, to Piedmont's distress, on retaining Venetia.

Napoleon could smile; he had gained Nice and Savoy for France. The French desertion broke Cavour's heart, although the decisive step towards a free Italy had been taken. Venetia became independent seven years later and the whole peninsula in 1870. While Austria was disappointed by her defeat, the war had added to A's reputation. He had fought bravely, given impartial advice and retained the respect of both sides when Franz Joseph used him as an intermediary at the peace talks. At the same time he had won the Tsar's admiration by accurately forecasting the dangers of support for France. Julia's adoration and love for her husband are touchingly shown in letters to her sister Sophia:

> HEILIGENBERG, 10th July, 1859
>
> You cannot imagine the enthusiasm for my Alexander which reigns here, and how proud they are of him. Since the armistice has been concluded. I breathe again, and hope for a re-union – but where and when? I do not know. I am consumed with excitement and impatience . . . O god, give us Peace!

> 25th July, 1859
>
> My beloved is coming back! Rejoice with me Sophie! He is in Vienna, and to-day he telegraphed that he will be in Frankfort early on Monday, and I am going to go there to meet him.
>
> The Grand Duke is preparing a splendid reception for his beloved brother – and here in our kindly Jugenheim joy and excitement reign; triumphal arches are being erected, and there are to be fireworks.

> 10th August, 1859
>
> . . . I was very proud, and yet very humble, to be sitting beside my hero, whom all were acclaiming. In Jugenheim the feeling of the people made our reception as touching as it was delightful! Our carriage literally disappeared under a rain of flowers so that we could hardly move . . .[12]

Despite her pride and affection for her husband Julia was mortified by his refusal to take her name of Battenberg when she was made a princess by the Grand Duke of Hesse at the end of the previous year.

After the peace was signed A, exhausted, planned to go to Warsaw, which was sensible; his friendship with his brother-in-law remained his best card. Hearing of his plans Franz Joseph asked him to pass through Vienna. He agreed and was asked to find out if the Tsar would agree to another conference. When A asked Alexander II if a meeting could be arranged with the Austrian Emperor he received the odd reply: 'My Austrian uniform is now in Warsaw and I've recently tried it on.' This sartorial news, when repeated, so delighted Franz Joseph that he promoted A to be a corps commander and gave him a Cross of the Order of Maria Theresa. Was this the first time that the bearer of news that a uniform had been removed from one city to another earned the informant both a medal and military advancement? The Tsar's reply raised A's stock, and made Austrian society realise it was unwise to continue to ostracise an unofficial ambassador's wife. Closed doors opened to Julia; the Verona hatchet was buried, she was invited to Schönbrunn,[13] and placed next to the Emperor. Her Austrian battle for recognition was won. Her placement was a famous victory.

A continued to stress the revolutionary nature of Napoleon's philosophy, hoping his diplomatic skill would encourage the Tsar to allow his family to return to his adopted homeland, Russia. He failed to realise his unofficial role had infuriated the Russian foreign minister, Gorcharov, who saw the pliable Tsar daily and ensured that A returned, disappointed, to his new command in Italy, only to find his promotion had made him unwelcome there.

As a German brother-in-law to the Tsar, he should have realised the Austrians would resent his advancement, but he had an irritating belief in his own rectitude, inherited by his son and grandson, which gave continual offence to the family's critics for over a hundred years. Four days after the death of Cavour, during a period of passionate mourning for the dead Italian hero, A tactlessly accepted an invitation to be the honoured guest at a large regimental celebration, and was surprised when he was accused in the Italian papers of insulting the memory of the late Italian hero. Sensitivity has never been a strong point of the German character; unfortunately it is a quality which cannot be learned.

General Benedek was also cold and unfriendly and A began to tire of life in Italy, which was not surprising as he was considered a tyrant by Venetians and was envied by his colleagues and superiors.

At the end of 1861 the Tsar, to ensure A didn't go on pestering him with requests to move back to Russia, gave him enough money to buy a palace in Darmstadt[14] and enlarge and join together his two farmhouses at Heiligenberg. In May 1862 A left Venetia for ever. Another possible reason for his resignation was the desire of Prussia to replace

Austria as the head of a unified Germany. To defend themselves from this threat the independent southern and eastern German states needed a leader. Who could be better than A, a passionate believer in the retention of the freedom of the individual, medium-sized German states?

NOTES

1. Corti, *Three Dynasties*, ch. 5, p. 77.
2. Ibid., ch. 5, p. 78.
3. Ibid., ch. 5, pp. 78–9.
4. Although Austria signed the Treaty on 2 December 1854 which infuriated Russia, she never carried out her commitments, which infuriated England and France.
5. Corti, *Three Dynasties*, ch. 6. p. 89.
6. Ibid., ch. 6, p. 90.
7. Napoleon III, with the ambition but without the genius of his legal uncle, had, after declaring himself Emperor in 1856, set out on a policy of aggrandisation. He saw his opportunity in northern Italy where Lombardy and Venice were bursting with hatred for their Austrian rulers and began to scheme with Cavour, chief minister to the King of Piedmont, to overthrow them; his price, the ceding of Nice and Savoy to France.
8. Corti, *Three Dynasties*, ch. 6, p. 95.
9. Ibid., ch. 6, p. 96.
10. Ibid., ch. 6, p. 112, quoting the Tsarina's letter to A.
11. Ibid., ch. 6, p. 112.
12. Marie of Battenberg, *Reminiscences*, pp. 12–13.
13. Corti, *Three Dynasties*, ch. 7, p. 130.
14. Ibid., ch. 7, p. 137.

5

MEANWHILE, what had happened to Julia and her children? She is a shadowy figure whose pregnancy when she married ensured the imprisonment of all but the most banal information about her early life. Her daughter's earliest memories in Italy unfavourably compare her mother's coldness with her father's charm:

> He was, and remained, the sunshine of our lives, not only in childhood, but in later life, and I cannot recall one single instant when he was other than loving, good, and kind to us. Of mamma we always stood a little in awe, because she was strict and made us speak French with her; she probably loved us all alike, but it was her habit to be always most tender with the youngest child, and I remember how we elder ones would sometimes comment upon this among ourselves. Praise from her always made a great impression on us.[1]

It is impossible for children to understand that a characteristic of their parents, which appears to them unkind or cruel, may be caused by sorrows or feelings beyond their comprehension. It is possible Julia's *froideur* to her children was caused by her love for her husband and her distress at his refusal to take her name. A kind man, it is possible he believed a change of identity would have confirmed the rumours of his illegitimacy.

Otherwise he was a loyal husband who never blamed his wife for the sacrifices he had made to marry her. At the same time he may have taken her courage for granted without comprehending her trials in the first years of their marriage. John Masefield wrote a novel, *ODTAA* – One Damn Thing after Another – and although Julia would never have used the abbreviation, the title describes the torments which nineteenth-century morality inflicted on a friendless stranger, frequently alone, often pregnant, in St Petersburg, Strasbourg, Switzerland, Austria and Italy. Fortunately she was clever and brave, but her marriage was, at the beginning, clouded by A's enforced idleness. His family carefully distanced themselves from the newly-married couple, and Julia knew her condition was responsible for the rift. Her embarrassment on arriving six months pregnant in a strange country, which had exported her husband in his youth, cannot be exaggerated. Her meeting with the 'slothful'[2] grand duke, who had tried to stop the marriage, and was planning to make her a countess and get her out of the country as soon as possible, can only have been a mortification. In Austria their banishment to Graz, where she had to keep company with a morganatic postmaster's daughter, was a further insult.

The last straw must have been when her husband decided to go alone to Russia for his sister's coronation, a decision which underlined his wife's 'inferior position'. Although she realised his visit was necessary to retain his sister and brother-in-law's affections, on which their future depended, her lonely vigil must have filled her with resentment. Until his journey they had been united by adversity; now her husband was 'recognised', while she had to remain alone in Verona, a garrison town surrounded by a hostile countryside, forbidding excursions and momentary escapes, where the dullness of life could only be mitigated by the traditional joys of confined communities: vendettas, petty quarrels, spiteful asides.

She could only have sat silent, embittered, when A, on his return after six weeks of celebrations, was asked about the magnificence of the seven-hour coronation of his brother-in-law and sister in the great church of St Peter and St Paul, and whether the Tsar had really marched 80,000 men past his wife, and if the fountains had flowed with wine and the onion domes gleamed with gold. Julia was both brave and discreet and her spirits never publicly wavered, even when A, elated by his change of circumstances, was tactless.

However, in their own home she may have shown bitterness, which encouraged him to take advantage of the new Tsar's affection and desire to use him as a diplomat. His acceptance separated them and ensured she spent more time alone. It is possible to imagine her walking lonely, pregnant, on the ramparts of Verona, avoided by the Italian nobility, who regarded her as an enemy, and the Austrian wives, over whom she claimed a precedence they were reluctant to concede. Elegant hints and conversational pauses would have told her they were aware of her forced marriage and her hasty, disgraced expulsion from Russia, while congratulations on her daughter's forwardness would have been conveyed in a manner hinting at knowledge of her premature pregnancy, an unforgivable sin, especially as her husband belonged to a semi-royal family while she could only claim as ancestors pastry cooks, tailors and pastors, professions despised by the military caste. Surely once again she relived the loneliness she had known when, after her mother and father's death she had, out of charity, been chosen as a lady-in-waiting to the late Tsarina. Such moments, despite her determination, caused iron to enter her soul, strengthening and narrowing her outlook, crushing her motherly instincts and making her determined to do all she could to ensure her children should not suffer the slights and ostracism which had blighted her life.

Her social sorrows made her decide not to burden them with her embarrassing relations, who unfortunately compounded the sin of 'unequal birth' with a passionate loyalty to Poland. She had very little Polish blood.[3] The myth often referred to her as 'von Hauke'. She was not a 'von'. Her father was made a Polish count four years before his death in 1829. Mountbatten always claimed his grandmother came from a martial family. This was partially true; Julia's grandfather Frederick Haucke [sic] was a soldier-servant-favourite of the celebrated sybarite Count Buol or 'Bruhl', (chief adviser and Svengali to Augustus II of Saxony, elected King of Poland),[4] in whose Dresden palace Frederick the Great found 800 dressing gowns, 1500 wigs and 200 pairs of shoes.[5] Haucke followed the Count from Saxony to Poland and stayed behind when his patron went home. After leaving the army he lived in Warsaw and started a pension for young men. His son, Julia's father Maurice Hauke [sic], volunteered to fight against Russia in 1794, and afterwards joined the Polish legion in Italy and fought for Napoleon at Mantua. In the Prussian campaign of 1806 he distinguished himself on the French side at the Battle of Friedland and was promoted to the rank of brigadier. His most distinguished feat was with only 3000 men holding Zamosc for a year, after the French retreat from Moscow, against 10,000 Russians. He only surrendered when provisions ran out.

In 1815 he became quartermaster in the Polish army, swore loyalty to Russia, and later became deputy minister for war. He was killed in the first hours of the nationalist insurrection against Russia of 1830. According to the *Polski Słownik Biograficzny*, (the Polish equivalent of the *Dictionary of National Biography*): General Hauke rode out with a few officers to see what was happening, and at about 8 p.m. in the main street outside the Radziwill Palace met a group of cadets who, after a brief discussion, shot both him and a colonel. Shortly afterwards his wife died, and to show appreciation of loyalty, the Tsar looked after his younger children and later made Julia a lady-in-waiting to his wife.

These pedestrian facts were not flattering enough for the Myth and the story was always retold, that *von* Hauke was killed defending the Grand Duke Constantine in front of his own wife and children.

The Hauke family originally came from Holland where they were called 'Haacken'. Afterwards they moved to Saxony where the spelling was changed to 'Haucke'. In Poland the name was finally altered to 'Hauke'. Considering the general's father's climb to affluence it is not surprising that the Myth, with its devotion to Charlemagne, avoided mentioning the family except for a few brief and inaccurate sentences about Maurice Hauke, whose fiery blood was doubtless responsible for the outstanding courage of Alexander, Sandro and Mountbatten. The snobbish neglect was ridiculous. Maurice Kazimierz Napoleon Hauke took the rebels' side on the night they killed his father. Afterwards he served with distinction in the Polish artillery, commanded the Polish legion in Tuscany, resigned, emigrated to America and died in 1852.

The next brother, Wladyslaw, also fought against Russia in 1831–2 but placed himself beyond the pale by marrying an actress in 1834. Another brother, Joseph, was killed fighting the Russians in 1831. Julia was embarrassed by her brothers' rebellious natures, and exasperated by her first cousin Josef Ludwik whom the Tsar appointed a cornet in the Red Hussars in the year she married Alexander. He fought for Russia bravely in the Caucasus and became a colonel when he was only twenty-eight. Unfortunately for Julia, he abandoned Russia in 1862, joined yet another Polish insurrection, became a successful guerrilla leader and national hero before his inevitable defeat. Years later he became a friend of Garibaldi and was given the command of the First Brigade of the Armée des Vosges which held

Burgundy against the Prussians for the Paris Commune, and was killed fighting near Dijon in 1871.[6] It would be difficult to find a more romantic career, and what idealist could hope for a finer death than to die fighting against Prussia? But at the time Julia's family's activities can only have caused her embarrassment.[7] They had to be forgotten and her children taught to belong to their father's world. Only her strong character enabled her to survive her humiliations and embarrassments.

Julia's only consolation in this time of trouble was her determination that her children should achieve material and marital success, which life had taught her were the criteria by which they would be judged. Although not an attentive mother, she and her obedient governess Adèle Bassing implanted ambitions into her sons with such fervour they became a religion, passed on by her son Louis to his son Mountbatten. It is probable the sorrows and frustrated ambitions she suffered while carrying her three elder sons entered their subconsciousness, and guided their lives.

If this is realised, the characters of A's sons and his grandson become more explicable. Mountbatten was not a free man but a prisoner of the fears and beliefs implanted in his childish mind by overheard conversations and ancestral voices, which, after the shock of his father's dismissal in 1914, could only be silenced by convincing himself it was his duty to maintain, even by manufacture and omission, the glories of the Battenbergs. Those who were later to find his conceit as unbearable as his snobbery, could not comprehend that behind his apparent certainty lay doubts and insecurities, and that his maturity was haunted by an obsessive fear of the public learning painful facts which his family pride told him must be contradicted or covered up. It is doubtful if he admitted the fears which lay below the confident surface of his public face, and made him cling for safety to his royal relations. This is understandable.

NOTES

1. Marie of Battenberg, *Reminiscences*, p. 7.
2. Mountbatten's own description. Hough, *Louis and Victoria*, ch. 1, p. 8.
3. I am indebted to Count Adam Zamoyski (member of a distinguished Polish family) who has generously given me the background and many details of the Hauke family.

4. It was the custom in Poland to choose their kings at a mass meeting of nobles.
5. Von Bülow, *Memoirs*, ch. 62, p. 603.
6. Information from Count Adam Zamoyski.
7. See Appendix 3, Members of the Hauke Family.

6

Julia's position improved in the 1860s, but she was still ignored by the King and Queen of Prussia. Despite her brother-in-law the Tsar's annual visits, I can find no trace of her visiting Russia. She was wise, as it would have stirred up unpleasant memories of the past in a country where her youthful shame was an amusing story; at home in Hesse she was safe. Luckily her eldest child, Marie, wrote in her memoirs an account of her childhood. The children were born in various countries: Marie in Strasbourg in February 1852 (the myth claimed in July on Lake Geneva),[1] Louis in Graz (Austria), 1854, Alexander (Sandro) in Verona (Italy) 1857, Henry (Liko) in Milan, 1858, and finally Franz Joseph in Padua in 1861. The next year they settled down in Hesse where the children spent their formative years. Marie was ten when the family came home, and vaguely remembered her life in Italy which she described in a germane sentence, 'I do not remember much of my parents in these years. We lived entirely to ourselves with Adèle (governess) . . .'[2] Their father must have been a rare visitor, unless he had taken leave of his senses. As Marie remembered: 'We saw papa nearly always in uniform and on horseback . . .' In Hesse they led an ordered life, spending the summer in the country and the winter, to begin with, in a wing of the old palace in Darmstadt and afterwards in the Tsar's gift, the Alexander Palace, finished in 1864. Marie had happy memories of children's dances, fancy dress balls, occasional operas, music lessons and home theatricals but again lamented 'we hardly ever saw our parents except at meal-times', and Adèle Bassing 'had the entire supervision of our nursery and schoolroom'.[3] Marie never ceased praising her father, in marked contrast to her mother whom she regarded with 'awe' and unaffectionate admiration. Even Mountbatten, dictating for some reason in the present tense, referred critically to his grandmother:

Experience of a wicked world has hardened her resolve; success has brought her new self-confidence. She shows little affection and softness towards her children and is seldom with them.[4]

In Darmstadt they had to study hard and Marie was not allowed to go for walks with her brothers.

The great occasion each year was the move to the country at the end of April. In the early 1860s Heiligenberg was still the same place A's mother had bought forty years before, to escape from her husband and bear her two youngest children. Marie in old age nostalgically described her early memories of her old home:

It stood four-square round the courtyard, in the midst of which, under the plane-trees, was a fountain. This courtyard played a great part in our family life. All the doors and windows opened on to it, and on every occasion, even the most trivial, we were to be seen there together. Heiligenberg . . . was simply a peasant's farm that belonged to a minister called Hofmann, and consisted of two little houses which lay facing one another, and were known as the 'front house' and the 'back house'. At that time the household buildings and the steward's offices completed the four sides of the courtyard, and it was only later that these were pulled down and replaced by new buildings . . . We children did not care for sitting about in the house when out of doors the birds were singing. And how we did enjoy our free hour, from ten to eleven! There was no holding us then, and, with our luncheon in our hands, we romped off to seek out our favourite places . . . I loved to slip away alone into the hazel-walk which, beginning below the gateway, wound its way into the ruins.[5]

All their pleasures were simple:

. . . though there was no lack of horses; it was considered too luxurious for us, and walking more suitable. All the intenser was our enjoyment of the farmcart party which took place every summer. Our friends were allowed to go with us, and all day long we delighted in the fun. Swaying and tumbling, we sat on the sacks which served us for seats; a peasant drove the cart, and we went merrily into the Odenwald. We had dinner either at Lichtenberg or at Rodenstein, and sometimes we met with little adventures, sudden thundershowers, or the like, and on our homeward way we sang Volkslieder, or snatched at plums from the trees as we went by.[6]

In 1864, after the house had been enlarged, A's sister the Tsarina, her family and an army of servants, paid annual series of visits. The disappointed, delicate woman, no longer loved by her husband, welcomed the simplicity of her old home in contrast to the exhausting formality of the Russian court. Her younger children were intertwined in age with Marie and her brothers and they lived happily together. The informality and friendliness of their lives is perfectly illustrated by one of their treats.

At twelve o'clock we rode donkeys to Felsberg, to show Alexander the Felsenmeer; mamma, Marie, Sergius, Alexis, our three boys, Arseneff, and Fraulein Tutshcheff. We set out in the loveliest weather, but at the foot of the Felsberg such a pelting rain came on that we arrived at the top wet to the skin, for not one of us had an umbrella. As soon as we got there all the boys were undressed and put into shirts belonging to the forester, while their clothes were taken to the kitchen to be dried. We girls, fortunately, had not got quite so wet, and so were not undressed. Then they brought us beer, coffee, and bread and cheese, and we all ate and drank just as much as ever we could, since owing to the pouring rain it was quite impossible to get back in time for our four o'clock dinner. When the rain left off a farm-cart was ordered, in which we drove home. The Tsar, the Tsarina, and all the company were already at table when we got back, and all ran out laughing into the courtyard to welcome us. It was a delightful party, and the funniest thing about it was that we never saw the object of our excursion, the Felsenmeer, at all.[7]

The children loved each other; Marie looked after them with the enthusiasm of a little mother, and made up for Julia's coldness and their father's absence. Their independence united them and they shared a comradeship not dissimilar to E. Nesbit's *Railway Children*.

In 1868, age caused the inevitable breakup; Louis, at the suggestion of the Duke of Edinburgh, went to England to prepare to join the British Navy. His mother and father had, to begin with, opposed the plan[8] but eventually gave in and allowed their son to leave home in

September with a blessing from the pastor. Marie's diary described her grief:

> The day of this dreadful separation! Over the heavy moments of farewell at Heiligenberg and at the station at Darmstadt I will draw a veil. Papa travelled with him.[9]

She came out the next year and soon obediently became engaged to an older but suitable, mediatised neighbour, Count Erbach-Schönberg, but her letters to Louis at sea only a few months before her wedding suggest her heart was more disturbed by her missing brother than her future husband. The traditional custom of marrying daughters out of the nursery ensured greater lifelong love between brothers and sisters than exists today, as those separated from their family before their childish links of pure affection had been broken, remained close to each other for their lives. At any rate Marie's letters make no bones about her passionate devotion to her brother:

> Heiligenberg, 8th October, 1870
> MY DEAREST HEART'S LOUIS,
> Now, thank God, the terrible farewell is over. However far we are from one another, our ardent love cannot on that account grow colder, and in thought I am always near you . . . And now, though our childhood is past, with its cheerful life, so free from care, in our parents' house, we still remain the old 'Puppi-Luli'. Now, I suppose, you are already on the ocean, and have left old Europe and its war behind – the only thing from which I, too, would fly. Our thoughts go with you to the New World.[10]

These are curious words for a girl to write shortly before her marriage, and suggest lukewarm feelings towards her prospective husband.

When in September 1866 Louis left Darmstadt in tears for England to prepare for his examinations in December, he was above the age at which entrants were accepted; but in his case the limit had been extended for six months or, as Mountbatten years later grandiloquently put it: 'As soon as it became known that a young German prince wanted to join the Royal Navy the well oiled cogs of privilege engaged smoothly and speedily.'[11] He was sent to a crammer run by a

Dr Burney at Alverstoke near Portsmouth. The arrangements made for the poor boy might have been planned to injure him: because of his rank Louis was not expected to mix much with the other boys and was to live with the Burney family and have his lessons in the house.[12]

The reaction of his schoolmates was predictable and the lonely, homesick boy wrote sadly home, but to his credit, despite his unhappiness, passed his exams. It is interesting to notice Louis was treated with far more favouritism than was later shown to the Dukes of Clarence and York, when they entered the Navy. The insistence by the morganatic Battenbergs on the rights of rank was caused by their awareness of the unimportance of their titles. King Edward's sons had no such doubts.

Louis's parents would have been wiser to have followed the example of Queen Victoria's close relation Prince Victor of Hohenlohe-Langenberg who also joined the British Navy but for many years called himself Count Gleichen.[13] The stupidity of his isolation at Dr Burney's was compounded when Louis was encouraged to accept an offer to serve as a midshipman on the frigate HMS *Ariadne*, which had recently been converted to carry the Prince and Princess of Wales on a tour of the Mediterranean. Before he signed on he went home, and again awoke his sister's grief:

> It was heartbreaking when his dear figure disappeared. He comes home now only as a guest. Each time we see him there is always the prospect of a parting to be endured. That's a bitter thought. Poor Sandro cried and sobbed for half an hour.[14]

Such a parting ill-prepared Louis for life aboard ship in quarters he considered 'a dark and stuffy hole'.[15] Neither had he been taught, unlike his companions, even the elementary laws of seamanship and didn't know how to 'sling a hammock, climb the rigging, or even to distinguish port from starboard'.[16] His ignorance ensured that he was an object of contemptuous attention, an agonising situation for the only German boy on a British boat. Not surprisingly, he was also disgusted by having to eat tough, salted beef and biscuits full of weevils. Ten years later the food had not improved:

> The food was appalling according to our modern standards. The biscuits, hard as bricks, were the tenement houses in which weevils

and maggots lived. Many people chewed the weevils and said they didn't taste any different from the biscuits, but some pernickity gourmands insisted on breaking their biscuits into small pieces, which they hammered on the table until the tenants fell out, and were duly executed; but the maggots were carefully removed and put into pill boxes, where they were fed and trained for the 'Maggot Derby'. This was not an annual race, but very often a daily one. The course was along the gunroom table, and the sides were lined with books to keep the racers on the proper path. The starting gate was a piece of wood across the course, behind which the maggots were arranged and kept in order by their owners. The start was made by the gate being lifted, and the owners were allowed to touch the maggots on the tail with a pencil as a whip, to start them on their way to try and win the Blue Ribbon of the 'Maggot Derby'.[17]

His diet improved when the royal party arrived; Louis was immediately asked to dinner. Later he accompanied the Prince in Cleopatrian luxury up the Nile. How could his shipmates – the senior midshipmen and the junior officers – not have resented his good fortune in frequently dining with the Prince and eating caviar, and pâté de foie gras instead of their filthy weevily rations? How could his preferential treatment not have caused hostility, accusations of royal favouritism and resentment, which his confusing double life prevented him from living down? He continued to mix with the royal party in Turkey, joined in the feast to mark the Prince's arrival in Constantinople, and afterwards rode with him into the Light Brigade's 'Valley of Death'.

As long as the royal party stayed on board the boy was protected, but at Brindisi the royal party left the *Ariadne* to travel home by train; Louis was left alone. Retribution followed. He was asked why his father and mother had different names? Why he had only been made a prince a few years earlier? His gutteral accent was mocked; he was sent aloft untrained, and terrified, and mercilessly bullied with the skill perfected in the nineteenth century by the British upper classes. The contrast with his happy childhood at Darmstadt was unbearable and he wrote home from Malta begging his father to withdraw him from the Navy.[18]

Worse was to come, on the voyage home they sailed through the Bay of Biscay: again in rough weather he was ordered into the rigging, a ghastly hazard to an unhappy, untrained boy.[19] Later he remembered, 'It was a constant terror to me.'[20] The reader may be amazed that his parents could have made such mistakes with their son and put him in a position in which he would inevitably suffer. But they were not a normal couple. His father, privately educated by General Frey, had no idea bullying was a cherished tradition in the British Navy. Julia's background on the other hand should have given her an intimate knowledge of the cruelties of upper-class adolescents.

But Adèle, the artful governess, may have persuaded Louis's mother – aware she was still fighting her war of acceptance by royal circles – that it would be a good idea if her eldest son caught the attention and won the friendship of the Prince and Princess of Wales. The plan succeeded, but Julia had unconsciously taken a tremendous risk not only by putting her son in a cruel, if privileged, position, but in allowing him, without training, to serve on a sailing ship. His career could easily have ended in disaster in the Bay of Biscay. One slip and his mother's ambitions would have been confounded. Luckily he escaped, miserable and shocked, but it was an unpleasant introduction to a naval career for a German boy helpless among adept English tormentors. His sister later wrote, 'He is the most German of us all.' This affinity with his homeland did him little good aboard the *Ariadne*.

Nor was life pleasant when the ship returned to London, where Louis found himself alone without friends. He was so unhappy he appealed in desperation to that strange mixture of kindliness and coarseness, the Prince of Wales, who, seeing he was at the end of his tether, due perhaps, to his own misguided kindness, advised him to stick it out for a bit longer![21] At the same time he arranged for him to go home on unofficial leave to Hesse. Marie at once saw how her brother had changed. 'He is far beyond his years. Already he is disillusioned about many things, which was inevitable, and the thought that soon, and for many years, he must leave us again, lies heavy on his heart.'[22]

He spent a few weeks in his beloved Germany, where he was welcomed as a hero; pride and happiness blotted out his unhappy memories.

His next posting was to the North American station where he served without the disadvantages of royal patronage. The change of scene, and perhaps a royal hint to the Admiralty of his sufferings on the *Ariadne*, caused the cessation of his torments. The life of a plain midshipman revived his love of the sea; he soon learned to climb aloft in the wildest weather; but scars remained. His initiation had made him cautious of his contemporaries and he clung to his friendship with the Prince of Wales. He never forgot his baptism by his upper-class shipmates on the *Ariadne*; his desperate plea to his parents from Malta; the shame of his rescue by the Prince in London. But despite these memories he sent his own two sons into the Navy, each believing Heiligenberg was their home, at a time when – as Mountbatten frequently pointed out – he was advocating the increase of British naval strength, believing war with Germany was inevitable. His insensitivity can be explained by the unconscious belief that the sufferings of his youth benefited his character, a common Victorian fallacy.

Two years later Sandro was sent to school as it was believed his gentleness and emotionalism made it necessary for him to leave home. The entrance of both boys to adult life was done in a manner which ensured painful experiences which affected their characters. The responsibility can only be laid at their parents' door. Until the Battenberg Archives are opened it is impossible to apportion blame, but A was always a visitor in his own household and while Julia was the stronger character, her interest in her children appeared confined to their birthdays. Adèle Bassing was the mistress of the children's fate. Did she, having already risked Louis's death to win the attention of the Prince of Wales, suggest Sandro's banishment to please Julia's ambitions, catch the Kaiser's eye and ensure her own authority remained unchallenged?

Sandro was awkward, and ten years earlier when his parents took him to Treviso they found him 'an extremely nervous child, difficult to manage'.[23] Our next glimpse of him is during swimming lessons when he was shut in a sort of 'hen coop' in a corner of the ladies' bathing pool 'where he shrieked piteously all day long'. When he was ten he solemnly gave his elder sister violin lessons. She wrote: 'he takes them very seriously, and I shall go on with them all the summer, because I believe it will be a great help to him.'[24] What a good, kind girl she must have been to suffer, for a whole summer the noise of a boy learning to play the violin.

There is no doubt Sandro's nervous sensitivity disconcerted his mother who desired her children to raise the status of her family. When in his thirteenth year he 'cried and sobbed for half an hour'[25] she decided he needed toughening up, and sent him in November 1870 to Schnepfenthal, 'the celebrated Salzmann Institute' approved by King William and Bismarck. This institution taught its pupils to believe in the Spartan-Prussian concept, that they should devote their lives to arms and the State; while the greatest glory for a German was to die for his country. Adèle may have agreed it was wise to court Prussia which since 1866 had become the dominant German power. We are given an account of Sandro's sufferings in a sad series of letters from Marie to Louis. She wrote in two styles, one unaffected, simple, the other stilted and insincere.

> I cannot let the box go without putting in a few words to you, accompanied by a piece of mignonette, whose fragrance will bring you a greeting from dear Heiligenberg.[26]

and

> This school has been chosen by our parents because it has been enormously praised by everyone on account of its strict views and good principles. There is a master for every five pupils, and there are only sixty boys altogether. The situation among the hills of Gotha must be charming.[27]

The unknown censor can only have been her mother or Adèle; one of them, was again leaning over Marie's shoulder, when she wrote her next letter:

> We have had two letters from Sandro; he seems happy and contented with his Spartan way of life, and has really no time to be homesick. He likes the Director Ausfeld very much, and the latter writes very satisfactorily of him to mamma. He is under supervision the whole day, and has an enormous amount to do, which, of course, is the best thing for him. Also that he gets no holidays is good for him, though I am afraid it will be very hard for him at Christmas.[28]

What innocent, loving young girl would have written that a beloved younger brother needed 'supervision', which was 'the best thing for him' or 'that he gets no holidays is good for him'?

But in January the truth broke out: the censor was absent:

He [Sandro] is really going through a very hard school. On Christmas Eve he had lessons till eight o'clock, and the box from home was not given him till the next day. Lessons began again on the 27th, and on New Year's Eve the entertainment (sic) took the form of a sermon. They were all so homesick that in the dormitory all night the sobbing never ceased. Sandro is pining away with homesickness. They have twenty-four degrees of cold there, and as the dormitory is unheated he cannot get warm at night and gets up in the morning frozen stiff. Moreover, he has been suffering for the last fortnight with an internal chill, so Ausfeld writes. Sandro himself never mentions a word of it; he never does complain, but his frightful homesickness is very evident . . .

Oh Luli of my heart! What a Christmas! You away on the wide ocean; Sandro unhappy at Schnepfenthal; the few of us who are left sad and melancholy under the Christmas tree but where on that evening was there joy? In the old palace it was dreadful; Uncle Karl tearful, all the children away, and sadness on every face![29]

On 25 February the censor was back again.

Poor Sandro is really passing through a hard school: now he has scarlet fever and has already been in bed three weeks . . . I must say the way he has borne the many privations and the homesickness of this very hard winter is admirable. He never complains and only speaks of what he thinks will give his parents pleasure.[30]

The last smug, ingratiating sentence suggests Adèle was the censor. Sandro's tough education was by no means exceptional; it was a nineteenth-century custom to send sensitive boys to rough schools to kill unhealthy symptoms of sensibility and artistic leanings. His sufferings lasted for three long years until his father, who loathed Prussia, decided he did not wish his son to become a military barbarian, and removed him to a more civilised academy in Saxony. For the rest of his life he suffered from insecurity and an inability to tell the truth, which affected his fortunes in later years. Were they the result of a sudden change from playing the violin to learning to be a good Prussian?

Fortunately, Liko (Henry), was no trouble; he was an 'ideal pupil', uncomplicated and unaffected by doubts or insecurity. Marie in a few words unconsciously brings him to life:

How joyously and with what a candid gaze did he meet life, as a boy, as a Schnepfenthal scholar, as cadet and Prussian officer. Among the perpetrators of merry pranks he was always foremost, full of fun and irrepressible.[31]

In other words he was a bumptious, tiresome boy.

The last child, the insignificant Franz Joseph, both in childhood and adult life, tried unsuccessfully to keep up with his more talented brothers.

Before leaving the young family, Adèle Bassing's peculiar position must be mentioned. Marie makes it perfectly plain she was influenced by her dominating governess, who stopped her going to parties unless she was asked as well, which was seldom as she was not, alas, a 'von Bassing'. Marie loyally praises her parents for putting up with their governess's vagaries. The memoirs suggest Julia wished to devote herself to her husband, and filled with ambition rather than motherly love, was willing to leave her children's upbringing to Adèle, confident she could turn them in the desired direction when it was necessary. She was right; Julia always influenced, and sometimes controlled, her children's lives. Adèle suffered the fate of her profession.

Marie's marriage was a sad affair. A gay, beautiful girl, she wrote lively, spontaneous diaries until she married, after which her husband's dullness deadened her recollections. Doubtless he was worthy and estimable, but there is no hint, in his wife's loyal memoirs of a shadow of a sense of humour. Gradually he snuffed the gaiety out of his pretty young wife. The charming girl who had spent her youth loving her younger brothers, became a tedious *hausfrau*, the second part of whose memoirs Cecil Beaton used as one of the sources of his mockery of German royalty in *My Royal Past*.[32]

NOTES
1. Marie of Battenberg, *Reminiscences*, pp. 7–8.
2. Ibid. pp. 7–8.
3. Ibid., pp. 7–9.
4. Hough, *Louis and Victoria*, ch. 1, p. 13.

5. Marie of Battenberg, *Reminiscences*, pp. 33–4.
6. Ibid., pp. 36–7.
7. Ibid., p. 47.
8. Mark Kerr, *Prince Louis of Battenberg*, Longmans, 1934, ch. 1, p. 7.
9. Marie of Battenberg, *Reminiscences*, p. 115.
10. Ibid., p. 144.
11. Hough, *Louis and Victoria*, ch. 3, p. 58.
12. Ibid., ch. 3, p. 69.
13. Sir Frederick Ponsonby, (Lord Sysonby) *Recollections of Three Reigns*, Eyre and Spottiswoode, 1951, p. 40.
14. Marie of Battenberg, *Reminiscences*, ch. 2, p. 11.
15. Kerr, *Battenberg*, ch. 2, p. 11.
16. Hough, *Louis and Victoria*, ch. 3, p. 62.
17. Kerr, *Battenberg*, pp. 12–13.
18. Hough, *Louis and Victoria*, ch. 3, p. 66.
19. Ibid.
20. Ibid.
21. Ibid., ch. 3, p. 66.
22. Marie of Battenberg, *Reminiscences*, p. 121.
23. Ibid., p. 15.
24. Ibid., p. 83.
25. Ibid., p. 120.
26. Ibid., p. 144.
27. Ibid., p. 145.
28. Ibid., p. 146.
29. Ibid., p. 146.
30. Ibid., p. 148.
31. Ibid., p. 33.
32. Information from the late Cecil Beaton.

7

A continued to be the Tsar's unofficial adviser and ambassador, until in 1866 events brought his career to an end, and made him for the rest of his life a frustrated spectator, instead of actor in the drama of European politics. Bismarck was responsible by goading Franz Joseph into declaring war on Prussia. Austria was supported by many of the medium-sized states, including Hesse-Darmstadt and a reluctant Baden, who preferred independence to absorption into Prussia, against whom they pledged their untrained armies. A was given command of the forces of Hesse, Baden and Württemberg. This was an impossible task as neither the soldiers nor their rulers wished to leave their own territory or to fight. The war was finished before they had stopped arguing; Prussia had defeated Austria at Königgrätz.

This decisive battle marked the second stage of Bismarck's consolidation of the German empire. His plans to create an empire began with his skilful entanglement of Austria with Schleswig-Holstein and ended with the defeat of Napoleon at Sedan. The battle of Königgrätz was a 'near-run thing'. Austria fought heroically and might have won if one of their manufacturers had not, a few years earlier, invented the breech-loading rifle, and if Franz Joseph's soldiers and not the Prussians, had been re-armed with it. The advantage to men who could quickly reload lying down, over opponents forced to stand up and methodically push powder and shot down their barrels, was one of the factors which changed the history of Europe, at any rate for a few years.

Another was the indecision of Russia and the conflicting desires of the Tsar, who hoped at the same time to see Austria taught a lesson for disloyalty in the Crimean War, and Prussia contained within her boundaries. When at last he realised the impossibility of this ideal he allowed his ministers to order troops to move towards the Prussian frontier. It was too late: Königgrätz was already lost. Had he given the order earlier the Crown Prince's men would have stayed in Prussia defending the eastern border, and could not have joined his father's army at a decisive moment. But in the long run a momentary check would have made little difference. Prussia had become an obedient, organised state, whose perfectly trained army moved with precision and speed under professional soldiers, promoted on merit. Austria remained buried in the past, relying on a charming aristocracy who lacked the new professionalism necessary to win nineteenth-century wars.

After the tragic death of Schwarzenberg, Franz Joseph had no statesmen to compete with Bismarck, who embodied the Prussians' hundred-year-old desire for conquest, and the triumph of order and military rule over the divided German federation. Frederick the Great had shown the way by utilising his soldiers' hereditary desire to sacrifice life and liberty at the orders of any strong leader. After Bismarck came to power it was merely a matter of time before efficiency overcame confusion. He was wholly motivated by personal ambition, despising, like Frederick the Great, his fellow countrymen.

This contradictory genius, the opposite of the ideal, obedient vassals with which he planned to populate Germany, was, despite his appearance, a sensitive, independent boy, who tried to evade military service, and loathed the idea of becoming a junior officer. A letter which he wrote as a young man to his friend Hans von Kleist-Retzow shows the depths of his sensitive, unJunkerlike mind:

The chief weapon with which evil assails me is not desire for external glory but a brutish sensuality, which leads me so close to the greatest sins that at times I doubt whether I shall ever gain access to God's mercy. At any rate, I am sure that the seed of God's word has not found fertile ground in my heart, laid waste as it has been from the days of my youth. Were it otherwise I could not be, as I am, the plaything of a temptation which even invades my moments of prayer. Whenever I am alone and unoccupied I have to struggle against visions of an abyss, the product of a depraved fantasy which leaps with astonishing agility from the consoling image of Him who suffered for our sins to new sinful thoughts ... I am often in hopeless despair over the ineffectiveness of my prayers. Comfort me, Hans, but burn this without speaking of it to anyone.[1]

His strongest weapon was his persuasive charm – not a Prussian characteristic – which few could resist, and his overwhelming personality. These qualities, allied to patience, ruthlessness and farsightedness, put him beyond comparison with his contemporaries.

The events which followed the victory of Königgrätz illustrated his genius. King William of Prussia, his blood up, supported von Moltke's plan to advance into Austria, crush the enemy and quarter Prussian troops in a demoralised Vienna. Bismarck disagreed and argued half the night after the battle, and for the next few days for clemency. The liberal Crown Prince was his only ally. The King and General Staff at first derided his simple argument that as north Germany had fallen into Prussian hands, the absorption of the remainder of the states was only a matter of time.

A decisive victory had been won; it was wise to pause, look ahead and understand if Austria was humiliated the new German empire would lie without an ally between the antagonistic states of France and Russia. What folly to create a third enemy in Austria when by generosity her friendship could be retained! This argument infuriated the vainglorious, weak King, who saw himself as a German Caesar riding into Vienna, his triumphant legions marching behind him. Eventually the power of Bismarck's personality overwhelmed his superiors and made them understand that in sparing Vienna he was playing a tactical game, not showing weakness to a beaten enemy.[2]

A immediately understood the effect the victory would have on his own career. It ensured the fragmented independent German states would be absorbed into Prussia and he would lose his independent position and cease to be an intermediary between friendly emperors. Bismarck's new empire had taken Austria's place as the leading German power, and *Realpolitik* replaced the aristocratic, diplomatic games of old Europe. A, with his old-fashioned pride, would not bow down to Bismarck – once when he met him he remarked condescendingly: 'I have not seen you for years.' He would not meet the King of Prussia either. These insults the Chancellor never forgot or forgave, and marked down not only A, but also his wife and family, as enemies to be destroyed. Fearless in battle, but filled with secret doubts, the great Chancellor saw every talented man who disagreed with him as a possible rival.

Unfortunately, at the same time A's brother-in-law the Tsar consummated his love for the beautiful Princess Dolgoruki. Her year-long resistance had driven the spoiled autocrat, used to obedient sub-missions, half-mad with frustration, and when at last she submitted the unexpected occurred; his love increased and for the rest of his life he elbowed the Tsarina quietly out of the way, to end her days in an upper storey of the Winter Palace, exactly above the apartment where she could hear her husband, his mistress and children talking and laughing. The Tsar's behaviour to his wife upset his brother-in-law. The winter of 1866 showed how their relationship had changed. In the spring A had been asked to accompany the Tsar to the World Exhibition in Paris, but when the time came the lover naturally wished to take his new mistress instead of his brother-in-law. Like all weak men he escaped from his commitment by avoiding mentioning the subject, and afterwards, ceased to use A as an unofficial ambassador and only occasionally sought his advice. With imperial tactlessness, he continued annually to visit him at Heiligenberg, bringing his wife and family, who amused themselves by dabbling in spiritualism. Besotted, he brought Princess Dolgoruki with him, housed her nearby so they could go for walks together. Unfortunately, the Tsar's young mistress resembled his niece Marie of Battenberg. The two were confused. Marie learned the dreadful truth and wrote years later: '. . . then something died in me.'[3] Despite this youthful blow she lived another fifty years.

A was comparatively young – only forty-three – when semi-retirement was forced on him. Naturally hardworking he missed the excitement of army and diplomatic life and looked back nostalgically to his past. He tried making money and once fell out with the Tsar by involving himself with Princess Dolgoruki's brother in a dubious transaction in Russian railway shares, a symptom of his decline. He visited Austria, Russia and England, which increased his melancholy by reminding him of his changed circumstances. He came to realise he had to live more and more through his children; luckily Louis and Liko by wise marriages fulfilled his wife's ambitions, which he gradually accepted as his own.

In 1875 A described himself as an old, dismantled hulk. This was an exaggeration. He was only fifty-two and was still a friend, if not a confidant, of the Tsar, Franz Joseph and Queen Victoria, who had admired him since their first meeting. The Queen's affection for the Battenberg family increased when her granddaughter Victoria of Hesse married her cousin A's son Louis in 1874, and despite her original fury, the ties were strengthened when her youngest daughter Beatrix married another of A's sons, Liko, at Whippingham, in the following year. Afterwards she considered the Battenbergs as part of the royal family, which added to the esteem in which A was held in England and West Germany.

Today he is a forgotten figure, occasionally mentioned in relation to his son. The publication of his hidden diary and letters would correct this error. He was an important 'reporter' for years of the inner circle of European affairs. Until his diaries are available it is only possible to generalise about his abilities. Of course he had faults and enemies, but the admiration felt for him by such diverse personalities as the peasants of Hesse, Napoleon III and Queen Victoria show his worth. Even von Bülow, who disliked the Battenbergs, stresses A's natural nobility, and when you consider his bravery in the Caucasus, and later at Montebello and Solferino, and the diplomatic honesty which won him the confidence of three emperors, it is possible to forget his tactlessness and the dishonourable role he played in the election of his son as Prince of Bulgaria. He passed on to his children and grandchildren the gift of leadership and the ability to inspire and convince. His brightest hour lay in his youth; his romance with Julia is the noble story of a young man who sacrificed high rank and a large fortune to save the honour of a lowly bred, pregnant girl.

To hide the frequently published facts of his birth and his splendid romance is bourgeois, unnecessary and prevents a wider appreciation of his character. Especially as today Julia has had the last laugh: her descendants are the heir to, and the king of, the two most important remaining thrones in Europe: England and Spain. The descendants of her enemies the Emperors of Russia, Austria, and Germany, have been scattered throneless, by the four winds.

NOTES
1. This suppressed passage is in Leonhard von Muralt, *Bismarck's Verantwortlichkeit*, Gottingen, 1935, pp. 89–90. Cited by Edward Crankshaw, *Bismarck*, Macmillan, 1981, pp. 72–3.
2. Crankshaw, *Bismarck*, ch. 13, pp. 216–18.
3. Marie of Battenberg, *Reminiscences*, p. 175.

8

I will write about the adult life of A's and Julia's children in the order of their deaths, not births, and begin with their second son Alexander who, to avoid confusion with two Tsars and his father, I shall call Sandro, a contentious figure in Europe when his elder brother Louis was still a junior British naval officer. Although he became a ruling prince, the highest rank reached by any male member of his family, the Kaiser's refusal to accept him as a brother-in-law underlined the inescapable fact that the Battenbergs, as 'morganatics', stood outside the magic inner circle of imperial Europe. Queen Victoria, after Alexander II's death, was the lone royal supporter of the family's ambitions.

Sandro, having survived the terrifying Schnepfenthal, turned into a dashing, good-looking young man but found service in the Hessian dragoons a cul-de-sac. It is probable that his father, aware of the limited opportunities available to a Hessian officer in peacetime, spoke to his sister the Tsarina; early in 1876 Sandro was offered and accepted with delight an invitation from his uncle the Tsar to join the Russian army. He received a friendly welcome in St Petersburg. A year later Russia declared war on Turkey. To explain why, it is necessary to give a short description of 'the Bulgarian question'.

The ethnic Bulgaria was and is an indefinable area. The original empire in the ninth century spread from the Black Sea to the Adriatic. Diminution, change and confusion followed, and at the end of the fifteenth century the Balkans became discontented but helpless provinces of the Ottoman Empire. The scattered Bulgars, after centuries of oppression, saw the chance of deliverance during the Russo-Turkish War of 1829. This hope soon faded and they remained subjects of the Sultan for another forty-seven rebellious years which ended in a general uprising on 2 May 1876 (new calendar). This was, as usual, put down by the Turks' traditional method of quietening discontent –

massacring dissidents. To their amazement this custom, which they had practised for hundreds of years without arousing the slightest interest in the outside world, caused feverish excitement in Britain, which after a long period of peace was bursting with Christian patriotism.

The massacres were originally mentioned by the *Spectator* on 3 June. Three weeks later the *Daily News* published a detailed account of the numbers of Bulgarians killed and quoting gruesome examples of Turkish brutality. As Disraeli believed it was necessary to maintain the Turkish Empire to contain Russia, he denied both reports. On 31 July 1826, while admitting a number of deaths, he dismissed accounts of Turkish barbarism as 'babble'. He soon had to eat his words when the atrocities were confirmed by reliable sources, and in August the *Daily News* published authentic details of the massacre in Batak, which caused such indignation that public opinion forced the government to appoint an investigator, an under-secretary at the Embassy in Constantinople, Mr Walter Baring, whose report was an unpleasant surprise.'[1] His description of Batak as 'the valley of the shadow of death' and the massacre as 'perhaps the most heinous crime that has stained the history of the present century' was not what his superiors had expected or desired.

Turkish nomenclature helped. It's impossible to imagine a more barbaric name for their irregular mounted troops than 'Bashibazouks'. The name 'Pomaks' suggests daggers rather than tribesmen. What could roll better off a liberal tongue than 'the massacre of fifteen thousand men, women and children by Achmet Aga at Batak'? With such names to play with the protestors, who had never been within hundreds of miles of the Balkans, had only to open their mouths to become orators. Lady Strangford,[2] one of those extraordinary, tiresome, enquiring Victorian women of limitless courage, went to Bulgaria and confirmed the slaughter. How many Bulgars were killed is difficult to say; claims varied from thirty to a hundred thousand. The Turks admitted to killing six thousand. The atrocities came at a time when educational reforms had altered the British class structure, and created an educated, moral, lower middle class, disgusted by barbarism. Sympathy for these unknown hillmen formerly regarded, if they were regarded at all, as bandits swept through the country. The Bulgarians were presented by the British press and the churches as the successors of our own spiritual ancestors who had died for their faith, crunched by the jaws of lions in the Colosseum (a popular subject with Victorian printers). No man could have relished the situation more than Gladstone. Disraeli was pro-Turkish, was he? Well, intelligent Christian voters must realise their Prime Minister was allying them to infidels and torturers! The Liberal leader published two tracts in the late summer of 1876 written in magnificent, if bizarre, Victorian, baroque English. What could be more amazing than his thundered belief[3] that 'there was not a criminal in a European gaol nor a cannibal in the South Sea Islands who was not horrified at the events in Bulgaria'. Oratory overwhelmed doubters and his peroration swept round the civilised world:

> Let the Turks now carry away their abuses in the only possible manner, namely by carrying off themselves. Their Zaptichs and their Mudirs, their Bimbashis and their Yuzbashis, their Kaimakams and their Pashas, one and all, bag and baggage, shall I hope clear out from the province they have desolated and profaned.[4]

What particularly pleased Gladstone, often surprisingly frank about his own hypocrisy, was the satisfaction of having both good and God on his side, and early in 1877 he wrote: 'Good ends can barely be achieved in politics without passion; and there is now for the first time for a good many years a virtuous passion.'[5] Wallowing in righteous indignation he told the House of Commons in May 1877:

> ... the 5,000,000 Bulgarians, cowed and beaten down to the ground, hardly venturing to look upward even to their Father in heaven, have extended their hands to you; they have sent you this petition, they have prayed for your help and protection. They have told you that they do not seek alliance with Russia, or with any foreign power, but that they seek to be delivered from an intolerable burden of woe and shame. That burden of woe and shame – the greatest that exists on God's earth – is one that we thought united Europe was about to remove; but to removing which, for the present, you seem to have no efficacious means of offering even the smallest practical contribution . . . I believe, for one, that the knell of Turkish tyranny in these provinces has sounded.[6]

That '5,000,000 Bulgarians' were extending 'their hands to you' and 'have prayed for your help and attention' would have amazed the supposed supplicants in their mountain fastnesses, as the majority of them had undoubtedly never heard of England. But the massacres stirred the muscular Christianity of England, and pushed Europe into a conference of the powers at Constantinople which suggested the Turks reformed their colonial habits. The Sultan of Turkey, Abdul Hamid, believing Disraeli was his friend, rejected such a ridiculous idea. Russia – moved by Pan Slavism and stirred by the historic dream of entering Constantinople – secured the neutrality of Prussia and a reluctant Austria by offering the bribe of Bosnia and Herzogovina, and embarked on a holy war.

As usual the Tsar's generals proved hopelessly incompetent (fortunately for them the Turkish army had even worse leaders)[7] and sent their private soldiers, practically slaves even after emancipation, to die like courageous flies. Despite initial losses it was believed the Russians were invincible, and that the corrupt Turks would soon suffer an overwhelming defeat. Suddenly things went wrong. The invading army, ill-supplied, ill-led, diseased, was held up for five months by Osman Pasha at Plevna, a defence which caused public opinion to change in Britain and Turkey to become an underdog hero. But when starvation at last forced the garrison to surrender, the war was over and the Tsar's army marched towards Constantinople.

This frightened England, and especially Austria, whose troop movements ostentatiously threatened the Russian flank. For the rest of his life Alexander II blamed Franz Joseph for his defeat, forgetting his soldiers were sick and exhausted, his Treasury empty, and that the British fleet had sailed into the Black Sea to prevent his advance on Constantinople.[8] Faced with a European war he could not win, his generals had no alternative but to halt in sight of their Eldorado.

The approach of the vast army of wild men from the north terrified the Sultan and his subjects, and the Turks quickly signed a peace at San Stefano, accepting the creation of a free Bulgaria, paying tribute to Turkey but ruled by a Christian government. The treaty caused dismay, and a wave of anti-Russian feeling swept through Britain, encouraged by fears that the Russian advance on Constantinople was part of a sinister plan by the Tsar to control the Suez Canal and conquer India. After all, as fiery British patriots pointed out, the Russian Empire was extending year by year, along the borders of

Persia and Afghanistan, towards Pamir and the northern frontier. These fears were colloquially expressed in a widely read pamphlet which began:

> The Eastern ogre commanded the southern entrance to Squire Romanov's estate. If the eastern ogre was killed Squire Romanov might get his gateway into his own hands and there would be no living beside him![9]

The public were impressed, and indeed the belief was not unreasonable as many Russian generals held the same view and believed that India could and should be brought under Russian rule.

Gladstone, to his amazement, found himself suddenly unpopular, and could rally only ninety Liberals to support him in the House of Commons when Disraeli proposed preparations for war, while the country sang:

> We don't want to fight
> but by jingo if we do
> we've got the men, we've got the guns
> we've got the money too.

An English journalist recalled in his old age the intensity of British feeling:

> I remember well the crowd of 70,000 or thereabouts that came together in Hyde Park one day when jingoism was at its height to protest against the Treaty of San Stefano. They shouted and sang, to their heart's content, 'The Russians shall not have Constantinople . . .' and in the exuberance of their spirits hurled dead cats and other objects high in the air. Prince Teck, as he was then called, was 'bonneted' in mistake for Schouvalov (the Russian Ambassador) but soon recognized and cheered, his battered hat brushed and handed back to him with profuse apologies.[10]

Arguments were bitter. A twentieth-century historian describes the passionate outbreak of British patriotism:

> When Plevna fell, and the Russians pressed forward in their headlong advance across the Balkans towards Constantinople, war fever

in England mounted to a new pitch. The very foundations of 'British interests' seemed to be in jeopardy. The British Empire in India would crack, perhaps crumble, when Russian troops stepped through the city walls of Constantinople. To prevent such disaster, and infinitely preferable, England must enter the war, to rescue the Sultan and his Empire, to drive back the Czar and his Cossack hordes. Thus spoke the 'war' party: the question was simple, war or no war, for Turkey against Russia, and the answer was easy – yes, with fervour. Any other response was base treachery to country, Queen and Empire.[11]

As usual in times of patriotic fervour, rudeness flourished. The Duke of Sutherland, who sponsored the Stafford House Committee to help wounded Turkish soldiers, accused Gladstone of being 'Russia's principal agent in England'. The editor of *Vanity Fair* was more personal; he remembered: '. . . years ago it was pointed out in these columns that Mr Gladstone had never been considered a gentleman by Society.'[12] Disraeli said of his great rival: 'The Right Honourable gentleman is almost a Bulgarian atrocity himself.' (The phrase has been variously remembered.)

The Liberal leader had his champion, E. A. Freeman, a Turco-loather who, when the Queen dined with Disraeli, wrote of her 'going ostentatiously to eat with Disraeli in his ghetto'. Nevertheless the patriotic mob and the conservative leaders – 'the toughs and the toffs' – were in the majority, and when a 'peace' party gathered to hear Mr Auberon Herbert address a meeting outside Apsley House, the speaker had his trousers pulled off and was nearly ducked in the Serpentine. Triumphant, the mob moved on to Mr Gladstone's house and broke his windows.[13]

The Austrian Emperor and his advisers were equally determined not to accept a peace, which established a powerful new Russo-influenced country on their southern border. As the likelihood of war increased the Tsar had to be persuaded by his generals that his army was not in a condition to fight England and Austria. The Russian Commander-in-Chief, the Grand Duke Nicholas, was emphatic: 'It would be impossible to save the sick, let alone the guns.' Furiously facing the inevitable the Tsar ordered Count Schouvalov to ask Bismarck to arrange a conference of the great powers.[14]

The idea pleased the German Chancellor who saw an opportunity of salvaging his policy of peaceful cooperation between the three empires of Austria, Germany and Russia. He suggested a congress in Berlin, which decided the Treaty of San Stefano should be rewritten.

The representatives then proceeded to carve up the newly conceived Bulgarian state without consideration for the desires of its inhabitants. Territory was whittled away; Rumania and Serbia took slices; Macedonia was returned to the Turks. Eventually only a reduced northern half of the originally conceived state remained; even this remnant had to recognise the Sultan's authority.

The southern, lopped-off half, called Eastern Roumelia, was given a Christian government and a Bulgarian-Greek governor who had instructions to obey Turkish orders. Disraeli, his foreign secretary Lord Salisbury, and Austria made the mistake of believing Bulgaria wished to become a province of the Tsar and provide Russia with a foothold in Europe. The opposite was the case; the new country was fiercely tribalistic and the last thing it wanted was to exchange the brutality of the Turks for the corrupt inefficiency of the Russians, whose advisers remained to help the selected ruler. The Treaty also ensured Bulgaria should be ruled by a Prince, excluding members of the reigning royal families of Germany, the United Kingdom, Austria, Italy or Russia, 'freely elected by the population, and confirmed by the Sublime Porte (Turkey) with the assent of the Powers'.[15]

Meanwhile, to confuse the Bulgarians, the territory was to be temporarily administered by a Russian commission backed by 50,000 troops, who were to be helped – no one explained how – by the Turks and the western powers, who had no troops in the country.

Satisfied, the delegates withdrew, leaving Russia furious at the disestablishment of a united Bulgaria, but retaining her gains in the Caucasus and Bessarabia. Disraeli received Cyprus as a new British colony, propped up Turkey and made the first inaccurate claim to have brought 'peace with honour' back from Berlin. On the other hand the artificially divided Bulgaria was left bitter and angry.

The Tsar agreed to withdraw what was left of the fever-decimated Russian army from the outskirts of Constantinople and to search for a prince to sit on the Bulgarian bonfire. The absurdity of the Congress treating Bulgaria and Eastern Roumelia as civilised powers can be judged by the crisis which arose over the headgear worn by Prince Alexander Vogorides,[16] the first governor, on his entrance into the Eastern Roumelian capital in May 1879:

His appearance there had been preceded by a discussion which in itself may seem trivial enough, but to which considerable importance was attached on both sides. The question was as to whether he should wear a Turkish fez or a European hat. The fez was construed by the Eastern Roumelians as a symbol of Turkish rule and Mohammedan predominance, and was therefore detested with a cordiality which bordered on fanaticism, if it did not actually overpass those limits. For the very same reason, the Turkish Government was naturally disinclined to give up that which the other side professed to regard as an evidence of the Porte's supremacy. The matter was debated with considerable animation; but the authorities at Constantinople insisted that, as Aleko Pasha was not an independent prince, but an Ottoman official, he must wear what it is customary for Ottoman officials to wear, and not a species of head-gear which it was plainly intimated would be used as a sign of disloyalty and insubordination. When, however, the Governor-General arrived at Philippopolis, it was found that he was wearing neither the fez nor an ordinary European hat, but the Bulgarian *kalpak*, or sheepskin cap. The Porte afterwards informed the Powers that the action of the Prince in thus substituting the kalpak for the fez was a violation of engagements previously entered into by him; and it was intimated that Aleko Pasha would be formally summoned to wear the fez, and to hoist the Turkish flag on the Government House, on pain of dismissal, combined with the sending of Ottoman troops into the province.[17]

NOTES

1. Stanley G. Evans, *Short History of Bulgaria*, Laurence Wishart, 1960, ch. 4, pp. 115–20.
2. See Valentine Baker's *Pasha's War in Bulgaria*, Sampson, Low Searle and Rivington, 2 vols, 1879. For description of this adventurous tiresome woman, vol. 2, pp. 12–13 etc.; Dorothy Anderson, *The Balkan Volunteers*, Hutchinson, 1968, continuous references.
3. William Ewart Gladstone, *Bulgarian Horrors and the Eastern Question*, 1876.
4. John Morley, *The Life of W. E. Gladstone*, vol. 2, Macmillan, 1906, book 7, ch. 8, pp. 159–62.
5. Evans, *Bulgaria*, ch. 4, p. 116.
6. House of Commons, 7 May 1877.
7. See Baker, *War in Bulgaria*.

8. Count Schouvalov (Russian Foreign Minister) quoted by J. F. Badderley, *Russia in the Eighties*, Longmans, 1921, pp. 368–9; Moneypenny and Buckle, *Disraeli*, vol 6, p. 190.

9. Evans, *Bulgaria*, ch. 4, p. 121.

10. Badderley, *Russia in the Eighties*, p. 2, 'Prince (Francis of) Teck', a penniless Württemberg morganatic, was the father of Queen Mary, the Marquis of Cambridge and the Earl of Athlone. On one occasion he had to escape to Florence to avoid his creditors.

11. Anderson, *The Balkan Volunteers*, ch. 15, p. 185.

12. Ibid., ch. 15, pp. 185–8.

13. Ibid.

14. Badderley, *Russia in the Eighties*, pp. 368–9.

15. English translation of the Treaty written in French in Evans, *A Short History of Bulgaria*, p. 115. Full French text, B. A. Sumner, *Russia and the Balkans 1870–80*, O.U.P., 1937.

16. A Bulgarian-Greek usually called 'Aleko Pasha'.

17. *Cassell's History of the Russo-Turkish War 1879–1880* vol. 2, p. 515.

9

SANDRO had distinguished himself in the war by fighting bravely; he had also tactlessly followed in his father's footsteps by writing indiscreet letters, deploring the organisation and leadership of the Russian army. Unfortunately he had seen the Tsar, at Plevna, gallop away at a false alarm, leaving King Carol of Romania to conduct the siege. His early idealism had been destroyed by the cruelty of the Bulgars who to his surprise excelled their late masters the Turks in this art.

After Plevna the Tsar rushed back to his mistress, Princess Dolgoruki, in St Petersburg, leaving his army to advance to the gates of Constantinople. Sandro, hearing his brother Louis was serving on board the Duke of Edinburgh's[1] ship HMS *Sultan*, recently returned from checking the Russian advance along the Black Sea, rode, with the insensitive tactlessness which went with Battenberg courage, into the Turkish capital to find him, although he must have known Britain and Russia were on the verge of war.

It is easy to imagine the amazement and alarm his presence in Russian uniform created in a city trembling with oriental fear. A huge crowd gathered and Sandro was forced to hide in the German Embassy. Louis soon heard of his arrival and rushed deliriously ashore, with an invitation to dine at sea with the Duke of Edinburgh[2] from whom he received an equally warm welcome. It never seemed to occur to either of the brothers or the Duke that it was odd for officers in the armed forces of countries on bad terms to meet together and discuss their joint – in the case of Louis and the Duke traitorous – sympathies. Sandro wrote to his parents describing their beliefs:

> A small boat very soon brought us to the *Sultan*, where I was received by Alfred and the whole ship's company with *extraordinary friendliness* . . . they all feel more Russian than the Russians, and make no secret of it.[3]

Later the brothers boarded the *Temeraire*, one of the newest 'secret' ships in the fleet, and dined with the Admiral, Sir Geoffrey Phipps-Hornby. The next day, as if above partisanship, they left for the Russian camp, where Sandro tactlessly took Louis to see the Turkish prisoners of war, as if they were animals in a zoo. The episode infuriated the British Ambassador who telegraphed an excitable report to London saying the young Battenbergs had endangered the peace negotiations; he did not say how. The Queen at once wrote an angry letter to the Duke of Edinburgh, whom she had never liked:

Alexander Battenberg may be very discreet & no doubt is very honourable, but *how* can *you* think that the *officers* & *men* of our Navy and in the Fleet of which you are a Captain will *ever believe* that the *important secrets* will not be divulged? Anyhow, will they ever trust you & Louis Battenberg? I own I should hardly believe you *capable* of such imprudence & want of (to say the least) discretion.[4]

The Queen's fury soon subsided. The British Ambassador was reprimanded for exaggeration, but meanwhile Phipps-Hornby had moved Louis to another ship. Sandro, upset, wrote to his Aunt the Tsarina, lamenting his brother's and the Duke of Edinburgh's humiliation. She replied, and in Billingsgate language described Queen Victoria as 'a crazy old hag'.[5] The 'hag' wrote in a more dignified manner to her eldest daughter in Germany:

Alas! you will share my sorrow and indignation when you hear that Affie has got into a sad scrape – which will I fear injure his future prospects in his profession. It is very terrible to have no sense of duty, no tact and I must add no sense of honour, but he never had. It was only yesterday that I heard the distressing circumstances, of which I will tell you more in a day or two![6]

1878 was a bad year for the Battenberg family. On top of the Queen's anger with Louis and Sandro, Julia annoyed Alice of Hesse by introducing a pretty, unmediatised woman, Caroline Willich,[7] to her brother-in-law Henry of Hesse. The two fell in love and wished to marry. Alice, the self-styled republican, dropped her liberal views when her brother-in-law was concerned and objected to an unsuitable union. That the Battenbergs, intent on advancement, should arouse in one year the irritation of both the Queen of England and one of her daughters was a considerable set-back, but a stroke of good fortune soon changed their luck. The Congress of Berlin had created a new Bulgarian princedom and A, encouraged by his wife, tested the water to see if the Tsar could give him this new demi-throne. Sadly he found Julia was unacceptable to the great powers. Changing his tactics he pushed forward his twenty-two-year-old son Sandro, in spite of the Tsarina considering him unsuitable. A argued, he was '. . . a favourite nephew of the Czar, the son of an Austrian general, closely connected with Russia through the campaign of 1877 and yet not a Russian'. His choice appeared to be not only a gesture to Beaconsfield, a compliment to Bismarck and an act of courtesy to Austria, but at the same time to promise delivery of a weak tool into Russian hands.[8]

By assuring him Sandro would be an ideal puppet prince A won over the Tsar and Giers, the Russian foreign secretary, to his son's cause despite the Tsarina's doubts. But he had to convince the Tsarevitch who wanted his brother-in-law Prince Waldemar of Denmark, who he said would work harder for Russia than 'the German' as he contemptuously called Sandro.[9] A insisted his son, who had fought for Bulgarian independence, was the best loyal candidate imaginable. This argument was intended to deceive the Tsar by pretending Sandro was a strong supporter of Russian supremacy in Bulgaria, when he was at the same time taking an anti-Russian line in England:

> Britain was at first somewhat suspicious; but there again Prince Alexander of Hesse was able to use the ties of relationship between his house and the Royal Family, for his nephew, Grand Duke Ludwig IV of Hesse, who had been ruling sovereign since 1877, was married to Princess Alice, Queen Victoria's daughter. Through this channel and through his son, [Louis] who was serving in the Royal Navy, Alexander succeeded in allaying all suspicions.[10]

Any doubts about A's double dealings are swept away by a letter written by the Grand Duke of Hesse:

The Grand Duke of Hesse to [his mother-in-law] Queen Victoria
> DARMSTADT, 8th May 1879
> DEAREST MAMA On my return I found the newly elected Prince

The main front of the Chateau Le Grancy near Lausanne, the home of the presumed ancestors of Prince Alexander of Hesse, his sister Marie, Empress of Russia, and all the Battenbergs.

Prince Alexander of Hesse and his wife Julia Hauke. He was forced to leave Russia to marry her. She was refused the right to call herself a Princess of Hesse and was created Countess, and later Princess, of Battenberg.

Tsar Alexander II of Russia (1818–1881). In 1841 he married Marie, sister of Alexander of Hesse. Unusually she went to Russia nearly a year before her marriage, followed a few months later by her brother Alexander. These unusual events were believed at the time to give credence to the belief that their father was Baron Senarclens von Grancy with whom their mother lived, openly separated from her husband, at Heiligenberg from 1820 until her death.

An undated collection of German princelings. Second from the right stands the Third Duke of Hesse, described by Mountbatten as "slothful', 'gross, eccentric and alarming'. The unkind criticisms are confirmed by his stance.

A symbol of the malaise of Austria. The mad Emperor Ferdinand I (abdicated in 1848). He amused Alexander of Hesse who visited him in Vienna on 26 March 1846 and wrote in his diary 'the Emperor is a pathetic object; not to put too fine a point on it, he is an idiot. He was very polite to me, but quite unintelligible. He wore our order of St. Louis on the clip of his watch, the cross hanging down to his knees.' Corti, *The Downfall of Three Dynasties*, p. 47.

The young Prince Louis of Battenberg,
Mountbatten's father.

Admiral of the Fleet. The Marquess of Milford Haven, father of Mountbatten.

Right: Prince Alexander of
Battenberg (1879–1886)
illustrating his family's weakness
for adornments. *Below*: A dramatic
picture of the forced abdication of
Prince Alexander of Battenberg in
Sofia on the night of 21 August
1886. As he was roused from his
bed by his valet shouting 'Fly,
before it is too late!', it is doubtful
if he would have had time to have
dressed himself in such a formal
manner!

of Bulgaria, prior to his departure for Livadia,[11] which took place to-day.

He requested me to beg you to entertain for him feelings of friendship, since he puts the highest value on the confidence shown him by England. Standing on the basis of the Berlin Treaty he will, above all things, try to raise Bulgaria – materially as well as morally – to a higher level and to strengthen her position, whilst he will himself keep aloof from trying political experiments.

He sets a great value on your being informed that he is *not Russian* in heart, and that he is *not* inclined to act as Russia's tool (*marionnette*). He is, therefore, rather vexed by the invitation to Livadia, as he sees it is but too natural that people will say he is gone to get his instructions, and as he is altogether likely to be regarded as a Russian vassal. He yielded at length, simply to avoid giving offence to the Emperor, and to avoid appearing ungrateful, since he and his family owe so much to the Emperor's kindness.

He certainly does not want to get instructions, but he may collect there very useful information, since Dondoukoff is there at present, and others who have hitherto ruled Bulgaria. If it can be done without being glaringly rude, he will refuse to receive the Bulgarian deputation at Livadia . . .

In conclusion I repeat his request: not to believe him to be a Russophile, but to have faith in his honest intentions, since he puts the highest value on the friendship of England.
LUDWIG.[12]

Despite the Grand Duke's doubts about Sandro receiving the deputation, the new prince not only went to Livadia but allowed himself to be introduced to the Bulgarian delegation by the Tsar with these words: 'From my hands receive your Prince, love him as I love him.'[13] Later, Sandro told his new subjects '. . . that he knew the unbounded gratitude Bulgaria felt for her liberator . . .'[14] Lastly before leaving Russia, Sandro had an interview with the Russian Foreign Secretary who impressed upon him that '. . . the newly chosen Prince . . . must never forget the great part Russia had played in his election.'[15] On none of these occasions did he express disagreement with the Tsar's Bulgarian policy.

The double dealing continued in Vienna, where Sandro told Count Hoyos, 'No one could expect the separation of Eastern Roumelia to continue permanently';[16] in Berlin, where Bismarck told him to strictly observe the Treaty of Berlin 'which separated the two Bulgarias'; in London, where the Queen, Salisbury and Beaconsfield told him not to be subservient to Russia. Poor young man; his father gave him no alternative to playing the chameleon. A and Julia's decision to send to Bulgaria the twenty-two-year-old, romantic, unrealistic, inexperienced son was unforgivable; to achieve this end they were prepared to undermine his future position by giving contradictory pledges to Russia, England and Germany.

Having sown misunderstandings Sandro wished to travel through Turkey to Bulgaria in order to meet the Sultan; at once his troubles began. Beaconsfield did not think it was wise for him to travel to Constantinople in a Russian ship. The Tsar insisted and had his way. The Sultan was angry, and only agreed to see the new Prince after a request from the British Ambassador. Sandro's reception was short and cold. The ancients would have found numerous ill omens in the journey to his new country. His ship was caught in a storm which made Sandro so violently sea-sick he was sure he had been poisoned when at last he staggered ashore half-dead at Varna; to be greeted disdainfully by the Russian representative Prince Dondukov-Korsakov.

It is possible to sympathise with Alexander II; he had no reason to doubt Sandro's loyalty. The Battenbergs were under an obligation to him. He had helped A, with money after his elopement, in Austria and Italy, and after his return to Germany, had paid for the building of a palace in Darmstadt and the enlargement of Heiligenberg. He had known Sandro since his childhood, kindly given him a commission in the Russian army, and had no idea his young nephew had been advised by Salisbury to work against Russian policy by collaborating with Turkey, or that his liberal beliefs would inevitably clash with Russia's plan to create a subject Bulgaria. It is not surprising that from the beginning everything went wrong. Sandro was annoyed on his arrival to learn that the Russians had already changed the constitution to ensure he was their prisoner. To increase his difficulties the Russian commander, the disappointed Prince Dondukov-Korsakov, who had hoped to be chosen prince, was antagonistic and jealous. When he heard Sandro had been chosen he at once stopped building what he had hoped would be his own palace, and built the ceiling so badly that when it rained, wet plaster collapsed on the new Prince's head. Sandro, frightened of being crushed to death, slept beneath a network of planks. These were mockingly called his 'wooden crown'.

This welcome made him feel helpless and furious; he further undermined his position by attacking the Russian generals and advisers who had remained to ensure Bulgaria became what would now be called a satellite state. Sandro naively did not see that he was asking for trouble in expecting Russia to change its policy with which he and his father had agreed when they perjured themselves to accept the princedom. Naturally the Tsar was furious. A heard of his anger and, alarmed, borrowed Louis from the British Navy and plucking Sandro out of Bulgaria, descended with his two sons on his brother-in-law in St Petersburg to try by force of charm to make peace. Their train was late; the Tsar politely waited for them in the Winter Palace: his good manners saved his life. Punctually at the time when the party should have been in the middle of dinner, terrorists blew up the dining room, killing over fifty[17] Finnish guards, garrisoned beneath. The Battenbergs' unpunctuality saved the Tsar's life; he showed no gratitude, and only gave Sandro useless reassurances instead of money.

The new Prince's position was desperate. He was in debt as he only had £24,000 a year to run the country, an inadequate sum. Wisely his parents told him to find a rich wife; obediently he fixed his eyes on the richest and most beautiful heiress in Russia, Princess Zenaïde Youssoupov.[18] Unfortunately, despite Sandro's good looks, she failed to see the fascination of living in Bulgaria and politely procrastinated. Empty-handed he returned home, where his Russian advisers promptly spread the rumour he was in the Tsar's service. Bulgaria as usual was alive with intrigue, and whatever Sandro tried to do was deliberately misunderstood or misinterpreted by advisers, whose corruption and carelessness of the appalling poverty in the country horrified the young innocent. But how could he ever have hoped to make Bulgaria independent of Russia, who had appointed him and on whom he was financially dependent? This he never understood and until his abdication he remained indignant that he wasn't given Russian money to confound Russian policies.

Neither was Russian influence his only problem. He had to deal with an elected patriotic National Assembly who (except for Slav extremists) were antipathetic to exterior interference. It's not necessary to dwell on Sandro's mistakes and his insistence on being called 'Your Highness' or 'Your Excellency', which annoyed both the Tsar and his subjects. His fundamental error was to believe he could rule a country where money bought loyalty, without money. The result was unending insurrection. He was also gullible, hotheaded and vain, and when told the country needed firm rule he saw himself as an authoritarian liberal. Instead of examining the motives of his advisers, he allowed them to persuade him to dismiss the Assembly and become an autocrat. He then excelled himself by choosing a stupid excuse for dismissing his Parliament – their refusal to grant him permission to aggrandise his seedy palace. Too late he found he had fallen into a Russian trap – Stanley Evans concisely describes his miscalculations:

> The *coup d'état* would not have been possible without Russia's connivance and the Russians who connived at it were not fools. They had not permitted it to happen for the greater glory of Vienna or Bismarck and the Prince soon found that, without an assembly, his Russian advisers had much greater power than heretofore. It was their nominees who built the first Bulgarian railway and they who determined its location. Soon the President of the Council, the Minister of War, the Chief of Police, the Governor of Sofia, and thirty senior army officers were all Russian, and to amend the situation, in June 1882, Alexander had to journey to Petrograd, only to succeed in changing the personnel, but not the policy of the Russian representatives.[19]

Sandro never recovered from his rash decision which haunted him for the rest of his reign. His political friends in the national Assembly were hurt and furious to find themselves ousted by corrupt and inefficient Russians: they believed their Prince had made a treacherous deal with the Tsar behind their backs, instead of understanding he was a stupid young man. His charm made him popular with the peasants; they admired his dashing looks and friendliness. Experience had taught them to expect nothing but self-interest from officials, and the new race of politicians.

The timing of his *coup d'état* was ill timed. Two months later his uncle, Alexander II, was assassinated; the new Tsar, the reactionary Alexander III, detested change and regarded his young cousin as a cheeky morganatic nobody, who as a child had irritatingly called him Mops. He thought his assumptions of authority impertinences and from the beginning of his reign encouraged the Russians in Bulgaria to throw out a prince who had put a pretended interest in his subjects above his loyalty to his late uncle who had given him the principality.

We get a glimpse of the embarrassing disloyalty of Sandro's officers and the poverty of his wild, unknown principality in the diary of his sister Marie Erbach, who, with her husband, visited his principality. They joined the Royal Yacht on the Danube, sailed through Romania and spent the first day sitting happily on deck, but that evening, when they entered Bulgarian waters, the guests were quickly sent below; Sandro had learned to his surprise that his river Navy was holding manoeuvres with live torpedoes: or in other words, planning to sink his yacht. Ignorant of her lucky escape Marie was delighted to find Sandro was loved by the peasants, a main source of his troubles. She did not understand the Tsar desired obedience, not popularity, for her erring brother.

On one uncomfortable outing, Sandro drove his sister and her husband to Sandrovo, his retreat on the Black Sea, by such a bad road they had to get down and walk. She describes the poverty and discomfort of his life:

> The next four days were unfortunately spoiled by the dreadful weather, and we had to make up our minds to bring our stay in Sandrovo to an end. But this was not to be managed so quickly, as first of all the furniture brought from Rustchuk, carpets, curtains, table services, etc. had to be returned thither in order to make the palace there habitable. It was certainly not comfortable – while without the storm raged and howled, and the rain came down in torrents, we sat freezing, huddled up in rugs in the cold rooms, which hour by hour became more bare and empty. At last only what was absolutely necessary was left us, but in spite of Sandro's urging it was found impossible to take our departure before the 1st October. Even in bed one could not get really warm, as the wind blew round our heads, and the night before we left the rain came through the roof on to Sandro's bed.[20]

It is not surprising that the young Prince found it difficult to persuade his family to visit him.

NOTES
1. Corti, *Three Dynasties*, ch. 10, pp. 240–1. Hough, *Louis and Victoria*, ch. 4, p. 89.

2. Second son of Queen Victoria, who married the daughter of Tsar Alexander II of Russia.

3. Corti, *Three Dynasties*, ch. 10, p. 241.

4. Hough, *Louis and Victoria*, ch. 4, p. 90.

5. Corti, *Three Dynasties*, ch. 10, p. 242.

6. Roger Fulford (ed.), *Darling Child*, Evans Bros., 1976, p. 23 (quoting Royal Archives). Fulford was unaware of the meaning of 'a sad scrape', but as the dates coincide, the reference can only refer to Prince Alfred taking Sandro aboard Britain's newest battleship.

7. Hough, *Louis and Victoria*, ch. 4, p. 91.

8. Count Egon Corti, *Alexander von Battenberg*, Cassell, 1954, p. 28.

9. Ibid., p. 37.

10. Ibid.

11. The Tsar's palace in the Crimea.

12. *The Letters and Journals of Queen Victoria*, edited by G. E. Buckle, vol. 3, 1879–1885, John Murray, 1928, p. 16.

13. Corti, *Alexander von Battenberg*, p. 39.

14. Ibid., p. 39.

15. Ibid., p. 40.

16. Ibid.

17. Reports of deaths as usual varied from one extreme to another. I have chosen a low number of casualties.

18. Later wife of Count Elston (who took her name) and mother of Prince Felix Youssoupov, killer of Rasputin.

19. Evans, *Bulgaria*, p. 132.

20. Marie of Battenberg, *Reminiscences*, pp. 184–215.

10

THE hatred between the cousins was accentuated when Russian agents tried unsuccessfully to kidnap Sandro in 1883: in the following years the Tsar's determination to unseat him became an obsession. When the plots failed Sandro thought he had routed his enemy; in fact, he had managed to survive. His optimism made him – when he was not depressed – consider himself a match for the Tsar. Unfortunately, his friends stuck a dagger of unkindness in his back when they supported the German Crown Princess's idea, first mentioned in 1883, that Sandro should marry her daughter Vicky.[1] Queen Victoria, excited by the romance, asked the Prince of Wales to try and persuade the German Ambassador, Count Hatzfeldt, to take Sandro's side against the Tsar. This was a dangerous initiative, as the Queen was making a request which would infuriate not only the Tsar but also Bismarck, who knew the Prince of Bulgaria's marriage with a Hohenzollern would jeopardise his policy of maintaining peaceful relations between the emperors of Russia, Austria and Germany. His anger was comprehensible. The only possible explanation of the Queen's meddling in German politics was to advance her granddaughter's unsuitable marriage. Bismarck's fury was increased by his correct assumption that the Queen had been involved in the affair by her daughter the Crown Princess. His dislike of the 'Englishwoman' was not, from a German point of view, as unreasonable as British historians have made out.

Sandro lived a lonely life in Bulgaria and escaped whenever he could to his relations for weddings, visits to Paris and the fashionable spas. He was depressed by the complications of survival and would undoubtedly have given up the thankless task if his father and mother had not begged him to stay. The strength of their fears can be measured by A's grovelling letter to Giers, the Russian foreign minister:

I guarantee the submission of the Prince, my son, to the person of Emperor Alexander, as I would my own. In spite of all the evil which may have been said about my son to His Majesty, I have persuaded him not to give up the hard task which has unfortunately fallen to his lot. But on the day it can be proved that he has lost the confidence of the Emperor and his Government, I shall be the first to advise him to abdicate. It is quite obvious that his position would be intolerable without the support of Russia.[2]

Shortly afterwards A also wrote to the Tsar, compounding the family's deceit:

I entreat you, Sasha, for the sake of friendship which unites us and of which you have given me such frequent proof, offer your hand in forgiveness to that young man who up to now has had to bear such heavy trials. He will always remain loyal to you and to Russia. I am as certain of him as I am of myself.[3]

The extent of father and son's deception can be judged by comparing A's letters to the Tsar with Sandro's letter to the Crown Prince Frederick:

All my efforts are now directed towards arousing Bulgarian national feeling, and using it as a protective rampart against Russian aggression. Russia nearly brought about my downfall once, but she will not be able to do so a second time. My position in the country is too strong; the Bulgarians are tough, and every step which is taken against me strengthens my position. Russia hates me because she fears me, but I rejoice in this hatred which I reciprocate with my whole heart, even if conditions force me to suppress my feelings for a few years.[4]

The Battenberg trickiness was ignored by Queen Victoria, and in a wild letter to Lord Granville[5] she argued 'a spoke' would have to be put in the Russian wheel, otherwise the Tsar would force the Prince to abdicate and put a Russian vassal in his place. When the foreign secretary paid no attention to her wishes she made the Prince of Wales try again and write to Bismarck's son Herbert (the German Ambassador in London):

104

My dear Count, my mother the Queen is most anxious that Germany should either intervene in St Petersburg on behalf of Prince Alexander of Bulgaria who is, after all, a German, or at least assist him with good advice.[6]

– a strange and unwise message when Sandro accepted the Princedom of Bulgaria he ceased to be a German citizen.

Herbert Bismarck replied tersely:

Germany has never interfered in the internal affairs of the Balkan States and Great Britain could do this much more easily as she has closer ties and interests there.

The Prince of Wales replied:

That is true, but what can we do with this Government? The Queen has tried her utmost to persuade her Ministers to intervene in St Petersburg, but in vain. She is very annoyed about it, but finds it impossible to make Lord Granville do anything. Nevertheless she feels that something should be done for the Prince of Bulgaria.[7]

Queen Victoria has long been praised for her common sense. It should be remembered that when family loyalties were threatened, her wisdom went out of the window. If Lord Granville had followed her advice Britain might have found itself at war with Russia. How it would have been waged is another matter; as Lord Dufferin[8] once commented: a war between the two countries would resemble 'a fight between a whale and an elephant', an interesting comment which raises the question of what the English and French armies could have done in the Crimean War if the Russians, rather than standing and fighting, had followed Kutsukov's[9] earlier tactics of withdrawal backed up by guerrilla warfare.

It is hard to excuse the interference. Queen Victoria and her daughter the German Crown Princess both showed they were prepared to risk damaging their countries' interests to promote a marriage, which was originally inspired by the Crown Princess, because of her affection for Sandro and the desire to irritate Bismarck and the Emperor, rather than on account of the lovers' feelings for each other.

Sandro was a practical wooer and was prepared to marry the silly, dramatic Vicky, as she was the best bargain he could get. He was bored to death, living uncomfortably in Bulgaria without a wife or money. After his failure with Princess Youssoupov, his mother had produced a rich German duchess; this plan fell through when Sandro discovered she was a simpleton. However, despite his pretended adoration for Vicky he let it be known he was prepared to marry any rich, available Habsburg heiress. His answer was a snub from Franz Joseph, making it clear he was not regarded as a suitable bridegroom for a Habsburg.[10] No other heiress or suitable princess being available, he had no alternative to Vicky, although a letter from Queen Victoria in September suggests her father, the ailing Crown Prince, was still unaware of his wife's plans, to which the Emperor would have strongly objected.

The Crown Princess spent her life fighting Bismarck. Was Vicky's secret engagement part of her campaign? Why did her mother so desperately want her to marry a prince whose mother had not been, and never could be, received at the respectable, old-fashioned Berlin court? She knew the Emperor and Empress would be horrified at the suggestion of such an unsuitable marriage, and that even her weak husband was not enthusiastic about the idea of his eldest daughter marrying a morganatic. Nothing daunted; she persistently wore him down, and by the end of 1883 won his consent that the pair should – without the Emperor and Bismarck being told – become secretly engaged. The Chancellor soon learned the truth and lost his temper. The last thing he wanted was to annoy Russia. Whatever his long-term intentions, he needed time and peace to unify and consolidate the new German Empire. Now this maddening Englishwoman was secretly planning to ally Germany to Bulgaria, exasperate the new Tsar and damage German foreign policy, all for the sake of a half-witted girl and a stupid young man. Bismarck hadn't the slightest use for Bulgaria: years before in the Reichstag he had declared he did not think German involvement in the Balkans was worth 'the healthy bones of a single Pomeranian grenadier',[11] certainly not the destruction of one of the fundamentals of German foreign policy. The Crown Princess's behaviour was so odd the suspicious Chancellor decided she must be carrying out a British plot conceived by that subtle schemer, Queen Victoria, for whose intrigues he had an exaggerated respect. He can't be blamed. Royal marriages were regarded as political alliances and it was maddening to needlessly infuriate the Tsar. His anger and suspicion increased in 1884 when Sandro's brother Liko became engaged to Queen Victoria's youngest daughter Beatrix; but he wasn't as angry as the German Emperor who wrote to him:

> We were absolutely startled last evening by a telegram from the Queen of England announcing the engagement of her youngest daughter to the third Battenberg son! To such depths has the Queen of an old and powerful dynasty descended to keep her daughter in the country ... My son [Crown Prince Frederick] says: 'It was somewhat difficult to have to recognise the eldest Battenberg as a nephew, but to have the third as a brother-in-law is too much!'[12]

Meanwhile the Empress Augusta's horror at the marriage of Princess Beatrix into a dubious family made her write a critical letter to the Queen[13] which is no longer in the Royal Archives at Windsor. Corti gives us a glimpse of its contents: 'The Empress said, *among other things*, that she had heard Henry of Battenberg was an insignificant little man, she did not know him, and did not care to have acquaintances of that sort.' The Queen told her daughter proudly, she had replied:

> I was very audacious and answered the last letter of the Empress full of hints and insinuations about the origin of the family which she supposed I did not know and that I did know and that the character of the young man and his brother and sister which was so excellent was what I considered first, and then that I could not understand how she could object so much to the family when she remembered that the father of her own son-in-law and his brothers and sister were the children of a Fraulein Geyesberg,[14] a very bad woman, and that they had been acknowledged by the whole of Europe as Princes of Baden.[15]

This letter is an interesting example of Queen Victoria's broadmindedness and showed she was aware of, and unshocked by, the doubts surrounding A's birth and the public scandal of von Grancy living with the Grand Duchess of Hesse. Unlike many of her contemporaries, she argued (despite her habit of making her grandchildren marry each other), that brains were more important than royal blood, and that only by marrying into families with *fresh blood* could the madness common in so many royal German families be checked. Her support for the Battenbergs and other morganatic families was curious. Was it a consequence of the shady background of her beloved husband's mother? Prince Albert was only four when she was dramatically expelled from Coburg for infidelity. Albert and his elder brother had little in common, the former being a model of virtue, the latter the reverse, boasting of more than forty illegitimate children and mercilessly bullying his wife.[16] The Queen's acceptance of the talented Battenbergs as husbands for a daughter and granddaughter was justified by events. The family produced in three generations three outstanding leaders of men, with whom their effete Hesse cousins compared unfavourably. In the present generation, Prince Philip and the King of Spain have further proved her decision was sensible. But at the time the Queen's approval of Liko's engagement to her daughter was incomprehensible to the imperial families of Europe.

NOTES

1. 'Vicky' was the affectionate abbreviation of the Princess Victoria of Prussia, eldest daughter of the Crown Princess. I will continue to refer to her by this diminutive to distinguish her from her mother and grandmother, both 'Victorias'. The former was also nicknamed 'Vicky'.

2. Corti, *Alexander von Battenberg*, ch. 5, pp. 98–9.

3. Ibid., ch. 5, pp. 99–100.

4. Ibid., ch. 5, p. 101.

5. *Queen Victoria to Earl Granville*, 12 October 1883, Letters, second series, vol. 2, p. 445.

6. Windelband, *Bismarck und die Europäischen Grossmachte, 1879–1885*, p. 521. A report from Herbert Bismarck in London of 3 November 1883.

7. Corti, *Alexander von Battenberg*, ch. 6, p. 96.

8. Later Marquess of Dufferin and Ava, at various times Ambassador to Russia and Turkey, Viceroy of India and Governor-General of Canada.

9. Commander of Russian forces which drove Napoleon out of Russia in 1812.

10. Austro-Hungarian Ambassador in Sofia. Baron Biegeleben's report on meeting with Sandro 27 June 1886 ends: 'The desire for Austria's support coincides entirely with the policy of the Prince and that of his illustrious father, and with his unbounded admiration for H.M. the Emperor, apart from the allusions made to me both here and in Jugenheim, regarding hopes for the Prince's marriage to a rich duchess which is unfortunately out of the question.' Vienna Archives.

11. Bismarck's speech, Reichstag, 19 February 1876.
12. *Letter of Emperor William to Bismarck*, 31 December 1884. Windelband, p. 616.
13. Corti, *Three Dynasties*, ch. 12, p. 305.
14. An unmediatised grand duchess of Baden, whose husband was considered unlikely to have been the father of her children, later a suspected murderess.
15. Fulford (ed.) *Beloved Mama*, p. 180, 17 January 1885, quoting from Royal Archives. The conclusion of this letter is published on p. 37.
16. There is a graphic picture of the coarse old sybarite in the memoirs of Marie, Queen of Romania. Marie Queen of Romania, *The Story of My Life*, vol. 1, Cassell, 1934, ch. 7, pp. 165–70.

11

A N opportunity for Tsar Alexander to vent his spleen on the
Battenbergs occurred at the marriage of the Grand Duke Serge
to Ella of Hesse in St Petersburg: Sandro was pointedly not
invited to the wedding, and his elder brother Louis, who had recently
married the bride's sister, Victoria, was publicly humiliated at the
wedding lunch, by being ostentatiously separated from his wife and
relations and placed at the bottom of the table, below the captain of his
ship.[1] This deliberate insult made his father remonstrate with the Tsar,
who replied it was due to what he had heard about the Battenbergs in
Germany. This cryptic sentence suggests his informant was Bismarck.

Sandro's flirtation with Vicky received a sharp check when he went
to see Bismarck in Berlin. The Chancellor was frank:

> He did not consider the Prince of Bulgaria her equal in rank and
> therefore not a suitable husband for a German Princess who would
> one day be the daughter of the Emperor. Was he not the son of a
> morganatic marriage? And had not the designation 'Battenberg'
> been taken from a small village in Hesse in order to give the family a
> name?[2]

In an interview with the Crown Princess and her husband, Bismarck
was even more brutal:

> To give the Bulgarians a Prussian Princess would be equivalent to
> throwing a marshal's baton over the walls of a besieged fortress.[3]

Sandro next visited Vicky's grandfather, the Emperor William I. His
reception was not friendly:

> I certainly do not always agree with everything the Russians do in
> Bulgaria . . . on the other hand, you, Prince Alexander, are to blame

to a certain extent in your relations with Russia, particularly the somewhat incorrect tone of your letters to the Czar. I advise you to make them less curt and more correct.

Sandro tried to argue:

But I was never so presumptuous as to write rude letters to Czar Alexander. Only when I received such letters from him did I reply a little more curtly. Only in personal letters did I write more confidentially as cousin to cousin, but I was never discourteous.

Sandro's excuse infuriated the Emperor, who shouted:

Cousin, cousin! An Emperor is an Emperor. My own son signs himself my 'most obedient servant' when he writes to me . . . I must tell Your Highness that I have heard that you are up to your eyes in debt and have had to humiliate yourself by taking a loan from European Jewry.[4]

Sandro said sadly he had very little money and ended by offering to resign. The Emperor replied: 'But I cannot risk Germany's friendship with Russia simply for the sake of Bulgaria. Very well then, go, it won't worry me.'

Typically his good nature came out when Sandro was leaving him; changing his tune the old man said kindly: 'But do not think that I have lost the personal interest I had in you formerly. I do not believe this slander, and as long as I am Emperor, you will certainly remain Prince of Bulgaria.'[5]

It had been a confusing, contradictory interview and showed the German Emperor was putty in Bismarck's hands. If his last words sounded reassuring, the Chancellor squashed Sandro's hopes when he stupidly simulated innocence about his engagement to Vicky (brave and dashing, he had scant respect for the truth). Bismarck was not prepared to put up with his evasions.

Well, as Your Highness appears to know so little about the matter, you will allow me to tell you there was serious talk of such a union, so much so that violent scenes took place in the palace; Her Imperial Highness, the Crown Princess, and the English Court are in favour of the marriage. His Imperial Highness, the Crown Prince, was *against* it; the Emperor and Empress have stated that they cannot agree to it. I, as Imperial Chancellor, have informed His Majesty that *Germany has no interest in Bulgaria, our interest is – Peace with Russia*. To ensure that it is absolutely necessary that Russia shall be convinced that we are not actively interested in the East. On the day a Prussian Princess becomes Princess of Bulgaria, Russia will grow suspicious and will no longer believe this assurance. In addition, *this marriage would interfere with my political interests*. This I will not permit and I have informed His Majesty that so long as I am Chancellor, this marriage will not take place; at the same time I have assured the Emperor he would find no successor to follow such a policy . . .

. . . I consider it my duty to speak plainly to Your Highness on this matter. His Majesty orders you to be present at Wiesbaden as he did not wish to see you in Berlin and I regret that you came here. In any case I cannot understand why you want to marry a Princess. Possibly Princess Beatrice or Princess Helene of Mecklenberg might be a suitable match for you. I would advise you to marry an Orthodox millionairess; that would stabilize your position in Bulgaria, *for ruling in the East means bribery and that requires money*. Nothing can be done honestly there. Anyhow, I think it is time you made up your mind whether you are a German or a Bulgarian. Up to now you have been a German, but with your departure that chapter must be closed. In your place I might have remained a German, for I can understand that it must be repugnant to an honest, upright character like yours to have to deal with Orientals. But if you wish to remain in Bulgaria you must submit to Russia for better for worse and even, if necessary, adopt an anti-German attitude.[6]

The interview ended with Bismarck's callous dismissal: 'After all, it is unimportant whether you go sooner or later. But go you will.'[7]

The young man must have been overwhelmed by the antagonistic, brutal old man sitting behind his huge desk, speaking slowly to allow each insulting truth to sink in. But Sandro had told lies, and invited correction by repeatedly contradicting himself about whether or not he had proposed to Vicky, even caddishly denying it to Baron Biegeleben, the Austro-Hungarian minister, in 1885:

The suggestion came from the German Crown Princess after we had been attracted to each other in Darmstadt last year, but that came to nothing through the refusal of Emperor William to give his consent.[8]

He repeated his denial to Count Karl Wedel, the German Military Attaché to Vienna in April 1885.[9] His denials confirm that the Crown Princess, not Sandro, had a passionate desire for the marriage to take place, dragging her mother into the argument, to confound Bismarck's policy. The only fair way to judge Bismarck's violent reaction to Queen Victoria's interference is to ask what Gladstone's reaction would have been if the Empress of Germany had meddled with our relations with France. It is not a difficult question to answer.

A little later the Queen made the Prince of Wales intervene again, exasperating the Chancellor who privately encouraged the Tsar to use Trojan horses to rid Europe of this threat to peace. Obediently, Russians spread rumours. Vicky's hand had been refused either because Sandro had a venereal disease or on account of his Turkish tastes. These rumours upset him; he realised he could not rely on the vacillating Crown Prince. In desperation he wrote to his father: 'I have had enough. Do help me to get out of Bulgaria decently.'[10] It was an embarrassing time for A and Julia; Bismarck took every opportunity to make the most unflattering comments concerning the origins of both of their families. The situation became more confused when Sandro again contradicted his father, who had recently promised his loyalty to Alexander III, by writing: 'You have no idea of the terrible hatred I bear the Czar and his Government.'[11] On another occasion he described the Tsar as a 'mad dog'.[12] But changing tactics on 14 April 1885 he wrote a sycophantic letter to the German Emperor: 'I am prepared to fulfil all the wishes of His Majesty the Emperor of Russia, on condition that these always come to me direct from His Majesty.'[13] Corti, without success, tries to present father and son as an honest pair!

While Sandro was busy digging his own grave by duplicity, he was unexpectedly saved by Eastern Roumelia, the southern half of Bulgaria, breaking away from Turkey. At the time, the Prince claimed unconvincingly he had tried to prevent the revolution. This is contradicted by his earlier letter to the Crown Prince Frederick: 'All my efforts are now directed to arousing Bulgarian national feeling.' If he was to retain the Bulgarians' patriotic loyalty he had no alternative to accepting integration.

The first reaction of the Russian press was to welcome the news; after all, the war of 1878 had been fought to unite Bulgaria. But by now the Tsar's hatred of his cousin was so intense anything he did was wrong. He also believed Sandro would not be supported by Britain. He was wrong again. When Russia insisted there could be no revision of the peace terms of San Stefano, England disagreed. In other words the two countries had changed places and now supported exactly opposite points of view to those they had nearly gone to war about seven years before.

The news of the Bulgarian unification was ecstatically greeted by the Crown Princess who believed it made Sandro a more eligible match. She wrote him a letter of twenty-eight pages, which must have made tedious reading at the busiest moment of his life.[14] As usual Vicky's emotions were expressed by her mother, who wrote the poor girl could not eat or sleep and 'regrets she cannot be at your side to share all the danger and excitement'. This was lucky for Sandro; our limited knowledge of the Princess suggests she was a scatterbrained, flighty girl under her infatuated mother's thumb. This is confirmed by the Crown Princess's gushing comment: 'Vicki wanted to run away, disguise herself as a man and go to war with you!!'[15] That the Crown Princess, not Vicky, wrote the letters, suggests she had an unrealised passion for Sandro.

The Tsar had turned his political somersault on account of his hatred of Sandro. Queen Victoria's intense feeling had persuaded Lord Salisbury to change his mind and admit he and Disraeli had misread the Bulgarian problem at the Congress of Berlin. British foreign policy in the Balkans was a series of gropes in the dark; Gladstone, Disraeli and Salisbury had not the slightest understanding of the mountainous area and were incapable of comprehending the 'Bulgarian question'. The union of the two Bulgarias caused a tremendous stir in Europe. The Queen expressed her fury at the British government's refusal to help Sandro in a series of violent letters.

In Turkey Abdul Hamid had no idea what to do. Fortunately Austria made up his mind for him, stating that Turkish intervention in Eastern Roumelia would be considered an act of war. This decision was made after a meeting of the three emperors at which Austria and the Tsar supported Serbia's invasion of Bulgaria. Bismarck, silent, amused, sat back to watch. The inspired Sandro, helped by the Tsar's withdrawal of his inefficient officers, amazed Europe by reorganising the young, excited Bulgarian army, filling the Russian gaps with fiery youths who had been taught to fight as soon as they could walk. In a brilliant Hannibalic campaign, he marched his army over the Bulgarian mountains, defeated the Serbians at Slivnica and advanced into Serbia. The despairing King of Serbia tried to resign and pass his responsibilities on to his baby son, who would hardly have been more useless than his father. He furiously cursed his prime minister who, not having a son to take his place, wished to retire into the army. At last the position became so dangerous Austria stopped the Bulgarians by threatening war. So ended a campaign which excited Germany and made Sandro a European hero. The Queen was delighted with her protégé's victory, but her pleasure was marred, according to A, because 'the newly published Almanach de Gotha had not placed the Battenberg family in the ranks of the reigning Princes.'[16]

Peace was followed by yet another conference. The great powers sat down to settle the future of Eastern Roumelia and again fudged the issue, deciding that while Eastern Roumelia could not join Bulgaria, Sandro could become the governor for five years, when his position would be reviewed. The decision infuriated the Bulgarians and undermined Sandro's position. His astonishing victory ensured his political eclipse.

The European governments were tired of a young man who threatened the peace of Europe. The new liberal Foreign Secretary Lord Rosebery said pessimistically to Sandro's sister Marie Erbach in London: 'there is not much more to be hoped for, unless God works another miracle.'[17] Bismarck was as determined as the Tsar to destroy Sandro, fearing the new German hero might one day return to Germany to lead the Liberal Party. King Carol of Romania regretfully realised Sandro had not the political skill to negotiate successfully with his European neighbours.

In the summer of 1886 Alexander III, encouraged by Bismarck, started plotting yet another revolution in Bulgaria. Sandro's desperation can be measured in July by a sad letter to his sister.

Dear Sister,
Beset on all sides like a hunted stag, overworked to such an extent that my eyes, for the first time in my life, refuse their office, I am only

now able to write to you once more. In a few days I must, in the fulfilment of my difficult task, make a political circuit of Roumelia. It will take twenty-nine days. God give me strength to go through with it. There is still much work before me. The Bulgars have little heart; it seems to me impossible to keep them contented. Of course all these evil ideas are the result of foreign promptings. But the Bulgars are really old enough to be able to tell true friends from false. How the situation stands today is difficult to determine, or how Russia's fight to dispossess me will end. I have always been more afraid of internal difficulties than of foreign ones. At present the former predominate. Until the autumn, that is to say, until the final settlement of the statute-revision question, my throne will be like a laid train of dynamite.[18]

The only thing which saved the lonely Prince from desperation was his belief in and admiration for the soldiers he had led to victory. His advisers warned him not to be optimistic and that the Struma Regiment and certain impressionable cadets were being bribed by his enemies. He refused, through self-satisfaction and vanity, to believe his blood brothers would betray him; naïvety was his undoing. On the night of 21 August he was woken by his valet running into his room crying, 'You are betrayed, they want to kill you! Fly, before it is too late!'[19]

Rebels surrounded Sandro and his brother Franz Joseph. They surrendered as drunken men prodded them with bayonets. When early next morning they left Sofia, the idealistic Prince saw to his horror, officers he had trusted and led to victory, calmly smoking as they watched him led away.[20] Their guards told their prisoners they were to be sent in the Royal Yacht down the Danube to Russia and would be shot if they tried to escape. On the two-day journey to the river they were shut up each night in dirty, hot little prisons full of bugs and fleas. Arriving at Rachovo they were immediately hustled out of sight into a hot, airless cabin. Their captors were worried; news had come from Sofia: loyalists had risen and the conspirators were on the defensive. The brothers knew nothing of either the counter-revolution or their planned fate as they sailed downstream, hidden, half-suffocated, in an airless hold.

To the world the yacht had vanished. Rumours excited Europe and terrified the English court. The confusion was so great that even the

Russians did not appear to know where Sandro was and when the brothers went ashore at the first Russian port, Reni, the temporary commander, a cavalry captain, hadn't the slightest idea what to do with his unexpected guests. The Tsar, who had persuaded himself Sandro was detested in Bulgaria and a joke in Europe, ordered him to return by train to Lemberg. He made a mistake. Sandro's disappearance and mysterious kidnapping had made him a hero both in Europe and Bulgaria, where the peasantry felt their patriotism had been insulted. They also dreaded his replacement by corrupt Russian administrators.

The successful counter-revolution was organised by one of Sandro's ex-ministers, Stambulov, a Russo-hater who roused Bulgaria with demands for the return of the stolen Prince and the unification of the country. The news of his success and the Russian contingent's discomfiture was passed on to Lemberg, to encourage their lost leader to hurry home.

His supporters did not realise Sandro's heart was broken. It is not surprising; for seven years he had ruled a country of illiterate savages. Frequent attempts had been made to kill him and he had been continually insulted and humiliated by Bismarck, the Emperor of Germany, and the Tsar, who had sneered at his morganatic background and his mother's low birth. In Bulgaria his Russian advisers had accused him of vicious habits. Events had been too much for him and when Eastern Roumelia rebelled in 1885 he was at the end of his tether. Serbia's declaration of war gave him new life and he had thrown his whole heart into creating and inspiring a patriotic army. He succeeded, and won a famous victory. His reward was to be kidnapped by his own soldiers. That was the last straw. Never again do we glimpse the brave prince. His backbone was broken; unfortunately his ambitious mother and obedient father would not accept this unwelcome truth. They insisted he should reclaim his principality, despite Sandro's tragic telegram to A from Lemberg: 'I am a broken man as a result of the inexpressible sufferings I have undergone.'[21]

Sandro's loyal Bulgarian supporters, unaware he had lost his nerve, increased their clamour for his return. The Crown Prince of Germany and Queen Victoria sent telegrams urging him to go back before it was too late. The Crown Princess persuaded herself now that Sandro was a European hero, Bismarck – who to keep his popularity had praised the

Prince's heroism – would allow him to marry her daughter. The tired man in Lemberg had one desire: to sleep.

Extracts from Queen Victoria's correspondence illustrate her intense and passionate interest in her son-in-law's brother. When he was abducted and his whereabouts unknown, her reaction in a letter to Lord Salisbury was frenetic and confused:

> BALMORAL CASTLE, 23rd August 1886
> ... This moment the Queen received Lord Salisbury's [he had succeeded Gladstone as P.M.] cypher.[22] Before speaking of the terrible personal trouble this is to us, and the cruel end of the exertions and self-sacrifice[23] of the poor dear young Prince, whose great abilities and bravery (far greater than those of any other ruler abroad) were the admiration of everyone – of her present as well as her late Government – she must speak of the very alarming aspects of affairs in a political and public sense! Lord Salisbury always said the Crown Princess's fears were exaggerated, that he thought things would come right, and now *here* the worst thing which *could* have *happened* for us and Turkey, has *taken place*! Russia is intriguing right and left, and we *must not* tamely swallow *everything* with a mere protest! Russia sets us at defiance! ... The most able and independent Prince Alexander of Bulgaria has been driven away, and we must not swallow *that* (meant as a slap in *our face*) without a *formal protest*, and *far more*, we should *insist* on a *Conference here*, and must not accept any Russian candidate, any wretched foolish Prince or Russian who will be proposed.[24]

In the same letter she suggested a replacement of ambassadors. Salisbury, in his reply of 10 September, tactfully agreed Sir Edward Thornton 'had not been much use' in Constantinople. The Prime Minister's treatment of this Ambassador – only six months off retirement – was not as servile as it looks. ornton's advice from St Petersburg had often been unworldly and misleading.

On 24 August the Queen wrote to the new Tory Foreign Secretary, who had succeeded the liberal Rosebery, from Balmoral with royal simplicity:

> BALMORAL, 24th August 1886
> The Queen thanks Lord Iddesleigh[25] for his very kind letter and for his sympathy, which indeed is much needed; for she is much

attached to the dear, brave, and so cruelly used Prince of Bulgaria, and she feels so much for the brother, her son-in-law, whom she loves as a son, while another brother is her grandson-in-law, who is a distinguished officer in her Navy. It is therefore a subject of intense personal interest to her as well as from a political point of view. Russia *must* be unmasked . . .[26]

Seldom has a constitutional monarch stated so plainly her belief that her personal wishes should transcend the national interest. Later when Sandro arrived in Lemberg the Queen's delight was almost uncontrollable and she packed off his brother Louis to Poland to help him. She also insisted on her pound of flesh, and Salisbury and Iddesleigh had to ignore a request to change the Ambassador in Russia, Sir Robert Morier. On 27 August the Foreign Secretary received another frantic telegram from the Queen:

(5.30 p.m.) – Received letter: highly approve. But not one minute must be lost! White[27] must be telegraphed to and sent off *at once* with some message or other, and *Lascelles*[28] *start at once* or all will be too late!

Dolgoruki is on his way. Have cyphered to Prince Louis who meets brother tonight to urge most strongly Prince Alexander's return, for peace of Europe, and we must stand by him.

Writing is too slow – Russia must not triumph. Morier must get leave too.[29]

This wild message was one of a series of notes from Windsor to which the Prime Minister replied comically on 27 August, 'Lord Salisbury with his humble duty respectfully acknowledges your Majesty's letters of the 25th and 26th.' He then hinted the Prince's condition had deteriorated:

. . . It is possible that he may be so disgusted with the treatment he has received, that he has given, or will give, a pledge to somebody, Russian or German, to give up the throne of Bulgaria and not to return there. This would be politically a very serious blow.[30]

On 29 August Salisbury firmly declined to move Sir Robert Morier from the British Embassy:

. . . No higher post could be given to him; and his term of office does not cease till 1889. To remove him would be looked on as a very harsh act both by the public and the profession; he would induce somebody in Parliament to declare that he was the victim of a backstairs intrigue; and the issue of a vote in the House of Commons would be very doubtful.[31]

Louis had taken the reluctant Sandro back to Bulgaria but the Queen was still not satisfied and, ignoring Bismarck, ungrammatically wrote to Salisbury:

BALMORAL CASTLE, 1st September 1886
All Germany is boiling over with indignation at the monstrous plot, and at the terrible treatment to which a reigning Prince and re-spected by all *but* Russians (by a *good many* of *them too*) the Paul-like Tsar's first cousin [has been subjected], and are furious with the language of the so-called official organs of the German Government.[32]

On 2 September, the power of the Queen's influence was shown. Lord Iddesleigh wrote to the ambassadors in Berlin and Vienna suggesting the great powers should give:

. . . open support of Prince Alexander, given in such a manner as to enable his Highness to devote himself without anxiety to the task of governing the country over which he has been placed by Europe. They desire to interchange views with the other Powers, and direct the Ambassadors to make a preliminary communication in this sense to the two Governments in question.[33]

The triumphant Queen sent back a delighted telegram, 'I approve most highly intended message to my Ambassadors at Berlin and Vienna.'[34]

Two days later in Berlin Sir Edward Malet received a crushing – and it must be admitted deserved – rebuff from the German Foreign Office when he suggested Germany should support a confrontation between Sandro and Russia. Before the Foreign Minister had time to think of a reply the situation had altered, disastrously. The Queen recorded in her journal of 4 September:

Found an alarming telegram from Sir F. Lascelles (very secret) saying he had seen Sandro, who, on finding disaffection was widespread, had determined to leave the country and appoint a Council of Regency. He will not formally abdicate, but hopes he will not be pressed to remain; he had announced his intention of leaving to Prince Bismarck, who consented to use his influence with the Tsar to secure an honourable retreat for *him*, and to prevent Russian occupation.[35]

The next day Sandro sent a telegram to the Queen:

Sofia, 6 September 1886 6 p.m. – I beg your Majesty to believe that I have only come to the decision of abdicating after mature deliberation. Three-fourths of all officers are mixed up in the conspiracy; the Opposition are likewise implicated; and the Ministry knew of the plot, which they did not seek to prevent, though they did not approve of it. The people and the soldiers are on my side, but supported alone by them I cannot govern. The whole Clergy is also implicated . . . I only returned to Bulgaria in order to be able to leave of my own free will. My remaining any longer would only cause a civil war, as, being betrayed by all, I could only maintain myself by suspending the constitution and decreeing summary executions.[36]

Sandro's state of mind showed how wise he was to resign and how *un*wise had been the campaign to force a man who had lost his nerve to remain. But the Queen would not give in and turned in fury on her ambassadors. Her letter from Balmoral on 8 September was spiteful and ill-informed:

Just heard from Crown Princess, whose information is alas! always correct, that Prince Alexander was to have been murdered on the ship, but the Tsar forbade it!! Also that Morier is much pleased now, and went about saying Prince was a liar, and British Government should never have supported him. Russians are astonished at his language, and think him very odd. My constant appeals for many months to have him recalled, or sent for on leave, were never listened to. Do so now or you will rue it. He does awful mischief.[37]

Even the loyal Lord Salisbury was having no more nonsense and on 9 September wrote firmly:

> Lord Salisbury's humble duty . . . All our information as to Sir R. Morier's misconduct with respect to Prince Alexander appears to come through Prince Bismarck, and he, as Sir E. Malet says, specially hates Sir R. Morier. On the other hand, Sir R. Morier's own reports, since we have been in office, have shown no ground in this respect; we have nothing against him except secret reports which we cannot quote, and which, passing through Prince Bismarck, may have been distorted; the harm he can do at St Petersburg is not great; but to recall him would be a very startling step, for which we could offer no justification.[38]

Events in Bulgaria emphasised the Queen's bad judgement in trying to force a confrontation with Russia. Sandro's decline had been rapid, and it was noticed he was under the influence of his elder brother, Louis, a naturalised British sailor of thirty-two, without any experience of Balkan politics or understanding of the volatile Bulgarian mind. He also had the family failing of acting quickly, believing speed made up for thought. When the Tsar announced he was sending Prince Dolgoruki to Bulgaria Louis panicked, and after an unwise conversation with the Russian consul concocted with the acquiescent Sandro a telegram to the Tsar:

> I thank your Majesty for the attitude taken by your representative in Rustchuk. His very presence at my reception showed me that the Imperial Government cannot sanction the revolutionary action taken against my person. I beg Your Majesty to instruct General Dolgoruki to get in touch with me personally as quickly as possible; I should be happy to give Your Majesty the final proof of the unchanging devotion which I feel for Your Majesty's illustrious person. As Russia gave me my Crown I am prepared to give it back into the hands of its Sovereign. Alexander.

Later, in a letter to the Queen, Louis tried to justify his mistake.

> I maintain that so far from being a mistake, the telegram was masterly in conception for it built a golden bridge for the Emperor.

One mistake I admit Sandro and I made: we imagined that the son of our noble aunt had still somewhere about him one remaining spark of gentlemanly and generous feeling that was of course a fatal mistake, but one which all men should honestly and truly forgive . . .[39]

This was a parsonic, silly justification; the telegram cost Sandro his principality. Alexander III had the mind and body of a butcher; gentility was a stranger to his nature. No promises would have moved him, except that Sandro was prepared to go. The brothers also followed another custom of the silent service and failed to mention the 'golden bridge' telegram to their father, Sandro's ministers or the supporters flocking to his standard. A mistake Louis wisely did not try and defend.

The Tsar could not believe his good fortune. For years he had tried to rid himself of this impudent, morganatic cousin, who dared to address him in a familiar manner, and repaid the kindness he and his father had lavished on the Battenbergs by frustrating Russian foreign policy, and breaking his own and his father's solemn promises of loyalty. The kidnapping had been a miscalculation; Sandro had risen like a phoenix from the ashes and become a Bulgarian hero. This made the Tsar so angry he was willing to fight, if necessary, both Austria and England to destroy his hated cousin.

Suddenly out of the blue came Sandro's telegram. His reply was brutally clear:

I have received Your Highness's telegram. I cannot countenance your return to Bulgaria as I foresee the disastrous results it entails for that sorely tried country.[41]

The Tsar acted quickly and published both telegrams in every European capital including Sofia, where Sandro's Bulgarian supporters heard for the first time their prince had resigned behind their backs. His chief supporter Stambulov was appalled. A terrible sentence of grief and condemnation burst from the shocked patriot's mouth:

This is the man for whom we have roused the whole of Bulgaria, have put our necks into the noose and brother has raised sword against brother, and he takes such a momentous decision without even telling us beforehand; he throws his crown at the feet of a foreign ruler and keeps us in the dark about it.[41]

In Berlin the Crown Princess implored her husband to beg Bismarck to help Sandro. He tried and was snubbed. In Hesse, A realised the mistake but it was too late to do anything. His son was a broken reed. On 3 September the Prince officially abdicated; circumstances had destroyed his volatile spirit. He had tried to serve his country but had been too young, idealistic, arrogant, above all inexperienced. Bismarck had been right; the task was too much for him. It was not in Sandro's nature to understand Bulgaria could only be ruled by subterfuge and calculated force.

On his way back to Austria, peasants in the villages came out to lament the passing of their Prince, touching his clothes as if he was a holy man. In this sad manner Sandro passed out of the troubled Bulgarian story. He was fondly remembered and in earlier days would have created a legend of 'the good prince', but in the mundane world of the 1880s his effect on the history of the Balkans was slight. Sandro's father should never have abased himself before the Tsar, put ambition before common sense and sent a rash, inexperienced boy of twenty-two to rule an uncivilised princedom brimming with confusion and hate.

A's second mistake was promising his son's submission to the Tsar, making him a prisoner of inefficiency, against which his liberal, hotheaded nature was sure to rebel. These commitments doomed his reign before it began.

The great powers found it difficult to find an independent successor to Sandro and for two years a series of delegations asked him to return. He considered and refused their offers. The last Bulgarian attempt was a request that A should rule Bulgaria to enable his son to succeed him. Sandro's father knew the Tsar's opinions too well even to consider the idea. After two years Ferdinand of Coburg became the new Prince. For a few years he nervously watched Sandro's movements. Unquestionably he made a better ruler than his predecessor; he was rich, ruthless, cunning: essential qualities for a prince in the Balkans.

NOTES
1. Captain Hawkes of the Royal Yacht *Osborne*.

2. Corti, *Alexander von Battenberg*, p. 116.

3. General von Schwienitz, German Ambassador in Moscow, *Denkwürdigkeiten des Botschafters*, Berlin, 1927, vol. 2, p. 271 (translation).

4. Corti, *Alexander von Battenberg*, ch. 7, pp. 119–21.

5. 'This sentence is in a report in Prince Alexander of Battenberg's own writing to Crown Prince Frederick William, in which he emphasizes the fact that the Emperor contradicted himself several times during this discussion. The whole description of this discussion is based upon this personal report and on the letter of Baron Biegeleben of 6 June 1884, which does not give the last sentence.' Corti, *Alexander von Battenberg*, ch. 7, p. 120.

6. Corti, *Alexander von Battenberg*, pp. 123–5.

7. Ibid.

8. Baron Biegeleben to Count Kalnoky, Sofia, 4 February 1885, Vienna State Archives.

9. Memorandum in Prince Alexander's own writing, Autumn 1885, cited Corti.

10. Corti, *Alexander von Battenberg*, ch. 7, p. 132.

11. Ibid., ch. 7, p. 141.

12. Ibid., ch. 7, p. 141.

13. Ibid., ch. 8, p. 155.

14. Corti, *Alexander von Battenberg*, ch. 8, p. 176.

15. Curiously enough, after her first husband had died, Vicky, in old age, ran away and married an ex-waiter called Alexander Subkov who beat her and made her ride on the back of his motorcycle. The marriage was not considered a success.

16. Prince Alexander of Hesse to Prince Alexander, 5 December 1885, cited Corti, *Three Dynasties*.

17. Marie of Battenberg, *Reminiscences*, 2 April 1886, p. 234.

18. Ibid., July 1886, p. 239.

19. Ibid., 21 August 1886, pp. 239–40.

20. The proposed kidnapping was known and approved by the Chief Minister, the head of the Bulgarian Church and senior officers. See Sandro's telegram to Queen Victoria, 6 September 1886, quoted on p. 121.

21. Corti, *Alexander von Battenberg*, ch. 12, p. 232. See also Salisbury's letter to Queen Victoria, 27 August 1886 in *Letters and Journals of Queen Victoria 1886–1901*, John Murray, 1928, vol. 1, p. 193; and Sandro's telegram to Queen Victoria, 6 September 1887 in Buckle (ed.), *Letters and Journals of Queen Victoria*, vol. 1, pp. 198–9.

22. The telegram said the F. O. had no idea of the whereabouts of the Prince of Bulgaria and thought it unwise to make any statement implying that

they thought the Prince finally overthrown. It might destroy his last chance.

23. By telegram the Queen altered this word to 'self-devotion'.
24. Buckle (ed.), *Letters and Journals of Queen Victoria*, vol. 1, pp. 180–81.
25. Formerly Sir Stafford Northcote.
26. Buckle (ed.), *Letters and Journals of Queen Victoria*, vol. 1, p. 186.
27. Sir William White had replaced Sir Edward Thornton in Constantinople.
28. Sir Frank Lascelles, *Chargé d'affaires* in Sofia on leave in England.
29. Buckle (ed.), *Letters and Journals of Queen Victoria*, vol. 1, p. 191.
30. Ibid.
31. Ibid., p. 195.
32. Ibid., p. 196.
33. Ibid., p. 197.
34. Ibid., p. 198.
35. Ibid., pp. 198–9.
36. Ibid., pp. 199–200.
37. Ibid., p. 203.
38. Ibid., pp. 203–4.
39. Ibid., vol. 1, p. 205.
40. Alexander III to Prince Alexander of Hesse, received 1 September 1886, in Corti, *Alexander von Battenberg*, quoting Hajek, p. 387.
41. Corti, *Alexander von Battenberg*, quoting Hajek, ch. 10, p. 242.

12

I N September Sandro returned to Darmstadt and received a rousing
welcome from the independent town which had never wished to be
merged in the Prussian empire. On the evening of his arrival
Lortzing's opera, *Waffenschmied*, was performed in his honour. Corti
described the scene:

> When Prince Alexander entered the box the entire audience rose and
> shouted wildly: 'Long live the hero of Slivnica!' The orchestra
> played the Bulgarian National Anthem *Schaume, Maritza* and
> everyone looked up entranced at the tall, slight, handsome and
> heroic figure of the man who had been through such hard times
> during recent years and who, in spite of all opposition, had drawn
> together and united the two halves of the Bulgarian people. Then
> silence reigned, the lights went out and Lortzing's melodies rang
> through the theatre.[1]

A distinguished audience had come to greet the returning hero,
including the Grand Duke of Hesse, his daughter and her husband the
Grand Duke Serge of Russia. Sandro was unmoved by the reception
but entranced by an actress, Johanna Loisinger, sitting in the opposite
box. He discovered she was not a *cocotte* but the daughter of a
secretary to an Austro-Hungarian general – her godfather – who
guided her career. She was beautiful, charming and chaste. Naturally
the affair was soon known in Darmstadt as Sandro called on her in the
interval, and afterwards took a box whenever she appeared on the
stage.

He had fallen in love and wished to give up Vicky, but was terrified
of Julia and the Crown Princess, who for different reasons were
determined on the marriage. Sandro tried to escape his commitment
and wrote to his brother, knowing Queen Victoria would see his letter:

'It is therefore impossible for me to make any fresh advances, and if anything is to come of the affair Frederick William of Prussia must take the first step.'[2] This was the first of many pleas for help, but there was little the Queen could do: Sandro now resembled a helpless sailing ship blown in a direction he did not wish to go by the Crown Princess's decision he should marry her daughter, whom she still saw as a future Princess or Queen. He vacillated, made flowery promises to the old Emperor William but could never screw up the moral courage to break off his engagement. Poor man, he had escaped from the wasps' nest of Bulgaria only to fall into the centre of a furious family storm, in which he was too frightened of his mother to admit his true love.

His position was made more difficult by the gradual deterioration of Vicky's father, the Crown Prince's, throat. On 10 November 1887 Queen Victoria's doctor, Sir Morell Mackenzie, admitted his first diagnosis that the Crown Prince did not have cancer was incorrect. The patient faced his limited future calmly, and bravely decided to retain his larynx. This ensured continual daily torture which he bore with courage. The effect on his wife was profound; she changed from a tiresome and frustrated wife to a desperate termagant, driven half mad by the possibility of missing the chance of becoming a reforming liberal Empress and losing an adored husband whom she was unable to help. Her despairing grief made her search for an outlet to mitigate her unhappiness and energy. She settled on her daughter's marriage to her unconscious love, Sandro, although it was obvious he no longer wished to marry Vicky. The Crown Princess refused to believe such an insult to her plans and her insistence on their marriage involved the Hohenzollerns in one of the most extraordinary royal matrimonial tussles of the nineteenth century.

The battle was fought between a frantic wife and a bully of a Chancellor over the body of a dying man. On Sandro's side, against the marriage, were (usually) himself, Bismarck, the old Emperor, the Crown Prince (spasmodically), Prince Henry of Prussia and the Grand Dukes of Hesse and Baden, and for the marriage were Julia, the Crown Princess, occasionally the weathercock Crown Prince – when he could be bullied into marital obedience, to begin with Queen Victoria, and, to confuse things, sometimes the unwilling prospective bridegroom, cowed by his mother and Crown Princess. What Vicky, who spent her youth in her mother's shadow, thought is unknown. Perhaps she was not certain herself. It is probable her weak brain was mesmerised by her mother's strong personality to believe she was in love with Sandro.

The Crown Princess's possessiveness was inherited from her father, Prince Albert, who immediately after her birth, hid her from everybody except his young wife in Windsor to allow him to gloat undisturbed over his new possession. Rumours quickly spread around London that the child was 'blind, misshapen or backward'. Fortunately, she was at last seen by Lady Lyttelton, 'pretty and in perfect health'.[3] Odd behaviour for a young father prompted perhaps by his own bitter childhood. His mother was banished from Coburg for immorality when Albert was four. The strangest part of the affair was Bismarck's fear that Sandro wished to marry Vicky, long after the romance was over and he had fallen in love with Johanna and made frequent genuine, if half-hearted, attempts to escape from his engagement.

However much the Crown Princess might play the ostrich, pretending ignorance of Sandro's love for Johanna, his new passion was common knowledge, and in June 1887 Vicky's brother Prince Henry of Prussia cornered him and said:

As you know my sister is very fond of you. My mother raves about you, and she wants you to marry my sister and so does Queen Victoria. My father is against it and what Their Majesties think about it you know already. This unhappy story has been a nightmare in our family for years and therefore I want to know – are you thinking of marrying my sister?'

'I do not know', replied the Prince, 'what right you have to call me to account like this?'

'As a brother who always was and still is against this marriage. Only this spring I told my sister that it can never take place. Well, what have you got to say?'

Sandro, as usual when he was in difficulties, lied; it is doubtful if by now he knew the difference between fact and fiction.

It is the second time in my life that this question has been put to me, the first time in 1885 by the Emperor in writing and now by you. I will answer your question as plainly as I answered the Emperor then. I have never asked for the Princess in marriage and therefore I cannot understand why I am being asked to renounce a marriage I could not possibly enter into. Princess Victoria is free to marry whom she wishes and I shall be the first to congratulate her if she becomes engaged to someone else.[4]

Despite this declaration the Crown Princess remained determined that at any cost Vicky should marry Sandro. He wrote to her emphatically denying what he had told Prince Henry:

I love your daughter truly and faithfully, I offered her my hand honourably and am prepared today, as I was four years ago, to keep my promise; I hoped I would be able to make your daughter happy but in the present situation, which has grown so terribly serious, I feel forced to ask Your Highness to help to bring this situation to an end. I therefore beg Your Imperial Highness to decide, without the slightest consideration for myself, the fate of the Princess, your daughter, and remain assured that to the end of my life I shall never forget how good you have always been to me.[5]

Typically the Crown Princess shut her eyes to his excuses, ignored his request to bring the engagement to an end, and seized on his first sentence, which she claimed showed he still wanted to marry Vicky. Ignoring Bismarck's opposition and her husband's failing health and peace of mind, she pursued her aims with the energy and determination of a fury.

Meanwhile Sandro lamely explained to Johanna that although he longed to marry her, he could only do so when he had broken off his engagement, which he declined to break. Was his moral cowardice due to his fear of his mother? His father left him alone, and for a long time did not take his son's affair seriously, remembering his own youth, and believing anyone who had spent seven years in Bulgaria deserved a holiday. Julia was worried. She had in her youth by guile or good fortune persuaded a minor royalty to marry her: why should not this actress do the same and ruin Sandro's life!

She had not been able to recover from the blow of her son's departure from Bulgaria; it was even said that she had remarked she would rather see him dead than fleeing from Bulgaria. Now all her ambitions for her child were centred on the great marriage in Berlin.

130

So she regarded his growing affection for Johanna with extremely mixed feelings. It was because the girl was so gifted and so beautiful, that she caused his mother increasing anxiety.[6]

To Julia the choice was simple; Sandro could either marry the Emperor's eldest daughter and regain his lost position or marry his actress and disappear. Remembering the slights of her own past her ambitions were understandable. She must have been exasperated that the chaste Johanna was usually chaperoned by her mother. The cancellation of Sandro's secret engagement would be a blow to her plans, which had been helped by her other sons' marriages to Hessian and English princesses, but the shadow of A's illegitimacy and morganatic marriage still hung over her mind.

A was old and ill and Julia knew his death would leave her exposed to those who only reluctantly recognised she was his wife. In Germany the imperial family (with the exception of the Crown Princess) still treated her as a woman whose past could neither be forgotten or forgiven. Worried, she continued to hope the marriage would take place, and would not recognise Sandro's new love affair, broken spirit and lack of ambition. Unfortunately her opportunities to control her son were limited. While it was easy to keep an eye on him in Heiligenberg and in the Alexander Palace, she could not follow him into the Darmstadt theatre where he nightly gazed at his love with indiscreet adoration. One evening he lost his head when Johanna tripped and knocked herself out. Leaping onto the stage, ignoring the astonished audience, he cried out: 'What has happened? Have you hurt yourself? Take my carriage and drive home, I beg of you.'[7]

The incident caused a tremendous sensation in Darmstadt and would have delighted gossips in Berlin if the capital had not been filled with rumours that at long last, the apparently immortal Emperor William I's life was 'drawing peacefully to its close'. He died on 9 March 1888 in his ninety-second year and his son took the incorrect title of Emperor Frederick III.[8]

The new 'possessed' Empress wrote to Sandro before her father-in-law was cold that she would make her husband settle the matter once and for all.[9] He was horrified by her letter and replied imploring her to decide Vicky's future without the slightest consideration of himself. He had lost his throne and was now poor and unimportant and he knew her son, the new Crown Prince William, did not like him. It was a

131

typically weak, if unavailing, cry for help and was ignored. The Empress replied telling him to write to the Emperor to ask if he could pay his respects. The idea momentarily revived Sandro's ambitions and he asked for an appointment, adding:

> I consider a public engagement unwise so soon after the death of his predecessor and I would prefer the new Emperor to decide first on my position and appoint me to a new post in the army. Then it would be easier for His Majesty to give his daughter to a German General than to an ex-Prince without definite social and political standing.[10]

Having changed direction and encouraged the Empress to believe he was still anxious to marry her daughter, he went on to say that as the Crown Prince was also opposed to the marriage, he did not understand how anyone could marry into a family which took every opportunity of showing its dislike of him.

At last in muddled desperation Sandro wrote to his brother Liko a letter which he hoped would convince the Queen he could not marry the sister of a future emperor who detested him. He achieved his object. The Queen wrote to her daughter:

> I can understand that in the painful uncertainty occasioned by the health of Fritz, you are anxious to settle and arrange everything of importance, but I beg of you not to act precipitately particularly in matters which are in direct opposition to the wishes of the late Emperor. By this I refer to the proposed marriage of Morette [Vicky] with Sandro. Above all, do not even consider such a step without William's consent. You must take him into account, for he is the Crown Prince and it would never do to conclude a marriage of which he did not approve.[11]

The Queen's bluntness did not change her daughter's mind but it made her realise she must hurry the marriage or, to put it brutally, her husband would die on her. His larynx was covered with spreading cancerous growths; he could hardly speak and had to write notes on small pieces of paper. In spite of his agony his wife gave him no peace, harassing him daily with constant requests to consent to the marriage.[12] He wrote to Sandro on 2 April asking him to come to

Charlottenburg. Bismarck heard of the invitation and retaliated, according to the unreliable Vicky, by priming the new Crown Prince William to vindictively announce, 'I will make things unpleasant for my mother, I will take it out of my parents for this.'[13]

The Crown Prince was not alone in his determination to stop his sister's marriage. His brother Henry also protested to their father when, to gain a moment's peace, he said he would make Sandro commander of the Brigade of Guards. The proposal was also criticised by the Grand Duke of Hesse, the head of Sandro's family, who begged the Emperor not to make such a contentious appointment. It was all too much for the drugged, painridden, dying man, who by now hardly knew where he was or what he was saying. He replied that he had not the slightest intention of doing what he had just proposed. But of course, alone with his wife, his courage faltered, and he told Bismarck on 31 March, 'I intend to grant the Order of Merit to Prince Alexander of Battenberg who is arriving here within the next few days to become engaged to my daughter. What do you say to that?'[14]

Bismarck said it was 'impossible' and repeated his objections: 'inequalities of birth' and the ill-effect the marriage would have on Russian relations, while it was true that the Tsar gave assurances he didn't care a 'fig' who Sandro married. On another occasion he told the Russian Ambassador 'I have no wish to interfere in Bulgaria; I don't want to send a single soldier there, but if Battenberg goes back I move!'[15]

The Chancellor finished by shouting that if the Emperor gave Sandro the Order of Merit he would resign. The Emperor wrote pathetically on his little piece of paper: 'What is to be done?' Bismarck replied: 'Countermand the invitation by telegram.'[16]

The poor man obediently obeying when the Empress, who was listening at the door, burst into the room demanding her daughter's heart should not be broken for reasons of state. The Emperor vainly tried to silence her and at last 'suddenly jumped up in great agitation, tore the bandage from his throat and tried to speak, but only the words "leave me alone" were clear.'[17]

The Empress, who it is to be hoped had a twinge of conscience at worrying her husband to death, left the room and the weathercock Emperor wrote: 'Battenberg will not come now, submit memorandum, discuss the matter with my wife.'[18] Nothing had been decided. What were Bismarck's motives? Originally he opposed the marriage, believing correctly it would infuriate the Tsar, if a half-German, half-English princess went to Bulgaria to support by her dowry her husband's opposition to Russian policy. This was a valid argument until Ferdinand succeeded Sandro. But Bismarck hated the Battenbergs and dreaded Sandro leading the Liberal opposition, a fear he retained even when it was obvious the broken man could no longer manage his own affairs, let alone a political party.

The Empress, by now distracted both by sorrow and her fixation, wrote an extraordinary letter to Sandro, suggesting a secret wedding, followed by a flight from Germany; adding that Vicky would not mind if he served in the Austrian army. This frightened Bismarck as he impatiently waited for the Emperor's death. To be safe he wrote a long, inaccurate memorandum of the ill effects of the marriage on German foreign policy and the dangerous advice Queen Victoria had given Sandro. He ended with his usual threat of resignation if the marriage took place.[19] The Empress reacted violently, and on 4 April told the Chamberlain to announce the engagement of her daughter, with her husband's consent, in eight days' time.[20] Crown Prince William, encouraged by Bismarck, wrote to Sandro:

> I consider it my duty to make my attitude in this matter quite clear. In my opinion it would be against the interests of the House of Hohenzollern and also of my country ... I will not leave Your Highness in any doubt as to my intentions. I shall regard everyone who works for this marriage not only as an enemy of my House, but also of my country, and will deal with him accordingly. I trust Your Highness will not force me to include you in this category.[21]

The Chancellor's next move in the bizarre game was to turn to the public for support, and on 5 April 1888 he gave Sandro as a thirty-first birthday present a formal proclamation in the *Kölnische Zeitung*, telling the nation to condemn the marriage as it would jeopardise German foreign policy if the Tsar's most hated adversary became the son-in-law of the German Emperor. He added for the tenth time he would resign if the marriage took place. For good measure he fired a second barrel in the *Grenzbote* attacking the Battenbergs' antecedents. Sadly Sandro wrote to Johanna on 7 April:

> My darling, I was nearly driven mad yesterday and today by people who kept coming to see me, and the last straw was the visit of the

134

Catholic bishop of Bulgaria. In addition, there was great excitement in the town about Bismarck's resignation by which means he hopes to stop my marriage. This resignation, which the dying Emperor cannot possibly accept has, I think, definitely put an end to my marriage.[22]

The Grand Duke of Hesse again came to the rescue and announced the marriage would not take place. On the same day Sandro wrote to Johanna: 'You looked too sweet again this evening . . . according to today's papers my marriage has been postponed indefinitely.'

The Empress was obliged to retreat but she was not beaten and forced her husband to talk to Bismarck again about the marriage. The Chancellor, whose cunning equalled his obstinacy, was prepared to prolong the discussion for a few weeks until the Emperor died, but he carefully refused to commit himself to any wedding. The Empress, as usual, read what she wanted into the meeting and wrote to Sandro telling him to marry Vicky secretly at Homburg in May. She added a lie, illustrating her unbalanced state: 'Bismarck had himself proposed that the wedding should take place without his knowledge and he would then hand in his resignation, but the Emperor would not be forced to accept it.'[23]

Bismarck was by now (and one can sympathise with him) furious. He suggested Queen Victoria should postpone her annual visit, which annoyed her; although being on this issue far more sensible than the Empress, she repeated her earlier warning to her daughter:

Do not consider the marriage without the full consent of William. It would be foolish to conclude a marriage contract to which he had not given his consent. Sandro's marriage might wreck all his chances in life.[24]

The tortured Emperor continued to sign state papers although by now he was nearly suffocated by the growths in his throat. However, another operation ensured him a few more weeks of suffering. This gave his wife the opportunity to badger him as he grew weaker and more pliant. On 12 April, in agony, besotted by morphia, he wrote in his will to his eldest son:

Should your mother or myself be suddenly called to depart this life, I hereby wish to state definitely that I give my full consent to the

135

marriage of your second sister with the ex-Prince of Bulgaria, Prince Alexander of Battenberg.[25]

He then wrote to Sandro, who replied that while he was ready to marry the Princess secretly, he would only do so in Germany. At the same time he again told Johanna how much he loved her. The affair was reported to the Prince of Wales by the British Military Attaché in Berlin, Colonel Swaine, who tactfully wrote, 'he is now reported to have *Ein Zartliches Verhaltniss* with a member of the histrionic art.'[26] The news was passed on to his mother; she made enquiries which confirmed it. The Queen was upset when she saw her daughter was making a fool of herself and decided to go to Charlottenburg, to see her dying son-in-law and to tell Bismarck she no longer supported the idea of the marriage:

> She arrived in Berlin on April 14th, 1888, and spent the whole day trying to explain matters to her daughter, advising her to give up the idea. It was no use, the Empress did not want to know it and therefore would not believe her mother. In spite of everything, she remained faithful to her idea. When the Queen received Bismarck the following day, she let him see that she had no more interest in the marriage and that she was possibly speaking also on behalf of her daughter ... The Chancellor was first overjoyed that she, and apparently also her daughter, the Empress, had dropped the idea of the marriage.[27]

The Mountbatten myth explains the meeting as a triumph for the Queen and a defeat for Bismarck. In fact she relieved the Chancellor by tacitly taking his side against her daughter, and according to Bülow said to the British Ambassador, Sir Edward Malet, 'I don't understand why my daughter could not get on with Prince Bismarck, I think him a very amiable man and we had a most charming conversation.'[28]

The Queen had realised the marriage was impossible without her grandson William's consent. The Empress secretly disagreed with her mother, and directly her back was turned wrote to Baroness von Stockmar:

> We must secure our daughter's happiness one way or another. We cannot turn back, neither for our own sakes nor for the sake of

others. Hatred, revenge and arrogance are making a family affair into a *cause célèbre* in order to bring about my destruction. If only we could have peace in this one matter, which is causing us all so much sorrow, and get it settled. Then we would be free to fight and work for other things. I would gladly jump into an abyss like Marcus Curtius and take the whole odium upon myself . . .[29]

At the same time Sandro was writing another of his ambiguous letters which, after giving reasons against his marriage, ended by saying he was prepared to wait. He was too late. On 15 June the Emperor died. Despite her obsession the Empress had adored her husband and in her possessive way wrote touchingly of his last moments:

I asked my dear one if he were tired, he nodded and said, 'Oh, very, very!' Gradually his dear eyes took on a different, oh, such an unforgettable plaintive look! We held a light up to his eyes but he did not blink at all; I raised his dear hand and he let it drop of itself! Vicky knelt by his side, her fair hair resting on his pillow, and she had her arms about him, crying bitterly and saying, 'Oh, dear Papa, Papa.' He no longer seemed conscious, coughed hard once more, took a deep breath three times, then gave an involuntary jerk and closed his eyes tight and convulsively as if something was hurting him! Then everything was quiet! I saw what had happened. He had left us, he had left me behind alone! I was seized with wild despair or I was turned to stone! I do not understand how I have the strength to write all this down. A pale greyness passed over his dear face! I took a withered laurel wreath down from the wall and laid it on the hero who had overcome all! I had given him this wreath when he returned home after the war with France; from the corner I fetched his service sword and rested it on his arm, folded his beloved hands, kissed them and his dear feet which were still quite warm! In this way I took my last farewell of the best husband in the world. Oh, why, why did I have to bear this?

I went away to my room, I had the strength for one farewell, but nothing more, I would have gone mad.[30]

This sad letter shows the strength of her feelings. It is interesting that a woman who was able to express her love for her husband with such haunting sincerity should have cruelly bullied and tormented him in the last months of his life. The Emperor dead, his son William immediately wrote to Sandro rudely announcing the marriage his father had asked him to arrange was off.

Sandro behaved in an extraordinary way, shut himself up in his room and wrote to his beloved Johanna:

> I have allowed my tears to flow without being able to prevent it; they were for the grave of my youthful dreams, the collapse of all for which I had striven and hoped for thirty years, the failure of all my military plans.[31]

Tactless words for a man to write to a girl he passionately wished to marry but an example of the way ambition and obedience to his mother ruled his life.

So ended the strange affair. Few came well out of the tragic comedy. Sandro was never able, despite his passion for the saintly, long-suffering Johanna, to make up his mind to finally break with Vicky for three reasons: his ingrained snobbery, the after-effects of his experiences in Bulgaria, and his fear of his mother. He was disloyal and deceitful in his letters, contradicted himself, changed his mind hourly, accepting the validity of his engagement one moment, denying it the next. He cried when he thought he would not be allowed to marry Johanna and cried again when he knew he could.

The Empress can be excused, but only by accepting that unhappiness had unhinged her mind, and made her devoid of pity for her husband. Bismarck showed his usual guile and the power of the press, and Queen Victoria belatedly showed sense. As for Vicky, she was a shadow of her mother's flame. Apparently she was flighty when young. Although her ghosted memoirs are unbelievable,[32] she appears to have been a weak instrument in the hands of an indomitable woman. That her broken heart was a figment of her mother's imagination is suggested by contemporaries, including Prince von Bülow, who remembered a visit to the court of Berlin in the spring of 1887:

> People were less interested in whether Prince Alexander would return to Bulgaria than in the question whether Victoria and Alexander would 'get each other' or not. After luncheon was over we went into the beautiful garden, where Princess Victoria was

playing lawn tennis with some of the gentlemen of the Crown Prince's court. While the Princess played tennis with all the grace or at least with all the energy with which Princess Nausicaa played ball, the Crown Princess poured out her sorrows to me. Her poor little daughter was so miserable she could neither eat nor sleep. She wept day and night at being prevented by the cruel policy of Prince Bismarck, from marrying her beloved Prince Alexander. She would either die of grief or commit suicide. At just the moment I heard these complaints Princess Victoria was winning her game with a masterly stroke of her racket, amid acclamations, so I could asure the Crown Princess, with a good conscience, that her daughter did not appear to be quite as unhappy as Ophelia or Juliet. The love affair between Alexander and Victoria soon came to an end after this. Both quickly consoled themselves. Princess Victoria was married in 1890, to the worthy Prince Adolph of Schaumburg Lippe.[33]

The drama suggests that it is doubtful if the Emperor Frederick, despite his good nature and magnificent looks, was the hero posterity has made of him. Was he, in Browning's words, 'a fine empty sheath of a man'? Long before his last illness, he often clashed with his wife, father, the Chancellor, and his eldest son and seldom won the point. In everyday dealings with his wife and Bismarck he deferred to each in turn despite their conflicting views. He resembled his father, who needed a strong guiding hand. But for his fatal illness he would have had to choose between his wife and the Chancellor. It has been accepted he would have chosen the Empress. On the other hand he was less rash than his son, and his pliable character resembled Lord Derby's, of whom Lloyd George said, 'He is like a cushion and bears the impression of the last person who sat on him.' It's doubtful if he could have immediately dismissed a chancellor he saw daily, while seeing less of his wife. Could he have resisted the strength of Bismarck's personality? It must be remembered his mother the Empress Augusta of Germany – a stronger character than her husband – loathed Bismarck for over a quarter of a century, but never succeeded in obtaining his dismissal. Would her successor have succeeded where she failed?

Until his illness, the Emperor and his wife were, to the outside world, 'travelling hopefully together'. Had he lived, would they have continued to do so? The battle with the Chancellor would have been titanic, and had the Empress replaced him as her husband's chief adviser, would she have been a disaster? Alternatively, had he chosen Bismarck, would she have driven her husband mad in his own home? I am inclined to believe, if the Emperor had continued in good health, a guilty secret would have made him always defer to his wife.

A recently published biography of Queen Victoria's physician, Sir James Reid,[34] by his granddaughter-in-law Michaela Reid, recalls an incident in R. Scott Stevenson's life of the Emperor Frederick's English surgeon, Sir Morell Mackenzie.[35] It throws a surprising light on Frederick and his wife's idyllic relationship by recalling a contemporary writer claimed Frederick had been unlucky enough to catch syphilis at the opening of the Suez Canal (in September 1869) from a beautiful Spanish girl, aptly named Dolores (Cada).[36] The Crown Princess, in the first stages of a pregnancy, had remained in Germany with her children. The symptoms of the disease appeared quickly and he was treated with apparent success by the Khedive's doctor: to trust an Egyptian doctor's knowledge and reassurances was unwise. After his return to Germany the Crown Prince looked ill and the Crown Princess wrote to her mother from Berlin on 2 April 1870:

> I am not quite happy about Fritz's health. He is over fatigued with perpetual *soirées*, standing in hot rooms for five hours together almost every night, in consequence of which he looks very yellow and his liver is a little out of order. He has a bad knee; a slight inflammation in the joint, Lengenbeck says – and is going to put a blister on it. Fritz looks thin and tired; but the Queen [of Prussia] will not admit the real reason which is his life which the King and Queen make him lead when he is here.[37]

Syphilis can affect the knee.
Queen Victoria innocently replied on 9 April:

> Would a change of air do him good? I would have offered sea bathing at Osborne in July for a fortnight but then I fear that for the liver the sea would be bad, or a fortnight or three weeks Highland air in August or September. In short if I can be of any use to one so dear to me – and so precious to thousands – I should be too glad and you would not grudge his being with me as you know that I should take the greatest care of him.[38]

It is doubtful if either a change of air or sea bathing at Osborne would have destroyed the venereal protozoa.

The calm tone of both letters suggests neither Frederick's wife nor her mother had heard of his romantic escapade, and its disastrous legacy. Fortunately for him he was, on his return from Suez, able to use first his wife's pregnancy, and then a prolonged absence on the French front (he commanded the 3rd Army in the Franco-German war) as excuses for discontinuing marital relations until he had recovered. But unfortunately at that time syphilis was frequently incurable, and lay dormant only to recur. The Crown Prince was to his family a nineteenth-century 'Bayard', and to Germany a liberal hero; he fought bravely both at Königgratz and Sedan but he was a moral coward, and far too frightened of his wife to admit he had strayed out of their Eden. It was typical of the character of this well-intentioned but weak man that he should have slept with her again in the summer of 1871, when he knew his cure was uncertain. Their reunion can be dated by the birth of his last surviving child, a girl, born on 22 April 1872. By any standards his conduct was reprehensible as he risked not only giving syphilis to his wife but to a possible child. It is inconceivable the Crown Princess would have risked her own health if she had known her husband was infected.

Their daughter Princess Margaret, married to Prince Frederick Charles of Hesse-Cassel, was luckily unaffected by the bacillus, but her son Christopher was a half-mad extremist, the associate and companion of Himmler. The wild seeds in his furious mind may have been planted by his unluckily tainted grandfather as they were in his elder brother, Prince Philip, a friend of Goering's, who was made a general of the Storm Troopers in 1933. An enthusiastic Nazi, he admired violence and was used as a sycophantic go-between between Hitler and Mussolini and Hitler and his cousin the Duke of Windsor. The latter connection may have saved him from imprisonment for after his release from Dachau he was immediately arrested on 9 April 1945 by the Americans as Target 53 in the Nazi hierarchy rounded up for interrogation. Successful British pressure prevented an embarrassing trial.

Shortly before his arrest King George VI sent his librarian and, of all people, Anthony Blunt, to retrieve secret papers considered damaging to the British royal family from his house, Friedrichshof. It is unlikely they, as suggested, related to Queen Victoria and likely they referred to Prince Philip's wooing of the Duke of Windsor with offers of a crown.

They are now buried in Windsor but as Blunt saw them it is likely that any interesting information was passed on to the Russians.[39]

The unfortunate Crown Prince's secret must have caused him unending fear and guilt. He appears to have had recurrent attacks. Not only the English doctor Sir Morell Mackenzie, but also Dr Moritz Schmidt, the Emperor of Germany's physician, and a Dr Krause from Berlin treated him for syphilis before trying to cure his cancerous throat.

He never risked becoming a father again. His adventure was disastrous for his wife; she worshipped her husband, and to be forced to live platonically with a man she passionately loved from the age of 32, would explain her neurotic, unbalanced behaviour, her unconscious passion for Sandro and her callous brutality to her dying husband. Without a frustrated private life would she have come to terms with Bismarck, or formed her unwise, passionate attachment to Sandro? Did Dolores ever know the harm she had done?[40]

NOTES

1. Corti, *Alexander von Battenberg*, ch. 11, p. 252.
2. Ibid., ch. 11, p. 253.
3. Daphne Bennett, *Vicky*, Collins and Harvill Press, 1971, ch. 1, pp. 23–4.
4. Corti, *Alexander von Battenberg*, ch. 11, pp. 263–4.
5. Ibid., p. 267.
6. Ibid., ch. 12, p. 272.
7. Ibid., ch. 12, p. 274.
8. He was either King Frederick II or the Emperor Frederick I.
9. Corti, *Alexander von Battenberg*, ch. 12, p. 277.
10. Ibid., p. 278.
11. Queen Victoria to Empress of Germany, 21 March 1888, quoted Corti, *Alexander von Battenberg*, ch. 12, p. 280.
12. Ibid., ch. 12, p. 283.
13. Bemberger, *Diary of the Crown Princess Victoria*, 1928, p. 434.
14. Corti, *Alexander von Battenberg*, ch. 12, p. 284.
15. Count Paul Schouvalov, Russian Ambassador in Germany, Badderley, *Russia in the Eighties*, ch. 18, p. 405.
16. Ibid., ch. 18, p. 407.
17. Corti, *Alexander von Battenberg*, p. 284. A variation of this ghastly scene was told to the British journalist, Badderley, by the Russian Ambassador, Count Schouvalov, after an interview with Bismarck who usually adorned any event with his own inventions. 'Bismarck was now raging, there was a terrible scene, and the Emperor Frederick at last gave

in. He telegraphed to Battenberg not to come to Berlin till further orders. Then the Empress Victoria came into the room. Her husband told her what had happened and she attacked him, saying: "You killed two of my children and now you want to kill another." What she meant I don't know. Two children died but I never heard their father killed them. The Emperor nearly choked, tore open his collar and would have rushed upon the Empress but that she fled out of the room. He then sank exhausted into a chair.' Badderley, *Russia in the Eighties*, p. 405.

18. Corti, *Alexander von Battenberg*, ch. 13, p. 285.
19. Bismarck to Emperor Frederick III, Berlin, 3 April 1888, *Gross Politik VI*, p. 282.
20. Corti, *Alexander von Battenberg*, ch. 12, p. 287.
21. Ibid., ch. 13, pp. 287–8.
22. Ibid., ch. 12, p. 289.
23. Ibid., ch. 12, p. 291.
24. Ibid., ch. 12, p. 292.
25. Copy made by Count Radolinsky of passage in Emperor Frederick's will. See Corti, *Alexander von Battenberg*, ch. 13, p. 293.
26. Sir Frederick Ponsonby, *Letters of Empress Frederick*, Macmillan, 1928, ch. 11, p. 299. Corti, *Alexander von Battenberg*, ch. 12, p. 294.
27. Corti, *Alexander von Battenberg*, ch. 13, pp. 294–5.
28. Von Bülow, *Memoirs*, vol. 4, ch. 44, p. 618.
29. Corti, *Alexander von Battenberg*, ch. 13, p. 295. The wild fanaticism displayed in this letter is to be found again in the letters of her niece, the last Tsarina, to her husband from 1914–16.
30. The Empress's own account in Count Egon Corti, *The English Empress*, Cassell, 1957, 'Through the Eyes of the Empress', p. 302.
31. Corti, *Alexander von Battenberg*, ch. 14, p. 299.
32. Hough, *Louis and Victoria*, p. 142.
33. Von Bülow, *Memoirs*, vol. 4, ch. 42, p. 605.
34. Michaela Reid, *Ask Sir James*, Hodder and Stoughton, 1987, Appendix 2, p. 261.
35. R. Scott Stevenson, *Morell Mackenzie*, Heinemann, 1946, pp. 105–18.
36. Jean de Bonnefon, *Drama Impériale*, Paris, 1888, quoted in Reid, *Ask Sir James*.
37. Roger Fulford (ed.), *Your Dear Letter*, Private Correspondence of Queen Victoria and the Crown Princess of Prussia, 1865–1871, from Royal Archives, Evans Bros, 1971, p. 273.
38. Ibid., p. 275.
39. John Costello, *Mask of Treachery* (document dossier of Anthony Blount), Collins, London, 1988, ch. 23, pp. 456–62.
40. See Appendix 4, pp. 242–5.

13

A T last Sandro thought he was free to marry his faithful, loving
Johanna, who had nobly put up with his continual whining he
might be forced to marry another woman. But obstacles
remained in their way. His father had cancer and he was sure his
mother would refuse to give her permission, arguing his marriage was
the funeral of a prince who could still, if he played his cards right, catch
a royal princess. Sandro tentatively trod in his father's footsteps and
applied to Franz Joseph for a general's commission in the Austro-
Hungarian army.

His letters at this period to Johanna are pathetic:

If I meet with refusal from Austria I shall go to America; are you
prepared to go with me? God grant that we may be spared that, I
would hate to go so far away from my home. Sweet Johanna, if only
you were already mine; I am so terribly unhappy; only the thought
of you gives me peace and confidence.

His request was refused with unflattering comments on the
Battenbergs[1] by the Archduke Albrecht. Unfortunately, the reply
coincided with A's last illness. Sandro no longer talked of America but
wrote to Johanna despairingly:

So all my paths are blocked; my future is black and hopeless and I
have to summon all my courage not to break down under the force
of circumstances. What shall I do now? Where shall I go? ...
Without any means at all I cannot pack my traps and wander out
into the world; to emigrate alone is more than I can bring myself to
do, and how should we live if you went with me?

Sandro was terrified of making the final decision. He no longer even
trusted Johanna, who had to reassure him of her love. But at last he

made up his mind and began to make preparations for their marriage. They were interrupted on 4 December 1888 by the death of his father.

After the funeral Sandro hid his plans from his mother and in January 1889 secretly persuaded the Grand Duke of Hesse to allow him to drop his Battenberg title and call himself Count Hartenau. His elopement was comic. Johanna took the first step in the spring, stopped working at the theatre and left by train for Mentone. Shortly afterwards Sandro went to Venice from where, having established a forwarding address, he moved to her hotel, wore large black spectacles and called himself Ernst. They did not sit together at the same table and met secretly, to walk towards the local abbatoir where, not surprisingly, they found themselves undisturbed.[2] Their love for each other must have been deep to transcend the sounds of bellowing cattle and air polluted by stinking skins. Fortunately the preliminaries were quickly settled and they married quietly on 6 February.

The Grand Duke of Hesse, to silence rumours, announced their wedding in a Government paper. The sensation was immense. Not only had the dowager Empress's desired son-in-law married an actress, but, Bismarck insisted, a threat to European peace had been removed. He could not contain his delight. His opinion of Sandro's weak character was confirmed. Like his father he had married beneath him. His bad Polish blood had come out; he would be no more trouble.

During the next year the married couple lived happily in Milan where a son was born in February 1890. Shortly afterwards Sandro entered the Austro-Hungarian army as a second colonel and was stationed at Graz, the town where his father had been posted with his newly-wed Julia many years before. Johanna had a daughter, and their happiness was only disturbed by his frequent gastric pains, a legacy of the Bulgarian campaign. Sandro died at the end of 1893, and disturbed his family as much in death as in his lifetime. His sister Marie, who had always loved him, hurried, too late, to his bedside, and years after in her memoirs gave an account (omitting any criticism of her mother) of Sandro's death:

Six months after our parting in Venice I received on 16th November a telegram from Graz: 'Count Hartenau dangerously ill.' We were in König and hurried off at once to Darmstadt to my mother, to persuade her to go with us to Graz. *She hesitated, and at last decided against the journey.* They were terrible hours until we at last found ourselves next day in the train – Gustav[3] and I.

At the station at Würzburg a telegram was handed to me . . . it was from Ernie, from Darmstadt. 'Sandro died early today – God give you strength.' . . . As if stunned I continued the journey all night long; in Vienna, in the morning, mourning had to be obtained. I stood silently by. At last towards evening we came to Graz . . .

Unknown people, Austrian aristocrats, friends of the Hartenau family, met us at the station. 'The Count died early this morning; the Countess has eaten nothing all day. She is ill; we depend upon you to help her to recover.' (The Countess had had, a month before, a little girl.)

We were driven through the town a long way out to the beautiful villa (its style reminded me of the palace in Sofia).

'Where is my brother? I wish to see him,' I whispered stumbling up the stairs.

In front of a door hung with black stood two 'Leichenbitter' – it was a 'first-class' funeral. 'Beg pardon, the coffin is already closed – the corpse is no longer to be seen' . . . I was pushed into an immense sky-blue apartment. Sandro's widow lay in bed . . . I had only seen her hitherto on the stage. I took her in my arms. I spent the evening with her. She accepted the long refused nourishment. From her and others I had the story of the last days.

Appendicitis – an operation no longer possible – a painful death . . . It was the anniversary of Slivnitza – Sandro was aware of it – delirium set in – he thought he was on the battlefield, gave the word of command – and died!

'Victory – victory!' were his last words . . .

My brothers were expected, but Louis,[4] who had met with an accident on board his ship, telegraphed he could not come. Liko and Franzjos did not arrive till the next evening.[5]

It was typical of Julia's adamantine character that she declined to go to her unforgiven son's funeral.

A few weeks earlier in Florence (Queen Victoria, unlike his mother, kindly received him), Sandro had made his sister swear he would be buried in Sofia. Four days after his death a delegation of two Bulgarian ministers arrived to take the corpse back to a State funeral. Nobody had thought of telling the broken-hearted widow that she was to lose not only her husband but also his body. Marie decided she had to be told and went into her sister-in-law's bedroom to break the news:

> I felt like an executioner as I sat down by the bedside of the poor woman, in order to inform her, on the very evening following the funeral ceremony, of the cruel fact that the removal of the body was contemplated. It was a frightful scene which now ensued. I remained firm, and explained that it was my sacred duty to fulfil my promise to Sandro, and tried to make it clear that it was no longer Count Hartenau, who had been interred in Graz, but the first Prince of Bulgaria, whom his people desired to have back. Gradually she calmed down, but wished to have Prince Ferdinand's promise that she also, when the time came, should be buried in Sofia. I persuaded her to abandon this idea by giving instances of other cases where the wives of celebrated men have not been laid beside their husbands, as in Westminster Abbey ... and in the end she consented to the removal.
>
> Deeply moved, I returned to the ministers, who gratefully kissed my hand.[6]

Marie's carelessness in not telling her broken-hearted sister-in-law, until the last minute, her husband's body was to be moved to Sofia confirms her insensitivity, as does her final comment, 'Deeply moved I returned to the ministers who gratefully kissed my hand.' A cruel, tactless sentence, illustrative of a woman who had learned to put order before kindness.

Julia's refusal to see her son after his marriage, conveniently forgetting her husband had saved her from banishment to the provinces for a similar moral crime, was cruel. But to her the past was dead, the present alone counted; Sandro had let her down twice and joined the untouchables. She could not, having gained respectability, forgive one who had imitated her own youthful behaviour and reminded her – and worse, the world – of her unmentionable history. Such hypocrisy is comprehensible: lying is a common and sometimes necessary sin to those with a past. Elderly sinners have always been the sternest critics of imitators of their past frailties. Julia's behaviour when Sandro lay dying, and her daughter Marie begged her in vain to see her son before it was too late, is another matter; cruelty at such a moment was unnatural, and leaves the impression that her hard, bourgeois mind was empty of pity or kindness.[7]

It is difficult to judge Sandro's character. He had not reached maturity when, at the age of twenty-two, he became a victim of his mother's drive for acceptance. It will be remembered, when she found him growing into a nervous, affectionate boy unfitted for the battle of life, she sent him to a Prussian school compared by the myth to Gordonstoun, but whose discipline was hardly dissimilar to that practised at Dotheboys Hall. Three years of indoctrination, followed by a short period in the Prussian army, overlaid his sensitivity with a veneer of arrogance and rudeness which antagonised his supporters in Germany and Bulgaria.

Julia's coldness created a flaw in her impressionable young son's character from which he never recovered. A hard-hearted mother either drives her children away or binds them to her by their hidden hopes to one day win her favour. She also creates emotional voids which makes them dependent on other women of strong character in whom they seek compensation. Sandro never won his mother's love and the vacuum was filled by the Crown Princess.

Another unfortunate and confusing part of his youth was the annual visit of his aunt the Empress of Russia and her children to Jugenheim. This caused A's children to be brought up for long periods with their Romanov cousins who, as they were staying in his father's house, had no alternative to treating them as equals. As a result the Battenberg children did not understand the difference between the status of morganatic and mediatised princes. This ignorance complicated their lives. When Sandro became Prince of Bulgaria he tried to recapture his childhood relationship with his cousin Alexander, known as 'Mops' in the nursery. This infuriated the Tsar and the Emperor of Germany. His elder sister Marie once lamented: 'When I became older I sometimes thought that my mother, independent and proud as she was, inculcated in us too strictly the duties of our position, while, on the other hand, impressing on us too little of the outward honour due to our exalted relatives and our relationship to them.'[8] Sandro only learned the cruel truth about the prejudice against morganatics in Germany when he tried to marry Vicky.

After a few years it was obvious to all, except Queen Victoria and her eldest daughter, that he was an inadequate ruler, who perpetually picked quarrels with the Tsar.

Another side of his character also ensured he would fall out with Russia: his genuine affection for the people fate had sent him to rule. This made him hate his Russian advisers for their careless habit of treating Bulgarians as expendable animals. Maxim Gorki's notebook gives an example of the type of Russian behaviour to conquered enemies which made Sandro oppose the Tsar's policies.

SUBSTITUTES FOR MONKEYS

Professor Z. the bacteriologist, once told me the following story.

'One day, talking to General B., I happened to mention that I was anxious to obtain some monkeys for my experiments. The general immediately said, quite seriously:

"What about Jews – wouldn't they do? I've got some Jews here, spies that are going to be hanged anyway – you're quite welcome to them if they are any use to you."

'And without waiting for an answer he sent his orderly to find out how many spies were awaiting execution.

'I tried to explain to His Excellency that men would not be suitable for my experiments, but he was quite unable to understand me, and opening his eyes very wide he said:

"Yes, but men are cleverer than monkeys, aren't they? If you inoculate a man with poison he will be able to tell you what he feels, whereas a monkey won't."

'Just then the orderly came in and reported that there was not a single Jew among the men arrested for spying – only Romanians and Bohemians.

"What a pity!" said the General. "I suppose Bohemians won't do either? . . . What a pity . . . !"'[9]

Who can blame a young German resenting such advisers? But it is ironic that Sandro's countrymen should have copied the Russian General's ideas in the last war.

Sandro had the charm of his father, brothers and nephew Mountbatten, but it is a dangerous quality when mixed with weakness, and though it made him loved by the peasants, his vacillations put up the backs of the Bulgarian politicians. His victory at Slivnica was a brilliant piece of organisation, the high point of his reign, but he had neither the stability, strength of character, or ability of his successor

Ferdinand to endure constant strain. His breakdown was caused by only four or five days' acute discomfort in dirty monasteries and a hot boat. Afterwards his energy vanished, and he became the reluctant tennis ball of the Crown Princess, without the strength of character to admit he was in love with another woman. Fortunately, he had four years of peaceful happiness before he died aged thirty-five.

THE ROMANCE OF THE MYTH

It is interesting to make a comparison between my account of Sandro's life after his abdication, and Mountbatten's myth. I wrote of Sandro's immediate love for Johanna, his weak attempts to extricate himself from his engagement to Vicky, the frenetic behaviour of the Crown Princess Frederick (later Empress) and her fixed determination Sandro should marry Vicky; the determination of Bismarck he should not; the rudeness of the future Kaiser William to the 'Battenberg morganatic'; and lastly the refusal of Julia to travel to see her dying son – all these events are the stuff of history and bring the dead to life. Yet the whole story is condensed in *Louis and Victoria* into a few lines dictated by Mountbatten, omitting any details which might discredit the happy family of 'Henty' Hesse characters frozen in the mind of a fourteen-year-old boy. The following four paragraphs, referring to the period after Sandro's abdication, show the effectiveness of omission and contortion of dates:

> Sandro never returned to Bulgaria alive, though his name, as the country's first Sovereign Prince, was revered by the liberal element and the peasants. Nor did this skilful and brave soldier ever fight again. His spirit never recovered after his abdication, his pride permanently wounded by what he regarded as his failure. He was as sickened by German as by Russian perfidy, and, like his father before him, offered his services to the Austrian Emperor. He gave up his princely titles and was granted the Hessian title Count Hartenau and given the command of a brigade.[10]
>
> The intense and *continuing*[11] love between Sandro and the lovely cousin Vicky developed into a tragic domestic and political issue. Even after Fritz's death in 1888, his widow, supported by the Queens,[12] conspired to bring about this marriage which Bismarck so implacably opposed. With Willie's accession to the German throne the chances for his sister's love match were even further

reduced, Bismarck and Kaiser Wilhelm seeking to discredit everything that his father had stood for.

Vicky's mother never recovered from her son's callousness. She had more feeling than her daughter. Louis and his wife tried to make peace with the young Kaiser, but in vain as Victoria wrote to the Queen, 'at Berlin people are only too glad to widen the breach'.

Sandro *at length* found solace in a beautiful opera singer, Johanna Loisinger, and married her in 1889. 'Oh, dear Sandro! it is a sad thing,' wrote the Queen. But for Sandro it was the happiest thing that had ever happened to him. For four years he lived at last in peace and harmony. Then he went down with appendicitis in November and died suddenly of peritonitis.[13]

This romantic version[14] was swallowed by Mountbatten's historians, and their varnished accounts ignore the malevolent opposition to the marriage by every member of the imperial families of Europe, excepting the Crown Princess, her weak husband and, to begin with, Queen Victoria. The disadvantages of A's birth are not mentioned, and the deliberate deception of the Tsar to gain the Bulgarian princedom is omitted and Julia's callousness is ignored, events are transposed and distorted, and the date of Sandro's love for Johanna changed.

It is impossible to tell when Mountbatten learned of the skeletons in the Battenberg cupboard which caused him to distort the lives of his grandfather and uncle, and hide away their papers in a vain attempt to bury recorded events. To know his grandfather's secret was bad enough, but to find in his uncle's life by Corti, published in German in 1921, accounts of the scorn poured on the Battenberg family at different times, by Tsar Alexander III, Bismarck, Emperor William I of Germany and his wife the Empress Augusta, William II, Bismarck and to a lesser extent Franz Joseph and the Habsburgs was too much. The revelations, if admitted, shattered the inspirations of Mountbatten's youth. He would not accept them and sank deeper into his inner world, all the dearer to him because it was threatened. Deliberately he encouraged himself to believe it was a virtue to cover up his own faults and those of his ancestors. His self-deception flawed his character if not his ability, made him many enemies and persuaded him to believe in old age in the impossibility that he had ever made a mistake. His behaviour is understandable. His unhappy time at Osborne accentuated his romantic attachment to his family's honour; only in retirement did this fault unbalance his mind.

NOTES

1. Archduke Albrecht to Count Kalnoky, 26 August 1888, Vienna Archives.
2. Corti, *Alexander von Battenberg*, ch. 14, p. 307.
3. Marie's husband, Count, later Prince Erbach.
4. His excuse was genuine; he had hurt his eye.
5. Marie of Battenberg, *Reminiscences*, pp. 263–4.
6. Ibid., p. 264.
7. In fairness to Julia, there are hints in her daughter's memoirs that her mind was frequently disturbed.
8. Marie of Battenberg, *Reminiscences*, p. 61.
9. Maxim Gorki, *Fragments of my Diary*, ch. 24, p. 246, Philip Allan, 1924.
10. He was made a second colonel.
11. This statement contradicts the fact that he fell in love with Johanna in 1886.
12. What Queens? The only Queen to be mixed up in the affair, Queen Victoria, after first supporting, later opposed the marriage and informed Bismarck of her change of heart before the Emperor Frederick died. There is no evidence the Empress ever conspired with any other Queens to bring about the marriage after her husband died. Her eldest son killed the idea immediately he succeeded.
13. No mention is made of his mother's refusal to see Sandro before or after his death, a striking omission and symptomatic of her unforgiving nature.
14. Those who wish to read the whole fairy tale should study Hough, *Mountbatten*, ch. 6, p. 135.

14

LIKO 1858–1896

THE history of A's third son Prince Henry of Battenberg (Liko) was both sad and funny. A strong, insensitive boy, he survived his Prussian upbringing in Schnepfenthal without suffering like his brother Sandro, and as a young man left Hesse, anxious by merit or marriage to enter the royal European family.

The Battenbergs had a bad year in 1883. Not only were Tsar Alexander and Bismarck furious at the idea of Sandro marrying a Hohenzollern, but in the winter when Louis became engaged to the Grand Duke of Hesse's daughter Victoria, their marriage was rudely opposed by the Hessian parliament, who refused to give her a dowry because she was marrying beneath her and would become a morganatic. This made it essential for Liko to revive the family fortunes by a splendid marriage. His prospects were not encouraging as, at the age of twenty-six, his only asset was a dashing appearance.

He began his army career in Saxony, before von Bülow[1] arranged his transfer to the King's Hussar regiment in Bonn, where his efficiency soon won him a transfer to the crack Garde du Corps in which he became a captain. A distinguished, if onerous career lay ahead of him in the German army, but he must have realised martial success lay in the future and that only by gaining a principality or minor kingdom, or by making an advantageous marriage, could he maintain the Battenberg momentum.

It wasn't easy. Europe was at peace, and as all the new princedoms and kingdoms had been snapped up by his brother and cousins, the easy road to a throne was blocked. Liko's choice of a royal bride was also limited; Nicholas I had turned his father and mother out of Russia, Alexander III detested Sandro and would not have dreamed of allowing any Battenberg to marry a Romanov. The outlook in Prussia was bleak. The Habsburgs' treatment of the family had veered from coldness to reluctant acceptance, to contempt for Sandro.[2] The only hope was England, but unfortunately all the Queen's daughters were married except the shy, fat, twenty-seven-year-old Princess Beatrice (a year older than Liko), whom her mother retained as her unmarried secretary.

What this unfortunate-looking young woman thought of her compulsory seclusion was not known but she bravely accepted her lot, and daily obediently read, wrote, walked or drove, according to her mother's whims. As it is likely a 'thin girl' was always longing to emerge from her ungainly body to love, marry and have children, her life cannot have been without regrets. She had been withdrawn from the marriage market at an early age when the Queen, fearful of losing such an efficient right arm, had forbidden her to dally with young men.

One of her few romantic memories, which may have drawn her to Liko, had been a short early friendship with his eldest brother Louis with whom she had once danced. The next evening she sat in silence, eyelids lowered, under orders from the Queen to frighten her possible admirer off. It was made plain that her life's work was to devote himself to her mother or, to put it politely, to put on 'the Windsor veil'. By 1884 the Queen had foolishly come to believe her daughter had given up all ideas of romantic escape, and was happily looking forward to reading books and taking down letters from her mother until death released her from bondage.

Julia's unhappy youth enabled her to understand that daughters, however plain, wished to marry and did not appreciate the idea of sacrificing their lives to their mothers. Why should Beatrice not have the dreams and hopes of every ageing girl? The good-looking, charming Liko, encouraged by his mother, seized his opportunity before and after Victoria's wedding in Darmstadt,[3] and set out to win the only royal prize available to him in 'blood conscious' Europe.

He could not have had a better chance as the Queen was distracted and worried by the imprisonment of Gordon in Khartoum and the death from haemophilia of her son the Duke of Albany. Worse, on the eve of her granddaughter's wedding she had been appalled to learn her daughter Alice's widower, Louis of Hesse, the bride's father, had secretly married his unmediatised mistress. The royal party was in an uproar, and Liko seized his chance to pay court to the fat young woman of Windsor.

Conceive how pleasant a change it must have been from reading aloud and taking down the Queen's querulous instructions to have suddenly found at her feet a dashing, young man wearing one dazzling uniform after another, gazing efficiently into her little eyes, fondly speaking of love and marriage. Liko was an experienced, efficient wooer and by the time the English party returned home the couple had come to an understanding or, as Mountbatten was later to euphorically put it, 'fallen in love', a phrase he used to justify marriages of convenience.

Considering the personalities and appearances of the pair it is highly unlikely Liko had lost his head; highly probable Beatrice had. He cannot be blamed for following the example of many ambitious younger sons, but he soon discovered he had fallen into a trap, and had not realised the price he would have to pay, or how violent would be the Queen's reaction against her daughter's engagement. The idea of the marriage seemed to her little short of disgraceful, not on account of the morganatic Battenberg blood – she had already championed Victoria's marriage to Louis – but because she wished to keep her youngest daughter as her companion and secretary. The idea the ungrateful girl should now leave her was unthinkable. Bitterly hurt, she declined for months to discuss the matter.

Beatrice's brothers and sisters, who knew what it was like to be closeted daily for hours with their mother, felt sorry for their sister; and as the anti-morganatic bias was weak in England and Louis was a great friend of the Prince of Wales, they tried to forward the 'love match' and persuade their mother to change her mind. The answer was no. 'I hate marriages, especially of my daughters,'[4] wrote the Queen, determined to keep her secretary; no arguments moved her. But her opposition weakened when, later in the year, she heard to her surprise that Liko was prepared to give up his army career and live at Windsor. It is probable she had not considered this possibility, her other German sons-in-law had obstinately insisted on their wives living abroad or in their own houses. This unexpected concession calmed her down but she still insisted the prisoner should be delivered bound hand and foot to Windsor.

Was the lover dismayed? Did he realise he had sold his freedom? Did he try to back out? Did his mother insist he married? These questions can only be answered by the hidden diary of Prince Alexander of Hesse and the Hartenau papers. All we know is Liko was told if he wished to marry Beatrice he had to give up his freedom and become a puppet at Windsor with the Queen holding the strings in her firm little hands.

Stalking at Balmoral was forbidden on consecutive days and Beatrice's future husband had to be in the house or garden to give her moral support; hunting was frowned upon, and as 'the shades of the prison house' began to close on the dashing young man, did he wonder if he was paying too high a price in order to satisfy his mother's ambitions? If so, it was too late to escape.

The Queen had no doubts about her absolute rights over her daughter and the necessity of subjugating her son-in-law. Her lack of feelings for anybody except herself is shown in a typical letter:

OSBORNE, 9th Jan. 1885
The Queen thanks the Duke of Grafton very much for his kind letter and good wishes for her beloved daughter Beatrice's betrothal. The Duke has known her from birth, and knows therefore *what* a devoted daughter she has ever been; he can therefore understand that it would have been *quite out of the question* for her ever to have left the Queen; and *she* would *never* have *wished* it herself, knowing well how *impossible* it was for her to leave her Mother.

Prince Henry of Battenberg is however ready to make England his home and the Princess will continue to live with the Queen as heretofore. He is very amiable, very unassuming and sensible, and in addition very good-looking.[5]

The pair were married at Whippingham Church near Osborne. Liko's theatrical white Prussian uniform looked out of place in the parish church and the Princess of Wales laughingly compared him to Lohengrin. Few of the Queen's German relations attended such an unsuitable wedding. The prison doors closed. We are given a hint of his feelings in a wedding photograph of the pair. To the left stands the bridegroom, splendid, bemedalled, beribboned (rewards for obedience), a magnificent picture of German manhood in his theatrical uniform and high boots, embodying the fascination of the Battenbergs. Behind his unnatural wedding mask can be glimpsed a personality created by nature to enjoy life and seek adventure. Despite his dazzling uniform he looks at the camera with an air of embarrassed detachment while his dumpy bride, to whom the best dressmakers and the finest jewels could not, even for a moment, give a jot of beauty, stares at him in silent admiration. When I first saw this photograph it struck a chord in my memory which weeks later fitted into place, and I was back in a restaurant in the Dordogne looking at a photograph of a good-looking, moustached young farmer, standing embarrassed in his best Sunday suit, holding at the end of a length of rope a prize, rosetted pig.

Undoubtedly they made a discordant-looking couple and unfortunately for Liko, since the sixteenth century, the marriage of a handsome, penniless young men for money or position to an older, ugly women has been a favourite comic theme in English literature and on the stage.

The pair became something of a joke. This distressed the proud young prisoner and it did not take him long to realise he was leading an unmanly and unbearably dull life. Where the Queen went Beatrice and himself had to go; at openings and inspections, the Prince could be seen lagging behind his mother-in-law and wife, his good looks accentuating her homeliness. The reality of living at Windsor may have been grimmer than Liko expected. Look for instance at three days in his life in May 1887:

10th May – Attended 'The Drawing Room', Buckingham Palace.
11th May – Visited the tombs in Westminster Abbey with the Queen and Princess Beatrice.
14th May – The Queen with Liko and Beatrice left Windsor at 3.30 for Paddington from where they drove to Mile End to open a 'people's palace'.
Afterwards they visited the Albert Docks and Mansion House and returned for dinner at 8.30.[6]

A little later they went to Balmoral to celebrate the Queen's birthday; one afternoon Liko had to stand with his wife and present a bunch of flowers to the Queen, before driving out to tea.

The next year he was taken to Florence for a month, from the end of March until the end of April. Afterwards the royal party went to Berlin where the German Emperor refused to give Liko the precedence of a royal highness. In 1889 he had to travel to Llangollen and sit for hours listening to Welsh choirs. True he was made a Knight of the Garter, a Royal Highness in England, Governor of the Isle of Wight, a privy councillor, etc., etc., but to his surprise – Germans take titles very seriously — each honour piled on him was a source of ribaldry in the English press. *Vanity Fair* cruelly summed up Liko's marriage gains:

> It is not vouchsafed to all of us to become demorganaticated, bridegrooms, Royal Highnesses, and Knights of the Garter in the twinkling of an eye.[7]

Soon he began to have love affairs, for which Mountbatten had a euphemism, 'picking flowers by the way'. But alas he always had to return to his Windsor prison where his wife talked, and talked, and talked. He introduced gaiety into the castle life, gave his bride a glimpse of romance, altered some of the Queen's habits, made meals more amusing, increased smoking facilities, but it was not enough. The fiery blood of the Battenbergs demanded action and adventure.

His family had no understanding of spiritual life; literature and the arts were strangers to their practical minds. As a result their last years were bitter, sad and empty. A, when he ceased to be the unofficial ambassador to the Tsar, did not know what to do with himself. His character deteriorated and he illegally speculated in Russian railway stocks with his brother-in-law's mistress's brother, and was persuaded by his wife to interfere with his sons' careers. He compromised Sandro before he went to Bulgaria and sent him back to probable death when his spirit was broken, all the while lamenting the pains of old age.

Sandro disintegrated before he left Bulgaria, and in idleness lost his manliness and became, in a few years, a weak, mindless imitation of the dashing youth who had threatened the peace of Europe.

In 1914 when Louis was dismissed from the Admiralty his only compensations were to catalogue medals, write a dull naval history of ships' names, paint banal pictures, and sit sticking stamps in an album, a sad expression on his noble face. Mountbatten in retirement tried to fill in his time by attending endless ceremonies and good works; it was not enough and he became obsessed with propping up the imaginary grandeur of the House of Hesse. This was an unsatisfactory alternative for active life and boredom made him bitterly turn in private on those superior to him in rank for whom he pretended affection.

'Prince Philip,' continued Mountbatten, 'is an absolute Mountbatten and not a bit Hanoverian, and his children have a degree of intelligence quite lacking in King George V, King George VI or any of those people at all. Prince Charles, too, is an absolute Mountbatten. The real intelligence in the royal family comes through my parents to Prince Philip and the children.

'The Queen, of course, is a marvellous person. Her ministers are always surprised at how well-informed she is. She is extremely sound – not brilliant – and that comes from her mother. There was great worthiness in King George V and even Edward VII, but that old Hanoverian line was becoming dimmer and dimmer so that they could not even pass their exams.'[8]

I will not comment on the taste of these opinions, which illustrate Mountbatten's desire to flaunt the superiority of his own inferior family,[9] but I will try and balance his unkind words about King George VI. When Winston Churchill lamented his death in the House of Commons, he ended with the words – I quote from memory – 'And after a day of sunshine and good sport, good night to those who loved him best; he fell asleep as every man who fears his God and nothing else must hope to do.' There was a long, sad pause of respectful silence: the feeling of the House and country was of affectionate regard and love for a man who, despite ill-health, had with his ideal Queen, restored the royal family's position after the short reign of Edward VIII, and had shortened his life by ceaselessly working for his country.

But at least the two Alexanders and the two Louis's were heroes of their times. Liko, plucked out of the army before he had won his spurs, had not only done nothing, there was nothing he could do, and it must have made him bitter to read of his brother's great victory in Bulgaria; no glory awaited him and he could see no future beyond trailing behind the skirts of two women or sitting disconsolately looking out of the window at the sodden Scotch hills, aware he was forbidden to go stalking in the rain.

Sections of the press were merciless and exploited the British dislike of foreigners near to the throne. Even Princess Beatrice's pregnancies were made a subject for scornful mirth.

Another Battenberg on the way! well!! well!! One cannot help drawing a comparison between the plague of rabbits in Australia and the plague of Battenbergs in Europe. And after all there is a close resemblance between the two visitations. The former, as well as the latter, 'gather where they have not strawed', are abominably prolific, and cause an amount of mischief which is in inverse proportion to their size and importance. Europe would gladly give £25,000 to a political Pasteur who would undertake to rid it of the Battenbunnies.[10]

After a time the tedium of this life and his constricted opportunities became unbearable, and he could not help comparing himself unfavourably with his brother Louis's thriving naval career. Too much was asked of a young man never cut out to be a courtier who, with Sandro, was sacrificed on the altar of his family's ambitions. Eventually he rebelled against his cushioned life, sailed in gales in the Solent and travelled against the Queen's wishes to Albania, an expedition which in those days could be compared to playing Russian roulette. He survived, but life became grimmer as the Queen got older and his wife plainer and more talkative.

In 1895 Julia died. Freed from her restraining influence, 'hotly pursued by a lady',[11] he could bear Windsor no longer and leapt into the mouth of death by going to serve in the campaign against the slave trader King Prempeh[12] (or Kwaka Dua III) of Ashanti on the Gold Coast, colloquially known as the White Man's Grave. It was his. Yet one cannot but feel he was fortunate as he could not, having broken his bonds, have returned to complete his life sentence at Windsor.

Beatrice was broken-hearted. Did she blame her mother? Did she ever realise the extent to which her adored husband, who had rescued her from spinsterdom, had chafed under tedious court constrictions? Did she wonder, in her long years of widowhood, if Liko would still have been alive if they had lived in their own home and not been confined in Windsor Castle? Did she resent her past servitude and realise her husband could, if the Queen had allowed it, have had a satisfactory career. After all, if Louis could belatedly join the British Navy, Liko could have joined the British Army and with his family's charm and talents, a successful career could have made his marriage endurable. Did Princess Beatrice ever dare to admit her selfish mother had destroyed her marriage by frustrating her husband's fiery spirits until he rebelled and died?

I ask these questions because one of my first memories is of a little old great-aunt[13] born in the dark ages of the 1850s. I remember hearing she lived in 'straightened' circumstances and thought that explained why she always sat bolt upright. Her appearance never varied; scanty false ringlets extended over her forehead in unsuccessful imitation of Queen Alexandra. Her kind, stiff, raddled old face was covered with layers of powder and rouge and she had – this fascinated me – only one eye. The other had been cut out while she lay conscious in an operating theatre, her eyelid raised. The remaining one wept copiously. I asked why, and my father told me it was unmercifully strained year after year, by ceaselessly reading to Princess Beatrice, for a pittance a year. Her story made a deep impression on my young mind, which increased later when I went to tea with my weeping aunt – now, by the by, a ghost at Pamflete, her childhood home in Devonshire. Time has not driven out of my mind the fat, garrulous old Princess with her pendulous cheeks, guttural voice and cross expression. I sat silent, paralysed with shyness and horror at the two-eyed torturer who would not stop talking.

The old pair lived on for many years and spent the early days of the war in a Sussex house where Miss Bulteel had in air raids to stumble downstairs to the air raid shelter carrying the cushions and bedclothes, unaided by the stronger, younger woman, who paid no attention to her lady-in-waiting's infirmities. Fortunately her last years were peaceful, as Princess Beatrice died in 1944. Perhaps my shocked feelings, which I retain to this day, have made me exaggerate the sufferings of a half-blind old woman, or was the Queen's youngest daughter taking revenge on a helpless symbol of her mother's power?

The Princess's unkindness was sometimes justified; she detested her sister, the one-eared Louise, Duchess of Argyll,[14] who had caught Liko's lascivious eye. Beatrice took revenge by asserting her sister was misbehaving with Arthur Bigge, Keeper of the Privy Purse. Furious Princess Louise wrote to the Queen.[15] After Liko's death she had her revenge, telling his widow 'that she alone had been his confidante and his wife Beatrice had been nothing to him.'[16]

The myth would not admit Liko married Beatrice for 'convenience' and makes up a cosy love story of the pair falling in love à la Cartland, but had to admit he could not stand the tedium of his position and in desperation broke out of his gilded cage to fight on the Gold Coast. Actually, it was not much of a war; no fighting took place and not one soldier was killed in action. Liko died of malaria aboard HMS *Blonde* and returned to England stowed below in a rum-filled can made of soldered biscuit tins. Poor man, it was typical of his bad luck that he should have chosen to fight and die in a bloodless war and end up in what was, to the Navy, a comic coffin. His widow can have received little consolation from the legend concerning the manner of his return to England. For many years after his death seamen would approach bartenders and ask in jovial voices for a 'tot of Prince 'Enery'.

FRANZ JOSEPH 1861–1924

Before telling Louis's story, it is necessary to break the death sequence and get rid of the fourth, youngest, least significant of the brothers, Franz Joseph. Born in Padua in 1861, he spent his life trying to emulate his brother Sandro; an exciting visit to Bulgaria had given him a taste for romance and intrigue. His character is familiar to both historians and novelists: the romantic plotter who believes he can win back his brother's princedom. He spent his life going to clandestine meetings, telling lies and living in limbo, uncertain of the difference between truth and invention. Two vignettes perfectly describe him: the first, from Sir Frederick Ponsonby's *Recollections of Three Reigns*, shows how unmercifully he was squashed by Queen Victoria despite her affection for his family:

No one was really kinder to bad shots as a rule than she was, although the head stalker came in every night to tell her exactly what each person out stalking or fishing had done. She always pretended not to know the result of the day's sport and asked for information. Prince Francis Joseph of Battenberg, who was a very bad shot, unlike his brother Prince Henry, unfortunately didn't know this. Having been out stalking, he proceeded to give a rambling account of his day's sport, quite unconscious that the Queen knew every detail. All would have been well if he had left it at that, but he went on to say that it was a pity everything was so badly done and that the stalkers did not know much about stalking. Then the Queen turned on him and rent him. She asked him how many shots he had had, and when he replied he could not remember, she asked whether he had seven, and had missed them all. She asked how far the stags were when he fired and he replied that he was no judge of distance, whereupon she said, 'I suppose about a hundred yards.' It then dawned on him that she knew exactly what had happened and he shut up like an umbrella.[17]

A second glimpse of this hopeless adventurer's life was recorded by Madam Balsan, born Miss Consuelo Vanderbilt, later a Duchess of Marlborough. In her autobiography she drew a graphic picture of her ambitious, old pug of a mother, hawking her around Europe in search of a grand husband:

We spent the whole of May and June in Paris, and I had five proposals of marriage. When I say I had, I mean that my mother informed me that five men had asked her for my hand . . . There was only one, a German prince, whose cause I was allowed to consider. Prince Francis Joseph was the youngest of the four handsome Battenberg Princes . . .

I met Prince Francis Joseph at an evening party given by Madame de Pourtalès in her house close to the Madeleine. That the Comtesse Mélanie de Pourtalès had been a famous beauty could still be seen. She was a typical *grande dame* and in her salons were to be found the *beau monde* of Paris. I felt lost as I entered that brilliant throng of statesmen, diplomats and elegant women, but my hostess with inimitable charm called me to her side and put me at ease. I sensed by the way she drew me out that her interest was not inspired purely by kindness to a little débutante and I wondered what lay behind it. Later in the course of the evening while I was with the Prince I saw my mother engrossed in conversation with our hostess; they were observing us with interest. Instinct suggested and made me fearful of some deep-laid plot . . .

The stage seemed set for a political intrigue and my hostess's ambitions to place her protégé on a throne showed signs of succeeding. I think that for a moment my mother's intentions to marry me to an English duke faltered! A royal crown glittered more brightly than a coronet! So the Prince continued his courtship unhindered, unfolding his ambitions to my apprehensive ears. It seemed I was but to exchange one bondage for another. Such a marriage could mean only unhappiness. Separated from my family and my friends, living in a provincial capital, ironbound in a strict etiquette, with a man whose views were those of a prejudiced German princeling – how could I reconcile myself to such a life? Only a great love could make such a marriage possible, and I felt aversion rather than attraction for the dapper man of the world for whom I realised I was only a means to an end. My mother on second thoughts decided to adhere to her former intentions and raised no objections when I confessed my feelings to her. So nothing more was heard of the project.[18]

Franz Joseph was a sad, silly shadow of a man, dapper rather than dashing, ineffective, charmless. Madame Balsan's straight-forward memory was not sensational enough for the myth; one of Mountbatten's pet authors, David Duff, dramatised the meeting in *Hessian Tapestry* and put words into the Prince's mouth which it is unlikely he used as they would have discouraged the heiress he was determined to inveigle into Bulgaria:

> But the Prince's cool confidence about his ambitions proved start-ling to the American heiress, and even the dull routine of afternoon tea in a stately home seemed preferable to bullets whining through the streets of Sofia and knives flashing in the cathedral . . .

Duff gave the reference for these thrilling words as *The Glitter and the Gold*, page 28, which I have quoted in full. There is no mention of whining bullets and flashing knives.

The only consolation Franz Joseph won from his plotting was a Montenegrin bride! An apple from the bottom of the royal barrel.

LOUIS 1854–1897

To understand Louis's adult naval career, it should be remembered his initial ill-treatment won him the lifelong friendship of the Prince of Wales, the undisputed leader of society, who had unwittingly caused his original ordeal. He found in him a protector who favourably influenced his future postings and encouraged him to take long periods of leave and half-pay. Louis was clever and attractive enough not to lose the respect of his patron's critical mother, Queen Victoria. Naturally his good fortune excited envy, cutting him off from the great majority of his contemporaries, who could not hope to meet him at Marlborough House or Sandringham. It was his acceptance of royal favours easing the hardships of his youthful naval career, and not the lack of culture in the Navy as his son suggested, which contributed to his scarcity of friends when at the end of his career he became First Sea Lord. Another reason was his professionalism, efficiency, and under-standing of the mechanism and foibles of every ship on which he served. He was full of ideas and understood the need for change and modernisation in the British Navy. This was not an advantage; many of his contemporaries considered such opinions sacrilege, especially coming from a full-blooded German whose home and roots remained in Hesse. That he was envied is not surprising, jealousy between generations has always been a natural part of life in every profession in the world, blinding the unsuccessful to the obvious virtues of those who have left them behind, and enabling them to blame nepotism as the cause of their own failure. Louis, as a midshipman, increased antagonism by three characteristics which throughout his career annoyed his own generation: charm, tactlessness and use of the royal family. Charm, like butter, should be thinly spread or it sickens. From the beginning of his first posting to the North American station, he was aware of this maxim and strictly kept his asset for social gatherings ashore; aboard he would retire to work, study or watch the sailors going about their various tasks, making notes of what he considered wasteful or impractical customs. From this period can be dated the beginning of his understanding of every detail of the daily running of ships, and the amount of work which could be expected from various members of his crews.

He rightly believed practical knowledge was essential for every officer, and brought up his sons to learn the same lessons. Their efficiency made both generations magnificent officers, with a detailed understanding of every seaman's job, a rarity which gained them the respect and admiration of their men. But at the beginning of his career, Louis's dedication to work irritated his fellow midshipmen, who believed he thought himself 'above' their recreations. This belief was fuelled by his successful social life ashore where he was plied with invitations. This was annoying but comprehensible as it was known he had won the Prince of Wales's favour; a visit of the Russian cruiser *Svetlana* to Havana in 1872 in which his first cousin the Grand Duke Alexis of Russia (in disgrace for secretly marrying a lady-in-waiting) was serving emphasised his close relationship to the Tsar.[19] Naturally it was irritating for the uninvited to know he was entertained in the richest households and courted by the prettiest girls, but this natural jealousy would have been mitigated if he had possessed the tact to join in his companions' youthful pleasures, a concession which would have made his privileged position more acceptable. Unfortunately he had a morganatic, Germanic respect for rank, and none of the quiet diffidence, popularity, and lack of snobbery of Prince George (later George V).

When he returned to England in 1874 to study at the Royal Naval College at Greenwich, he flung himself with zest into society and soon fulfilled his mother's wish that he should become a close friend of the Prince of Wales. For the second, but not the last, time in his naval career he suffered from his hedonistic life in royal circles and was reprimanded for idleness by the Admiral in Charge, Sir Astley Cooper Key.[20] This check made him work harder and succeed in his final exams (he always appeared to effortlessly pass his tests). He came first in seamanship: 'the best study ever' Mountbatten later modestly claimed (his son had no need to exaggerate, his father was a brilliant sailor), and equal first in gunnery. But in the French exam he did badly as his examiner, a Frenchman, had a strong dislike of Germany who had violated his beloved Paris only three years before.

Louis's successes at Greenwich were noticed by the Prince of Wales and he was asked to visit India with the rank of orderly officer in the winter of 1875–6. The party was to sail on the *Serapis*. Mountbatten later described to Hough his father's feelings:

Louis thought the invitation over very carefully. The last tour had been a great mistake. But now he had been in the service for six years, he was no longer a greenhorn, he was much more self-assured and much more accepted by his generation of naval officers. This, surely, could not damage him as the earlier tour had done? He accepted gratefully; and then went off to enjoy himself buying all the kit and uniforms he would require for the occasion. Second to wearing uniforms, Louis liked best to buy them.[21]

While the last sentence shows Mountbatten's loving identification with his father, it also illustrates Louis's insensitivity to his fellow officers' feelings. He should not have forgotten his début on the *Ariadne* six years before, or that his life ashore in America and Canada had been very different from that of his shipmates, and that before, during and after his term at Greenwich, he had been a constant guest of the Prince of Wales in London and the country, and that it looked odd for a sailor to go on a land tour of central India. It was a sign of weakness that he could not see such a jaunt would encourage his critics to believe he was more of a courtier than a sailor. The Prince of Wales himself thought so, and when in India he heard Louis had been offered a place on the Duke of Edinburgh's ship the *Sultan*, he said, 'You would do much better to get a little half-pay and spend the season with me at Marlborough House.' Louis wisely refused the offer but unwisely accepted the Duke's, again laying himself open to criticism. Apart from enjoying himself in Malta playing polo (it's impossible not to notice how often in the next generation his son Mountbatten replayed his father's life) Louis was favoured again as the Duke of Edinburgh had promised his father he would be treated as an unofficial flag lieutenant, a privilege to which he was not entitled. According to Kerr he carried out naval duties, but in *Louis and Victoria* he found he was 'to act as a naval ADC and equerry'.[22] Variants are common in the saga. Both agree he messed with the Duke, unlike the other officers.

Mountbatten later claimed 'Louis was by now despairing of ever being treated normally and of getting on in his career like everyone else.'[23] This was an unfair complaint, as he had chosen to accept royal patronage and had been to sea three times out of four with royalty. How could he claim he was not getting the same chance as 'anyone else' when he had accepted postings which distanced him daily from his fellow officers? He, not they, dined nightly with the 'touchy and quirky' heavy drinking Duke. Louis only had himself to blame. If only he had left his career to the Admiralty he would have had the same chance as everybody else. However, his love of royalty was shaken on this posting by his royal Captain, nicknamed 'Matilda', who, bad-tempered and often drunk,[24] was hardly on speaking terms with his commander, who considered him at times incapable of running his ship.

A dissatisfied Louis was either under or overworked, and was vastly relieved when the Fleet was ordered to the Golden Horn to check the Russian advance on Constantinople. In my account of Sandro's career I described the meeting of the two brothers in Constantinople, their return to the *Sultan*, their joint visit to the *Temeraire*, the Queen's rage and Louis's abrupt move from the *Sultan* to another ship.

He was then ordered back to England where, to his surprise, he found the climate had changed and he was in favour again. The Queen had asked her secretary Sir Henry Ponsonby to write to W. H. Smith, the First Lord of the Admiralty:

Osborne
April 10 1878

Dear Mr Smith

The Queen is informed that the Duke of Edinburgh is surprised and annoyed at the sudden removal of Prince Louis of Battenberg from the 'Sultan' without H.R.H. having been informed of it. H.M. who fully approved of the transfer of Prince Louis – had understood that this would have been done in the usual manner and believed that my order to the office was always sent through the Capt. of the Ship. But as H.R.H. had no notice of it, the transfer has the semblance of being made for some reason.

The Queen hopes you will be able to satisfy the Duke of Edinburgh that such was not the case, and to explain to H.R.H. the reason which made this move desirable.[25]

This set the First Lord a difficult task as it was impossible to politely explain to the Duke that the Queen's anger had been the reason for Louis's move. However, the implications were plain: (1) the Queen had been correct to rebuke her son and Louis, and (2) they had been forgiven. The Tsarina was less charitable and wrote to her brother that Sandro had been victimised by the old fool who was calmer now 'she had indulged her spleen'. She continued: 'Marie [her daughter] declares that you only have to give her [the Queen] a good fright to draw in her horns.'[26]

It is now clear what happened. The Queen's children had grown up, and the older ones knew how to get round their mother and quieten her violent reactions. They were knit together by the loyalty of strictly brought up families, and although Alfred was not popular, none of them wished to see him publicly humiliated, a dangerous precedent. Neither did the Prince of Wales wish to see his young friend Louis's career ruined by a youthful indiscretion. To lessen the Queen's anger they asked what harm the incident had caused. Was not Admiral Phipps-Hornby to blame for allowing Sandro on his ship? Had not the excitable British ambassador exaggerated the effects of a harmless meeting and made Alfred and Louis scapegoats? There was enough truth in their defence to make the Queen have second thoughts about publicly humiliating one of her children, however much she disliked him.[27]

Bored by the fracas, the Queen agreed to shift the blame. The

Ambassador and Phipps-Hornby received polite reprimands while the First Lord W. H. Smith assured Louis that the past would not be held against him, and he was to be given an opportunity to lead an 'ordinary' officer's life on the battleship *Agincourt*, stationed in the Mediterranean. At last his pretended ambitions were fulfilled, he was to be treated as a normal sailor, but not for long; the Duke of Connaught became engaged to Princess Marie Louise of Prussia and planned to honeymoon in the Mediterranean on the Royal Yacht *Osborne*. He asked Louis to come with him as a lieutenant and friend. Despite his good intentions the invitation was too good to be missed, and Louis returned to an easy royal berth.

After the trip, which could not conceivably have been called a test of seamanship, the *Osborne* was put into dock for repairs and Louis hung about hunting, shooting and dancing, often in the company of the Prince of Wales with whom he went to Plymouth to lay the foundation stone of the Eddystone Lighthouse which was, Mountbatten recalled later, 'one of the few serious duties of that summer of 1879'.[28]

When the *Osborne* came out of dock Louis took the Prince of Wales to Kiel, and afterwards to visit the Grand Duke of Hesse, in Darmstadt. Louis again showed acute insensitivity, in not understanding why he was not immediately offered another appointment. It does not seem to have occurred to him that to have left the *Agincourt* to sail off on a honeymoon cruise and to have followed it up with a trip to Germany with the heir to the throne was unwise, if he wished to be taken seriously. It is not surprising the Admiralty was fed up with the spoiled, if able, young German.

His next serious occupation was a love affair with Lillie Langtry, which resulted in a baby whose living female descendants have maintained the family's tradition of beauty. This frightened his family, and as the well-informed Queen was still unsure of his intentions and did not want a handsome temptation hanging around her daughter Beatrice, the Admiralty posted Louis to the *Inconstant*, Lord Clanwilliam's flagship of a 'flying squadron' of five ships whose intention was to go round the world without using their engines, to prove the continuing importance of sail.

This Canutian dream was typical of the conservative attitude of the services to change. Sail was, to many old sailors, what the horse was to the army. On board one of the other ships, HMS *Bacchante*, sailed the

Prince of Wales's two sons, Albert and George. Mountbatten later wrote, 'It would also be an experience for the service's new raw royal recruits.' This was inaccurate as they had already sailed in the *Bacchante* to the West Indies and Spain.

On both occasions they had been accompanied by their amazing tutor, the Rev. John Neale Dalton, later a Canon, and father of Hugh, who knew everything about everything. For some reason he originally took a dislike to the *Bacchante*, claiming it was unsafe, and wished his charges moved onto HMS *Newcastle*, the last wooden frigate in service. The Admiralty, to prove Dalton wrong, sent the Captain of the *Bacchante*, Lord Charles Scott, to sea to find a severe storm and see if his ship capsized.[29] Fortunately he found a storm, but remained afloat, and also safely survived the hurricanes of the Caribbean and the huge waves in the Bay of Biscay. Dalton then suggested the separation of the two Princes to avoid both drowning if their ship was sunk. How he could then have taught more than one of them he didn't explain. It was about the only time in his life he was silent about anything; he usually suffocated his listeners with detailed, tedious displays of irrelevant knowledge.

All went well until the Fleet was caught in a storm between Cape Town and Australia when the *Bacchante*'s rudder broke. The Admiral was worried the royal brothers had sunk, but eventually they arrived safely in Western Australia. Mountbatten blames Lord Charles Scott, arguing he was 'incapable of dealing with a crisis', and states the Princes' lives were only saved by the commander taking over the ship. He concluded his account of the Princes' escape with these words:

After this it could be said that the Princes had had sufficient sea experiences for the time being and they were transferred to the *Inconstant* for their own safety until they went home separately.[30]

This alteration of the truth was caused by Mountbatten's need to include his father in any situation in which the royal family was involved. While it is true that the Princes transferred to Louis's ship, when the *Bacchante* was being repaired, this could not have taken long, as later the *Bacchante* towed the *Inconstant*[31] through a becalmed sea and the Princes returned to England in her. They were welcomed home by the Prince and Princess of Wales in Swanage Bay on 5 August 1882, and later by Queen Victoria at Cowes.[32] The reader wishing to know more about this extraordinary journey can if he wishes read Dalton's 750,000 word journal which, he claimed, was stimulated by the two usually silent Princes' comments, a pretext which gave him an excuse to dwell endlessly on every single thought which thronged his head. A more amusing alternative is to read ten brilliantly funny pages, describing the voyage, by Kenneth Rose in his life of King George V.[33] Mountbatten's alteration of facts was an affectionate attempt to prove Louis's closeness to King George V, but it's rather bad luck for Lord Charles Scott to go down in history as such a deplorable captain that the young Princes had to be snatched out of his incapable hands.

On the homeward journey, the little Fleet broke up at Gibraltar. The Princes went home and Louis sailed to give Ahmed Arabi's rebels a lesson at Alexandria. Naval officers in 1882 were thirsting for blood. For years they had been hanging about like sportsmen waiting for the rain to stop so they could go out shooting; here at last was their opportunity.

The famous bombardment of Alexandria was the result of a nationalistic rebellion against the Turkish colonial rulers of Egypt, and to a lesser degree against England and France, the Sultan's allies, who were trying by a system of dual control, to solve Egypt's insoluble economic problems. The uprising was not surprising considering the appalling poverty of the agricultural community and the insatiable greed of their Turkish rulers. Lady Duff Gordon described the general malaise in 1867:

I cannot describe the misery here now – every day some new tax. Every beast, camel, cow, sheep, donkey and horse is made to pay. The fellaheen can no longer eat bread; they are living on barley-meal mixed with water, and raw green stuff, vetches, & c. The taxation makes life almost impossible: a tax on every crop, on every animal first, and again when it is sold in the market; on every man, on charcoal, on butter, on salt ... The people in Upper Egypt are running away by wholesale, utterly unable to pay the new taxes and do the work exacted. Even here (Cairo) the beating for the year's taxes is awful.[34]

The original plan was that if negotiations failed the British and French governments would bombard Alexandria. But Paris had second thoughts, and ordered their fleet not to join in.

Negotiations broke down and the bombardment began on 11 June 1882. The Alexandrian forts, fortunately manned by untrained gunners, fired back unsuccessfully with their strange mixture of muzzle loading and antique guns. Nor were the Royal Navy marksmen impressive; their 3198 explosive shells only destroyed 28 emplacements. The fleet would have suffered badly if it had been faced with a modern artillery. The Egyptians soon ran away and gave the Navy practice without retaliation. The casualties in the British Fleet, which was hit by 75 missiles, counting stone cannonballs, were 6 dead, 27 wounded. The bombardment, lauded by the war-starved newspapers as an heroic epic, was hardly more dangerous than shooting pheasants with Arab sportsmen today.

The Fleet was now faced with Lord Dufferin's 'elephant and whale' problem. What was to be done after the forts had been silenced with only a force of 450 Marines and 150 Blue Jackets to send ashore? Bravely the puny force landed on 13 June at the mercy of Ahmed's uncounted thousands. Captain Fisher of the *Inflexible* described their good fortune:

I landed on the 14th [sic] to take possession of the forts and city, and the two following days were the most anxious ones I have ever spent in my life, as our force was quite inadequate. None of us slept a wink for three days and were regularly done up when the General (Sir A. Alison) arrived with his troops. As it turns out, I believe our preparations and activities kept [Ahmed] Arabi from attacking us, as he made certain we had a much larger force at our command.[35]

It was true the danger was over, but once in, Britain couldn't get out of Egypt, and this was the beginning of a relationship which ended at Suez in 1956.

Unfortunately the *Inconstant*, with Louis aboard, arrived the day after the bombardment. A month later he wrote the Prince of Wales a letter which gives interesting clues to his relationship with the heir to the throne, and explains his unpopularity as a young man with senior officers. After describing his sailors digging a canal, and numerous false alarms, he refers to Captain Lord Charles Beresford who had earlier offered him a job in the naval police force:

It would have been very much better if he had left months ago. That trip to the Head Quarters was a mistake. Everyone here foretold him how it would end. I suppose you will see him when he gets home as I see by the papers that you are to be back from the continent about now.[36]

He ended with some very polite sentences referring to the Prince of Wales' family:

Last night I also received a telegram from Louis (of Hesse) in answer to mine. I am so glad for his sake that you and the Princess were with him on his birthday. He says 'I hope you will join Naval Brigade' . . . I have this minute been interrupted by such a jolly letter from your younger son. Please tell him how delighted I am to have it and that I'll answer it in a few days.[37]

Louis then complained Admiral Seymour had turned down a request made by the Duke of Connaught that he should be put ashore in charge of some 'Gatlings', and alternatively should see active service as the ADC to a general.

My request was refused point blank, in, I may say, a very rude manner without giving any reason. Even Capt. Fitzgerald, who's not the most polite of men, was astonished. From the foregoing it would seem that I am Admiral Seymour's *bête noire* – but why? I keep on asking myself that question, as we have ever been the best of friends on shore – I never served with him – and he received me on arrival most cordially, saying that I should yet have a chance of seeing fighting etc . . .

Please give my most respectful love to the Princess and my best love to the young ladies who I am glad to hear have not forgotten their faithful 'peacock' – also needless to say to your dear sons.[38]

This letter with his references to the Prince's children is sycophantic, while for Louis to describe himself to the Prince's daughters as their 'faithful "peacock"' was both familiar and embarrassing.

Louis did not seem to realise that Seymour had other things to think about than whether or not a young lieutenant should fight ashore. He was unwise to repeatedly ask to be moved from a mundane if useful job to become a privileged ADC. His criticisms of Beresford and Admiral Seymour, or Ocean Swell, as Mountbatten jovially called him, were disloyal, and suggest he was prepared to sneak on senior officers behind their backs in order to keep his royal patron well informed: an unattractive trait. Louis was in a bad temper at missing the action and reacted like a spoilt child. If he hoped to influence the royal family against his admiral he was mistaken. Admiral Seymour was created Lord Alcester for his management of the bombardment. Considering the opposition it was the cheapest peerage ever earned, but the action was enormously enjoyed by the British public.

When the sport was over, Louis was welcomed back into the 'prince's set', for a few more months' social excitement.

NOTES

1. Von Bülow, *Memoirs*, vol. 4, ch. 42, p. 304.
2. Report of Baron Biegeleben, Austro–Hungarian Ambassador in Sofia, to Vienna. Quoted Corti, *Alexander von Battenberg*, pp. 215–17.
3. The Queen and Princess Beatrice arrived in Darmstadt on 17 April. The marriage was to be on 30 April as the more convenient May was considered by the Queen to be 'a cursed month'. They were back in Windsor on 14 May. Liko had plenty of time.
4. Fulford (ed.), *Beloved Mama*, p. 176, quoting Royal Archives.
5. Buckle (ed.), *Letters and Journals of Queen Victoria*, vol. 3, p. 593.
6. Ibid., May 1887.
7. *Vanity Fair*, 1 August 1885.
8. Hough, *Mountbatten*, p. 86.
9. See Appendix 3.
10. *Society*, May 1889.
11. David Duff, *Hessian Tapestry*, David and Charles, 1979, ch. 22, p. 243, quoting Marquis of Carisbrooke.
12. *Encyclopaedia Britannica*, 1926 ed. See Ashanti Wars.
13. Miss Bessie Bulteel, 1855–1948, lady-in-waiting in turn to Queen Victoria, the Queen of Spain, and Princess Beatrice.
14. Her ear was lost in a sledge accident in Canada.
15. Reid, *Ask Sir James*, ch. 6, p. 103.
16. Kenneth Rose, *Kings, Queens and Courtiers*, Weidenfeld and Nicolson, 1985, p. 181.
17. Ponsonby, *Three Reigns*, ch. 4, p. 59.
18. Consuelo Vanderbilt Balsan, *The Glitter and the Gold*, Windmill Press, 1953, p. 28.

19. Information from Count Alexis Tessier, a direct descendant of the Grand Duke Alexis and his secret wife.

20. Hough, *Louis and Victoria*, p. 75.

21. Ibid., p. 76.

22. Contrast Hough, *Louis and Victoria*, ch. 4, p. 87 with Kerr, *Prince Louis of Battenberg*, ch. 4, p. 63.

23. Hough, *Louis and Victoria*, ch. 4, pp. 87–8.

24. The Duke of Edinburgh, later Duke of Coburg, a chronic drunkard, defied medical advice. See Reid, *Ask Sir James*, ch. 6, pp. 108–9.

25. Royal Archives, E53/61, Queen Victoria to W. H. Smith, 10 April 1878.

26. Corti, *Three Dynasties*, ch. 10, pp. 242–3 quoted Hough, *Louis and Victoria*, ch. 4, p. 91.

27. See Queen's letter to her daughter Victoria of Prussia, p. 95.

28. Hough, *Louis and Victoria*, ch. 4, p. 94.

29. Kenneth Rose, *King George V*, Weidenfeld and Nicolson, 1983, ch. 1, p. 19, quoting Sir Henry Ponsonby's Memorandum.

30. Hough, *Louis and Victoria*, p. 101. No mention of Scott's hopelessness was made by Wemyss, Dalton or Kerr.

31. Kerr, *Prince Louis of Battenberg*, pp. 79–86.

32. Lady Wester Wemyss (ed.), *Life and Letters of Lord Wester Wemyss*, ch. 2, p. 29.

33. Rose, *King George V*, ch. 1, pp. 6–15.

34. Lady Duff Gordon, *Last Letters from Egypt*, London, 1867.

35. Arthur J. Marder (ed.), *Fear God and Dread Nought: Letters of Lord Fisher*, Cape, 1952, ch. 3, p. 107.

36. Letter from Prince Louis of Battenberg to the Prince of Wales, Royal Archives, T8/T1.

37. Ibid.

38. Ibid.

15

In 1883 Louis joined the Royal Yacht, *Victoria and Albert*, and became engaged to his cousin Victoria of Hesse, a clever, talkative (Queen Victoria considered her a gasbag),[1] opinionated, socialistic young woman. The Grand Duke of Hesse was unenthusiastic about his daughter's engagement, but Queen Victoria, who had always loved her eldest granddaughter, was delighted.

As the Royal Yacht was being refitted Louis was yet again granted leave. The marriage celebrations in 1884 were, as I wrote earlier, marred by Victoria's father marrying his mistress. This infuriated the Queen. What made her even angrier was a telegram from the Empress Augusta, summoning her son William home from mixing with such polluted company. The affair caused a great sensation and even in 1972 Mountbatten fulminated: '. . . the Grand Duke [of Hesse] was more hell bent than ever on his suicide course of action.'[2] A comic comment as his grandmother had by Victorian standards behaved as badly as Madame de Kolemine!

Eventually it was decided to buy the woman off. A sad decision, as the poor Grand Duke had lived with and loved her for years. She was stupider, but kinder and nicer to him than his dead wife Alice, who was quickly bored by his pedestrian mind. Ninety years later Mountbatten unblushingly tied himself into knots to whitewash the Hesse honour, and vainly try to prove the Queen's power:

'That dreadful woman', as the Queen now described Mme de Kolemine, had long since retreated to Moscow, but she took with her all the Grand Duke's love letters, and early in June Queen Victoria got wind of blackmail threats. These came to nothing, and it is not difficult to imagine the scale of the counterthreats if she should do [sic] any such thing.

In fact Mme de Kolemine did herself rather well in spite of her blackmailing failure. After despatching to everyone of influence at first importunate and then threatening letters, she was granted a title and given a large annual allowance. This did not cease when she married M. de Bacharacht, another Russian diplomat, nor when the Grand Duke died and she outlived him by many years.[3]

How much simpler for Mountbatten to have admitted that Madame de Kolemine successfully blackmailed the Grand Duke and received a title and a large pension!

Louis, on leave, admitted his appointment to the *Victoria and Albert* was a 'mighty fine loaf'[4] which left him plenty of time with his bride. They took a house in Sussex before going to Russia for Victoria's sister's marriage to Serge.[5] The bride Ella had already refused both the Crown Prince Frederick's eldest son William and the Prince of Baden. Perhaps she married the Grand Duke because his character was at total variance with hers. She was a good woman; he was a notorious sadist who, as Governor of Moscow, mercilessly persecuted the Jews. I have already described the wedding in Sandro's life, and how the Tsar, to insult the Battenbergs, placed Louis at the bottom table.

Louis' service on the Royal Yacht between September 1883 and September 1885 was, to say the least, spasmodic. He led a carefree life, only disturbed by the birth of a daughter, Alice, and the amusement caused in England by his penniless brother's engagement and marriage to Princess Beatrice. The marriage separated Prince Louis still further from his brother officers, as Liko lived at Windsor and soon won the Queen's ear.

These halcyon days were interrupted in 1886 by his fatal visit to Lemberg to escort his reluctant brother back to Bulgaria. There he composed the silly telegram which ensured Sandro's abdication, his stupidity emphasised his incomprehension of the feelings and re-actions of both his own generation and his relations. It is worth mentioning that his lack of diplomacy was often inspired by his determination to believe he could get what he wanted, a trait he passed on to his son. Certainly he never strayed from the road to success, and the winning back of the family's position forfeited by his father's marriage. As this could only be achieved in the nineteenth century by close relationships with royal or imperial families, Louis basked at Windsor and Sandringham with a clear conscience, ignoring his contemporaries' understandable resentment which increased when on

30 August 1885 he was promoted to the rank of commander. Two days later he went on half-pay for twenty-three months (excepting two weeks on shore duty in the middle). At the end of this period he was appointed to HMS *Dreadnought*.

Such apparent favouritism to a German prince was grist to the mill of the Irish MPs. On 1 August 1887 Mr Redmond asked in the House of Commons:

I beg to ask the First Lord of the Admiralty a Question of which I have given him private Notice – namely, Whether it is a fact that a German Prince – Prince Louis of Battenberg – has been appointed to the command of Her Majesty's Ship *Dreadnought*, over the heads of some 30 British officers who stood before him for promotion and, if this be so, will the noble Lord state what are his qualifications for that position above those of the officers in question; and, what are the reasons of the Government in giving him such an extraordinary mark of favour over officers of longer service?

The First Lord, Lord George Hamilton, replied, in an exchange which shows how little the House of Commons has changed in the last hundred years:

That is not the Question of which the hon. Member gave me Notice. That question was, whether Prince Louis of Battenberg had been appointed Commander of the Dreadnought . . . I have been looking this afternoon into the qualifications of the officers eligible for that appointment, and, in my judgment, Prince Louis, by his past experience and record of service, is best qualified to perform the duties.[6]

The next day Mr Pickersgill (Bethnal Green) rose to 'beg to give Notice that if Prince Louis of Battenberg is appointed, I shall move that his salary be disallowed'. Sir Edmund Commerell (Southampton) tried to put in a good word:

Mr Speaker, with reference to the Question addressed to the First Lord of the Admiralty, I beg leave to say that Prince Louis of Battenberg served as lieutenant under my command, and a more competent officer – [Cries of Order!][7]

Mr Redmond later returned to the subject and asked the First Lord of the Admiralty:

'Whether, in view of the appointment of Prince Louis of Battenberg to the command of the *Dreadnought*, he will state the date when Prince Louis became a British subject; how long he has served in the Navy; and, what are his experiences and qualifications for the post; and, whether a German has ever before been placed in command of a British man-of-war, over the heads of British officers equally qualified?'

Mr Conybeare (Cornwall, Camborne) also asked, 'Whether it is true that Prince Louis of Battenberg has been appointed to the command of HMS *Dreadnought*; and, what special qualifications have entitled a foreigner to be promoted over the heads of some 30 British officers?'[8]

Lord George again defended his decision but Louis's record had invited these unpleasant and embarrassing questions. Despite this he thought criticism unfair and believed he had done his duty, and as part of a hierarchy, had naturally been favourably treated which was, after all, what hierarchies were for. He could not understand that Englishmen, although they had a German queen, did not like Germans, and while officers were perfectly willing to put up with the promotion by the Queen of her son the Duke of Edinburgh, they couldn't see why a German princeling from 'a half-attainted stall' should join them, neglect the customs of his generation, cultivate the royal family, take privileged leaves, go years on half-pay, and, to top it all, continue to regard Germany as his home.

Louis's miscomprehension of British insularity lasted for the whole of his naval career. He wrote to his mother in 1873, 'I shall never feel quite at home in the British Navy . . .'[9] This remained true for many years and, when Admiral Seymour refused him permission to fight in Alexandria, he took it as a personal affront. Nor can he have enjoyed being abused in the House of Commons, and reading mocking articles in the newspapers stressing how the imperial European families had boycotted the wedding of his brother to the Queen's dumpy daughter.

The trouble was that Louis, as a young man, was a snobbish, blinkered opportunist who had worked far harder than his contemporaries realised, but whose appointment as commander of HMS

Dreadnought looked at the time like undeserved favouritism of a royal toady.

This is borne out by a study of his postings between 1879 and 1889. Mark Kerr, in *Battenberg*, compiled a chronology of Louis's postings taken from the badly written official records. Opposite this page compare the list Mountbatten gave to Hough, which tried to hide his father's long periods of half-pay and royal employment by omitting the dates from Kerr's list. The reason for this omission was that Louis's paid leaves made a mockery of his naval career. It must also be remembered that this lax period followed his first ten years of service when he sailed constantly with or under members of the royal family.

ADMIRAL MARK KERR'S CHRONOLOGY COMPILED FROM OFFICIAL RECORDS OF SERVICE OF PRINCE LOUIS 1879–89, PUBLISHED 1934	LORD MOUNTBATTEN'S ALTERNATIVE CHRONOLOGY IN LOUIS AND VICTORIA, PUBLISHED 1974
29 October 1879	25 April 1879 Prince Louis appointed *Osborne* (Royal Yacht)
Half-pay 10 months	*Omitted 10 months' leave on half-pay*
24 August 1880 Appointed *Inconstant*	24 August 1880 PL appointed *Inconstant* (Flying Squadron)
7 November 1882 Appointed *Duke of Wellington*	17 November 1882 PL appointed *Duke of Wellington*
14 December 1882 Half-pay 9 months	*Omitted 9 months' leave on half-pay*
14 September 1883 Appointed *Victoria and Albert* (Royal Yacht)	14 September 1883 PL appointed *Victoria and Albert* (Royal Yacht) *For extra leave see Hough*, Louis and Victoria, *p. 122*
30 April 1884 Married HGDH Princess Victoria of Hesse	30 April 1884 Victoria and Louis married *For extra leave see Hough*, Louis and

	Victoria, *pp. 122–3*, *Kerr*, Battenberg, *ch. 5*, *p. 108* [At least 7 weeks]
25 February 1885 Princess Alice born	25 February 1885 Princess Alice born
30 August 1885 Promoted Commander	30 August 1885 PL promoted Commander
1 September 1885 Half-pay 11 months, 1 week	1 September 1885 PL on half-pay

No leave period mentioned

In effect PL took approximately 2 years' leave with a break of two weeks between 1 September 1885 and 28 August 1887

6 August 1886 Appointed *Cambridge* (2 weeks' land service at Milford Haven)	
20 August 1886 Half-pay 11 months 1 week	
29 July 1887 Appointed *Dreadnought*	29 July 1887 Appointed *Dreadnought*

Omitted 8 months 1 week leave on half-pay

25 January 1889 Half-pay 8 months, 1 week	
13 July 1889 Princess Louise born	13 July 1889 Princess Louise born
3 October 1889 Appointed *Scout*	3 October 1889 PL appointed to command HMS *Scout*

Total Period on Half-pay Leave:
49 months 3 weeks from 29
October 1879 to 3 October 1889

It will be seen by comparing the two lists that Lord Mountbatten, out of loyalty to his father, omitted the following three periods of half-pay leave:

29 October 1879 to 24 August 1880	10 months
14 December 1882 to 14 September 1883	9 months
25 January 1889 to 3 October 1889	8 months 1 week

altogether amounting to two years, three and a half months. To this should be added his two years of admitted leave, plus two other periods of leave when the Royal Yacht *Victoria and Albert* was in dock in 1883, and he was married. Altogether in ten years he had approximately four and a half years' leave, spent two years on the Royal Yachts and served approximately three and a half years on ships of the line. Such a record did not make Prince Louis popular as while it was not unusual for promising young sailors to take two or three years' leave, the combination of royal patronage and his long periods on half-pay made it appear he was trading on his friendship with the royal family.

PRINCE LOUIS'S NINE POSTINGS CONNECTED WITH THE ROYAL FAMILY

HMS *Ariadne*	1869	Prince and Princess of Wales aboard. Included trips up the Nile and to Constantinople.
HMS *Serapis*	1875–6	Indian tour of Prince of Wales. Included a 7000-mile land trip around India.
HMS *Sultan*	1876–8	Captain, the Duke of Edinburgh. Included Louis's visit to Russian lines with his brother.
Royal Yacht *Osborne*	1879	Louis sailed as lieutenant on a royal yacht during Mediterranean honeymoon of Duke of Connaught.
Royal Yacht *Osborne*	1879	Louis accompanied Prince of Wales to Cherbourg and on land trip to Hesse.
HMS *Inconstant*	1880–2	Served on HMS *Inconstant*, a ship in Lord Clanwilliam's flotilla which sailed around the world. The Prince of Wales's two eldest sons sailed with the fleet and at one moment moved to the *Inconstant*.
Royal Yacht *Victoria and Albert*	1883–5	At the beginning of this posting the *Victoria and Albert* was in dry dock and Prince Louis lived near Chichester before and after his marriage in 1884.
HMS *Dreadnought*	1887–9	The *Dreadnought* was under the command of the Duke of Edinburgh, C-in-C of the Mediterranean Fleet.

		His wife had been Louis's sister Marie's best childhood friend.
HMS *Cambrian* (in command)	1894–7	For three years guardship to the Queen when wintering at Nice. That Louis realised his record was something of a joke is shown by his reply to a royal suggestion his next command should be the Royal Yacht *Osborne*. Hough with M's authority wrote: 'He gently explained to the Queen that it would be the end of his real naval career if he accepted this appointment. Already they were calling the *Cambrian* Prince Louis's yacht because it was so often on royal affairs.' (Hough, *Louis and Victoria*, ch. 7, p. 193)

Louis's life was made more difficult by his wife's behaviour, which was odd by Victorian standards. Her chief disadvantage at every stage of her life was her ceaseless prattle which bored even her best friends.[10] She was in the vanguard of the feminist movement, treated her husband as an equal, and rebelled against the tedium of garrison life, and the expected subjection of a wife to her husband.

During their first married period at Malta, which lasted from 1888 to 1892, Victoria paid visits to Russia, many times to Germany, and once or twice to England. It was a restless way of life and she wondered sometimes whether it was harmful to her young children to grow up without roots.[11]

Her behaviour suggests selfish detachment rather than motherly concern: her absences cannot have helped her children to feel secure: her coldness to her husband worried the Queen.

Let me again ask you to remember that your *1st duty* is to your dear and most devoted *Husband* to whom you can *never* be kind *enough* & to whom I think a *little* more *tenderness* is due sometimes.[12]

Louis also suffered from her untidiness, a contrast to his 'immaculate presentation'. Even her son admitted she had 'careless – almost slovenly – ways', and, although he tried hard, couldn't pretend it was a love match on her side.

She suffered from a strange, undiagnosed illness immediately before her marriage which Mountbatten claimed was attributable to her knowledge that her father was about to make an unsuitable secret match. Was it fear of physical contact? Queen Victoria, given to sentimentality about the relationship of engaged couples, was realistic when her granddaughter became engaged.

Letter to Crown Princess of Germany

Windsor Castle,
June 15. 1883

Many affte. thanks for 2 dear letters of the 21st and 23rd. You are, I see pleased at the Engagement of Victoria of H. with Louis Battenberg. I thought she wld. not have married at all – nor wld. she if she had had to leave her poor Father she said, but as she will not have to do that – I am very glad she has found a person, kind, good & clever & whom she knows thoroughly well. Of course people who care only for 'gt. matches' & C., will not like it. – But they do not make happiness – & Louis says they will be quite comfortable . . .[13]

For the Queen to use the phrase 'whom she knows thoroughly well' without mentioning the word love is illuminating. But it is also interesting to read Victoria had told her father she would continue to live partially in Hesse. Why? A younger brother and sister remained at home and she knew her father had a favourite mistress. Was she providing an escape route to her old home when marriage became distasteful to her? If so, she frequently used it. Her lack of vanity, total disregard of 'appearance', coldness to her husband and neglect of her young children all suggest she was an intellectual, rather than a sensual woman.

On Louis's side it had been a marriage of convenience in accordance with his mother's wishes. If Julia had ever hoped he would catch Princess Beatrice the idea had been effectively squashed by the Queen. But to marry the daughter of the Grand Duke of Hesse and Alice of England was a desirable match. It was time he settled down, now that he had established himself in the inner circles of the English royal family and luckily avoided a scandal with Lillie Langtry, which could have deterred the mothers of other possible brides. Certainly Louis and Victoria got on reasonably well despite his irritation with her unfeminine untidiness. Since he was not in love with her, her coldness did not hurt his feelings. He had got what he and his mother wanted; a wife with good connections. Her frigid independence suited him better than a clinging woman, lamenting his absences at sea; as it was he was free to concentrate on his work and make his own amusements.

NOTES

1. Hough, *Louis and Victoria*, ch. 4, p. 108.
2. Ibid., p. 118.
3. Ibid., p. 123.
4. Kerr, *Prince Louis of Battenberg*, ch. 5, p. 108.
5. Fourth son of Tsar Alexander II.
6. *Hansard*, 1 August 1887.
7. Ibid., 2 August 1887.
8. Ibid., 2 August 1887.
9. Hough, *Louis and Victoria*, ch. 3, p. 73.
10. For Princess Alice Countess of Athlone's description of Victoria's indiscretions see pp. 18–19.
11. Hough, *Louis and Victoria*, ch. 7, p. 167.
12. Ibid., ch. 5, p. 134. Queen Victoria to Princess Louis of Battenberg, 21 August 1885.
13. Royal Archives RA U32, quoted in Fulford (ed.), *Beloved Mama*, p. 141.

16

WHEN Louis joined the *Dreadnought* the criticism voiced in the House of Commons was repeated in the Navy, for again Louis agreed to serve under his wife's uncle, the Duke of Edinburgh, the new Commander-in-Chief in Malta, who lived in the island's palace. We get a glimpse of the garden's splendour in his daughter Marie of Romania's florid reminiscences:

> Oh, the sweetness, the beauty, the enchantment! And still all those gardens beyond, beckoning to you from behind high walls. Stepping through small openings from one to another, you advanced into joy, and everywhere flowers, fragrance, sunshine, and the buzzing of a myriad wings. Unknown worlds to be discovered. Mystery. Shady groves and little canals of water running beneath dark evergreen branches, and what violets! Light blue double ones, larger than any we had ever seen, and others deeply purple, half hidden amongst their fragrant leaves. Oh, the joy, the joy, the joy![1]

Mountbatten, in a typical euphoric mood, described the Edinburghs' life:

> There were 'drawing rooms', dinner parties and balls at San Antonio, Malta's equivalent of Buckingham Palace with the Duke and Duchess of Edinburgh as the 'reigning King and Queen'.[2]

Louis led a privileged life on shore. It helped that his sister, as a girl, had been the Duchess's best friend. At the same time he continued his studies and joined in the tasks of the lower deck. What could be more different than Marie's impression of her father's garden than his account of loading coal:

We have had a heavy job coaling from a collier alongside us. From Saturday, 4.30 a.m. until Monday forenoon I was in my clothes, having my meals almost always standing, and only lying down on the deck, all dirty and greasy, for an hour's sleep at a time. It was very hard on the men, who worked incessantly, two halves relieving each other every two hours night and day and, having to work all through Sunday, they required a good deal of humouring. The heat was intense, and with a burning sun.

On the third day I was so worn out that I could hardly drag myself along. We hoisted in close on 1,000 tons; that is 11,000 bags which had to be filled, then hoisted in, emptied, and sent back for refilling. I wonder what a Lieutenant-Colonel of the British Army would say if he was expected to do that in time of peace as a matter of ordinary routine?[3]

The Battenberg habit of joining in the dirty work at sea was one of the sources of their popularity with their crews, but it would have been wiser if Louis had insisted on serving under another commander-in-chief in a less favoured command. He declined to serve on the China station. In 1889 his father died; again he went on half-pay although this is not recorded in Mountbatten's chronology. In the same year the Duke of Edinburgh was relieved by Sir George Tryon, famous in naval history for sinking his flagship the *Victoria* off Tripoli, and drowning himself and 357 members of his crew.

In October Louis was given the command of a torpedo cruiser the *Scout*, but the feeling in the Admiralty against his 'idle past' remained and he was not promoted. In 1891 the Queen made up her mind it was time he was given a push and wrote to Lord George Hamilton, First Lord of the Admiralty:

She hopes and expects that Prince Louis of Battenberg, to whose merits everyone who knows the service well can testify, will get his promotion at the end of the year ... There is a *belief* that the Admiralty are afraid of promoting Officers who are Princes on account of the radical attacks of low papers & scurrilous further delay in giving him what he deserves.[4]

It's doubtful if this letter was kept secret. The Queen's interference would have been resented, as she was telling the First Lord of the

Admiralty to advance the career of an officer who had far less experience than normal. That the Queen was right in her judgement of Louis's capability is irrelevant. She was demanding that he, at the age of thirty-seven, should be pushed forward over the heads of his contemporaries and seniors who had served for long periods in faraway stations, while he, after his youthful posting to North America, never left British waters or the Mediterranean.

Lord George capitulated. At the end of the year Louis became a captain, and in the following year was given the command of the cruiser *Andromache* for the summer manoeuvres. But his opportunity to show his ability was shortlived; in 1892 Louis became deputy inspector general of fortifications and head of the Mobilization Department, and as Kerr points out, this led to other responsibilities:

> Soon after taking up his appointment, Prince Louis was made Naval Advisor to the War Office, and he became the Chief Secretary to a joint Naval and Military Committee of Defence . . . The Deputy Inspector General of Fortifications acted as the Senior Secretary who, when Prince Louis joined, deputed him to do his work as he had too much other business, to attend to.[5]

His position was important, the Kaiser, having dismissed Bismarck, was rearming and behaving in a wild, irresponsible manner, forcing Britain, France and Russia to reassess their friendship and commitments. The committee was one of the first to study the question of the reorganisation of both the army and the navy, the defence of the British Empire, the repelling of an invasion of England, the future of submarines and torpedoes, and the general colonial defence system. Discussion on such a wide variety of subjects was naturally vague, but Louis surprised the other members by his tact and efficiency. He was also practical and:

> . . . invented a Course Indicator, a most useful instrument, which was adopted by the Admiralty in December 1894, two years after he had invented it. This became the standard instrument throughout the British Navy, and was also adapted for use of the Air Force during the Great War.[6]

This invention showed his practical ingenuity and later stimulated his son's interest in inventions. The committee had three further purposes: to modernise equipment, prepare for war and create cooperation between the two services. Louis surprised the army representatives by the unbiased way in which he tried to see their point of view. His success was helped by his impartial German background; the British Army and the Royal Navy had been at loggerheads for years as sons followed fathers into the polarised services. The fatal journey to Bulgaria had also taught him the dangers of over-confidence.

His past behaviour had given him the reputation of being withdrawn, difficult and a privileged snob, but his soldier-colleagues respected his cooperation.

When he returned to sea as captain of the *Cambrian* in 1894, he won the enthusiasm of those who served under him by his knowledge, ingenuity and flair.

As expected, his ship was chosen for three years in succession as the guardian ship of the Queen, when she stayed at Cannes. The choice naturally gave rise to further complaints of favouritism. These were silenced by the ship's performance, which Kerr later described:

The *Cambrian*, second-class cruiser, was commissioned by Captain H.S.H. Prince Louis of Battenberg on October 16, 1894, with myself as Second-in-Command, and Osmond de B. Brock as Gunnery Lieutenant, for the Mediterranean Station.

This was really a remarkable commission, as the ship was inspected by four different Admirals, all of whom stated that they had never before given a ship such a good inspection report. She was the smallest ship on the station, but by the end of the commission she held every cup. She made the record time for anchor drills of all kinds, and the record for a small cruiser's coaling, and in games was at the top of the Fleet.[7]

Louis's undoubted success was caused by his sense of order which enabled him, uninfluenced by sentiment or the weight of tradition, to realise that the British Navy had been, when he joined it, a motley, badly trained assembly of vessels unfit for action, commanded by elderly captains who resisted change and looked back nostalgically to the glories of sail. Many of these old timers believed in a code of discipline, which was another name for brutality. Improvements came slowly, old habits lingered on, and conditions below deck remained cramped, airless and dirty. A low standard of living was considered good enough for ratings whose officers had suffered identical discomforts as midshipmen with the addition of such merciless jokes as the cutting of newcomers' hammock strings.

Unlike many of his contemporaries, he understood reasonable complaints which caused many sailors every year to desert in foreign ports. He treated his own crews strictly but humanely; the number of educated sailors was rising annually and he was before his time in thinking of their intolerable conditions, and did all he could by the use of white paint, to brighten and lighten their quarters. He understood that while Princess Marie might cry out in her father's garden in Malta 'the joy, the joy, the joy', there was little joy for a decent seaman in Valetta; the women of the port were revolting and there were few other recreations on the stony little island. Louis realised that the general indifference to the seamen's off-duty hours was callous, and he created opportunities for them to take part in competitions and games.

His reforms were assisted, perhaps suggested, by Mark Kerr who served under him as a midshipman on the *Inconstant*, on land in the naval brigade at Alexandria, as his second-in-command on the *Cambrian* and the *Implacable*, and finally as his captain on HMS *Drake* in 1905. A perky, efficient little sailor with the enthusiasm of a sports master, he agreed with Doctor Arnold that growing boys had to be kept busy. Fortunately he lived in an age when technology was in its infancy and athleticism was considered a proof of leadership. He had little difficulty making Louis accept his belief 'that officers who were good at games were nearly always excellent at handling men and producing efficiency in those under them.'[8] Louis allowed him to search for officers of this type in the Royal Naval College at Dartmouth and 'make selections of the "games" kind that I thought suitable and he would ask for them to be appointed and the result was a really first class company'. Singular as it may appear today, the policy worked wonders, and the band of athletic heroes increased the ship's competitive morale. The *Cambrian* not only won every competition but had an extraordinarily low percentage of ratings punished.[9]

When Kerr was given his first command in 1909 he continued the recruiting system he had perfected under his old captain:

We had a wonderful lot of officers, and at rugby football they were supreme: Wodehouse, Lieutenant, afterwards captain of England;

Oakley, midshipman, afterwards half-back for England, with four others who played for the Navy, and eight who played for the United Services, was first-rate for putting the *Invincible* at the top of the Fleet in shooting, steaming and games, and this ... they succeeded in doing.[10]

Louis's humanity improved the lives and morale of his crews; they soon preferred playing organised games to catching clap and getting drunk in Maltese brothels. Kerr was artlessly pleased with himself and while his brisk gamesmanship seems amusing today, it was a blessing to neglected sailors in a dirty Mediterranean port. Even his self-satisfaction was infectious: 'I started playing cricket as captain of the men's team with the assistance of two officers and for the first time they won a few matches.'[11] The older generation of officers were surprised how well the public school spirit worked on Louis's ships. His reforms won him many young supporters, who annually increased in numbers to balance his critical contemporaries and seniors who, remembering his pampered past, were disinclined to believe that his character had changed.

The work of a captain in peace time was seldom inspiring, but Kerr drew a vivid picture of Louis's popularity when he left HMS *Drake* in 1907:

He then shook hands with all the officers and made a short speech, and as he turned to go down the gangway the whole ship's company rushed over the other one on to the Mole, and formed a double line of men from the *Drake*'s gangway to the *Venerable*, through which the Admiral walked, the men saluting as he passed them: a farewell far more impressive and affectionate (as it was entirely unrehearsed and spontaneous) than any other I have ever seen given, and the silence was made more eloquent than any cheering could have been.[12]

Kerr also praised his sense of honour, and loyalty to both superiors and inferiors. But was he loyal to his homeland Germany? Because of his affection for Heiligenberg he never bought a house in England and made himself unpopular by continuing to take his leaves, even in 1914, in Germany with whom Britain was on the verge of war.

The Admiralty realised in the 1890s that as Louis spent a large portion of his leave with his German and Russian relations 'he could be of great value to the Navy's Intelligence Department'[13] or, to put it bluntly, he would make a useful spy. Opportunities occurred, and when in 1894 the Kaiser invited him to visit a new squadron in the North Sea, he made a full report to the Secretary of the Admiralty, and was congratulated for his useful work. Was it honourable to spy on his first cousins? The answer is not easy. Changelings cannot escape divided loyalties and Louis may have believed there was nothing wrong in passing on information freely given to him.

It should also be remembered that he remained all his life a Hessian rather than a Prusso-German. The difference was considerable. The two countries had fought each other when Louis was twelve. His father had commanded the beaten Hessian forces; his son had witnessed his sad return followed by the humiliation of a Prussian occupation, a loss of territory and payment of a large fine. From that moment his father detested Bismarck. The feeling was mutual and the Chancellor waged a vendetta against Sandro. This persecution confirmed Louis's acute dislike of Prussia's military ambitions. But while his background makes it easy to understand why he was untroubled at passing on confidential information given to him by close relations about the German and Russian Navies, it does not explain why he could not see that making his home in Germany delighted British critics. It is also interesting to wonder why, as he had planned for many years to fight A's war against Germany, he didn't consider the difficulties he was creating for his sons, by bringing them up to regard Heiligenberg as their home, and at the same time planning to send them into the British Navy. The young Mountbatten's Hessian upbringing planted in the boy a great and confusing love for his youthful surroundings. Even after fighting two wars in the British Navy, against his father's homeland, he was never happier than when he returned to Hesse, or proudly signed his name in German in the old town of Battenberg which had given his pregnant grandmother a name in 1851.

In 1896 the Queen offered Louis the command of the Royal Yacht. He refused, and explained that to qualify for promotion he had to complete his period of service on the *Cambrian* before serving on a larger ship. It is worth noting his mother died in 1895.

Louis's refusal to continue to be a sailor-courtier symbolised his decision to remain in the Navy and work. This was the first step to

The Emperor Frederick III of Germany, formerly the Crown Prince, and the Empress. The latter, the eldest daughter of Queen Victoria, developed a passionate wish her daughter should marry (against her father- and mother-in-law's wishes) Alexander of Battenberg. She persecuted her dying husband to agree to the match which would have ensured Bismarck's resignation. Her letters were as fanatical as those of the last Tsarina's, her niece.

Prince Alexander of Battenberg's love, Princess Victoria (Vicky) of Prussia, and her final husband, a waiter, Zoubkoff.

RUINED SISTER
OF EX-KAISER.

TRAGIC SALE OF HER TREASURES.

DEBTS OF A WAITER'S WIFE.

"Daily Express" Correspondent.

BERLIN, Tuesday, Oct. 15.
"Frau Alexander Zoubkoff, née Princess Victoria of Prussia, has failed to satisfy her creditors. Her property and effects must, therefore, now be sold by auction."

Herr Schultze, Bailiff of Cologne, nervously made this announcement this morning as, with beads of perspiration pouring from his forehead, he opened the sale by auction in the Schaumburg Palace at Bonn of the treasures of Frau Alexander Zoubkoff, the ex-Kaiser's sister, whom romance in the shape of a young Russian waiter has driven, in less than eighteen months, to financial ruin.

The bailiff took up his stand before the vast crowd of nondescript-looking persons who had flocked to share in the spoils of the Hohenzollern princess' humiliation, in the same spot in the great Schaumburg Hall of Mirrors where in the days of her glory the princess had been wont to welcome to her home the mightiest rulers and most lovely princesses of the courts of Europe.

ZOUBKOFF'S ARREST.

At the very moment that Herr Schultze raised his hammer to knock down the first lot—a magnificent old English teapot—Alexander Zoubkoff, hounded from country to country, was just being arrested by the French police at Deidenheim, on the Franco-Luxembourg frontier, as he was trying surreptitiously to cross into France.

Precious pieces of old London silver, many of them stamped with the Royal Arms of England, failed most remarkably to achieve the prices that had been expected by expert valuers as their due.

A great oval baroque soup tureen stamped "London 1770," which had been inherited by Frau Zoubkoff's mother from Queen Victoria, changed hands for a paltry £300. It had been expected to fetch at least £1,000.

A particularly poignant moment came when a silver statue of the Emperor Frederick, the Princess' father, was offered for sale, but failed to raise a bid. Eventually it was practically given away at half its starting price for £5—a sum which its value in silver exceeded.

It is now considered absolutely impossible that the proceeds from the sale of her treasures will suffice to meet Frau Zoubkoff's debts, which are estimated to be close on £50,000.

The ex-Kaiser's sister will, therefore, be left penniless and at the mercy of her Hohenzollern relatives, who, embittered by the disgrace that they consider she has brought on their house by her marriage to the waiter, will not be over-anxious to support her

---

Princess Victoria of Prussia, married in 1890 to Prince Adolph of Schaumburg-Lippe. She was unofficially engaged to Prince Alexander of Battenberg, first Prince of Bulgaria (finally Count Hartenau). She was always a scatter-brained idiot. A cutting from the *Daily Express* of 1929 shows the scant sympathy given to those who broke 'the blood laws' of Europe.

Alexander III of Russia (1845–1894) and his wife, sister of our Queen Alexandra. This personification of autocracy was deliberately deceived by his uncle Alexander of Hesse and his cousin Alexander of Battenberg, first Prince of Bulgaria. A blood snob, he looked down on his morganatic cousin, never forgave his deceitfulness and finally broke him.

Bismarck in old age. He despised and feared the Battenbergs and was determined Alexander should not marry Princess Victoria of Prussia.

The remarkable Austrian Emperor Franz Joseph (1848–1916) refused to allow a Habsburg to marry a Battenberg.

Mounthatten's uncle, Louis V of Hesse (1868–1938). He was an heroic, bemedalled peacetime soldier but when war broke out his martial enthusiasm faded and he ran a hospital train! During the war he acted as an intermediary—seeking peace—between the Kaiser and the Tsar. For some reason his son Louis, Mountbatten and his grandaughter-in-law believed it necessary to hide this fact!

Prince Henry of Battenberg (Liko, 1858–96), third son of Prince Alexander of Hesse, married Princess Beatrice (1857–1944), youngest daughter of Queen Victoria. The marriage of this theatrical, morganatic Prince to the plain English Princess caused anger and many spiteful jokes among Europe's imperial families.

A foretaste of things to come. The last Kaiser, William, as a boy celebrating death. Even the grim-faced woman is carrying a gun.

Admiral Lord Charles Beresford, son of the Marquess of Waterford. An opponent of Fisher and Battenberg, he failed to understand that by 1907 the latter was on his side, and continued to work up antagonism against his nationality. He became the leader of a section of the Navy which opposed Fisher's plans. He called Fisher 'the mulatto' and was supported by the Prince of Wales.

Admiral Lord Fisher, First Sea Lord 1904–10 and 1914–15. He was originally a friend of Prince Louis of Battenberg, but in 1907 his organisation of the fleets split the Navy and lost him Battenberg's esteem. To put it politely, he was unbalanced.

The young Mountbatten. At this time he was Prince Louis of Battenberg.

Lord Mountbatten in old age.

becoming the First Sea Lord, and showed the pleasure-loving young snob of the 1870s and the arrogant 'absent on half-pay' sailor of the 1880s was dead and buried. Like many men with quick minds he was as bad a junior officer as he was a good admiral. Beneath his calm lay insecurity; although he was a darling of the English court and married to the Queen's granddaughter, he knew his paternal grandfather's legitimacy was suspect and that his father had married a pregnant nobody.

This weakness encouraged his friendship with the increasingly powerful Prince of Wales, who had been an extravagant, uncultured young man (his character improved with age), whose *nouveau riche* friends enabled him to live the ostentatious life of a greedy Croesus. He liked rich food, plush hotels, women, gambling, racing, money, plutocrats and disliked art or aesthetics of any kind; in short he was a sybaritic Philistine. A vein of coarse unkindness lay below his jovial exterior. An example was his treatment of his friend, the sycophantic Christopher Sykes, whose houses he used for his own convenience.

The baiting began in the 1870s. One night, in a good mood, the Prince of Wales poured a glass of brandy over Sykes's head. The victim after a moment replied, 'As Your Royal Highness pleases.' The unexpected reply made his royal patron nearly choke with laughter. He had discovered a wonderful new game, Sykes's nephew and namesake wrote:

The Prince's simple taste liked enlargement. In place of the glass a full bottle was substituted, and another royal discovery was that even funnier effects could be conjured by pouring the precious liquid not on to his hair, but down his friend's neck. Amid screams of sycophantic laughter the Prince invented an entirely new diversion. Christopher was hurled underneath the billiard-table while the Prince and his faithful courtiers prevented his escape by spearing at him with billiard-cues. And there were further elaborations of the sousing theme. Watering cans were introduced into Christopher's bedroom and his couch sprinkled by the royal hand. New parlour games were evolved from the Prince's simple but inventive mind: while smoking a cigar he would invite Christopher to gaze into his eyes in order to see the smoke coming out of them, and while Christopher was thus obediently engaged, the Prince would thrust the burning end on to his friend's unguarded hand. And the basis of the joke never weakened. To pour brandy down the neck of some roaring drunk sot of a courtier was one thing; but Christopher remained the statuesque figure he had been on the great night of the brandy glass. He never failed his audience. Never. His hat would be knocked off, the cigar would be applied, the soda-water pumped over his head, and he would incline, and murmur: 'As Your Royal Highness pleases.'[14]

Did Louis enjoy such jests? If so he had come a long way from the gentle youth his sister portrayed in her memoirs.

Fortunately the Prince of Wales had a serious side to his character. Tactfully, he considered himself a Britisher, although he was a pure bred German; he detested his nephew the Kaiser and saw clearly the necessity of cooperation with France to balance German power. Louis suffered and benefited from his patronage. The Prince started him off on the wrong foot in the Navy, saved him from bullying and encouraged him for years to neglect his naval duties. But having failed to turn him into a social butterfly, he had the sense to appreciate his natural talents, and support him – when the old Queen's interest in life was waning – for the position of Assistant Director of Intelligence from 1899 to 1901.

This posting gave Louis his opportunity. He took it, and to begin with was on good terms with Sir John Fisher, the most powerful personality in the Navy, who at that time commanded the Mediterranean Fleet. Both men desired reform, and the extent of Louis's influence can be read in his correspondence with Fisher on the creation of Osborne and Dartmouth, gunnery practice, a naval staff and the reorganisation of the various fleets. This was their honeymoon. The two did not always agree in the stormy days which lay ahead.

NOTES

1. Marie Queen of Romania, *The Story of My Life*, vol. 1, p. 107.
2. Hough, *Louis and Victoria*, ch. 7, p. 165.
3. Kerr, *Prince Louis of Battenberg*, p. 111.
4. Royal Archives, E5 6/45, QV to Lord George Hamilton, 5 September 1891. Quoted in Hough, *Louis and Victoria*, ch. 7, p. 171.
5. Kerr, *Prince Louis of Battenberg*, p. 116.
6. Ibid., p. 119.
7. Mark Kerr, *Land, Sea, and Air*, ch. 5, p. 89.
8. Kerr, *Prince Louis of Battenberg*, ch. 7, p. 142.

9. Ibid., ch. 6, p. 122.
10. Kerr, *Land, Sea, and Air*, p. 147.
11. Ibid., p. 144.
12. Ibid., pp. 143–4.
13. Hough, *Louis and Victoria*, ch. 7, p. 178.
14. Christopher Sykes, *Four Studies in Loyalty*, Collins, 1946, pp. 28–9.

17

FROM 1904 to 1910 a series of unique events disturbed the life of the Royal Navy. Leaks were given to the press; junior officers were bewildered; senior officers took sides. The King supported one party; the Prince of Wales the other. Careers were made and broken. The whole country watched agog; Louis's enemies came into the open.

In order to understand his subsequent difficulties it is necessary to assess the personalities involved in this astonishing drama. The trouble began with the appointment in 1904 of Fisher as First Sea Lord. His enemies had hoped he had lost his chance when the dull Lord Walter Kerr was preferred to him in 1899. But when the Boer War illuminated the army's deficiencies, politicians of both parties realised the need for realism at the Admiralty. Fisher, a forceful personality, looked the right man to prepare Britain for war with Germany. His plans, conceived before he came to power, were concisely described by his biographer, Arthur J. Marder:

(1) introduction of the nucleus crew system; (2) the scrapping of obsolete warships; (3) the redistribution of the fleets in accordance with modern requirements; and (4) the introduction of the all-big-gun type of battleship and cruiser. The first three were announced, and the fourth foreshadowed, in an Admiralty memorandum of December 6th, 1904. The first three were closely interdependent. Each was part of a whole.

The nucleus crew system, which enabled ships to be put on the reserve list, partially manned, ready to go to sea in an emergency, was, with certain reservations, accepted by the Navy as an economic reform, but the scrapping of 154 ships in 1905, the strange redistribution of the fleets and concentration on the building of a new Navy of

all-big-gun Dreadnoughts and Invincibles was immediately opposed
by traditionalists. It is probable the opposition would have been muted
if Fisher's plans had been introduced in a less arbitrary way, but he was
a fighter and a bully who believed in trampling on rather than winning
over the opposition, a foolproof method of making enemies. A friend,
later an enemy (Fisher could not stand a word of criticism), Captain
Hedworth Lambton,[1] expressed senior officers' fears about Fisher's
bad manners in a letter to Lord Selborne[2] written on 28 January 1904:

> Because one likes and admires a man it is no reason he should be
> a headstrong autocrat. Between *you* and *me* I know Charlie B
> [Admiral Lord Charles Beresford] has remonstrated with one
> friend[3] at his arbitrary methods – he (1st Sea Lord) is setting the
> whole service against your administration. All the good he does is
> nullified by the tactless manner he does it. Officers are treated with
> less consideration than Lipton would deal with a grocery clerk . . .[4]

A short description of Fisher's character is necessary if his great
virtues and failings are to be understood. He was born in 1841 and
entered the Navy without the advantage of either belonging to the
landed gentry or a naval family. His father, descended from four
generations of country parsons, was an unsuccessful soldier and
afterwards an equally unsuccessful rubber planter in Ceylon, before
ending up as an inspector of police in the same colony.

Fisher's ugly face had an 'oriental cast', a gift to his enemies and
cartoonists. He joined the Royal Naval College in 1854 and as a boy
distinguished himself in China. In October 1859 when he was eighteen
he had a correspondence with a motherly friend, Mrs Edmund Warden, the wife of the manager of a Shanghai company. His letters
illustrate his sensitivity, bitterness, touchiness and inability to forgive
and forget, weaknesses which increased with age and warped his
judgement.

KANAGAWA
October 22nd (1859)

. . . Now, while I think of it, Mams, I want to ask you something that
has *annoyed me very much*, REALLY. When I asked you if I could
get anything for you, you said NO, and after that you went and
asked Hills to get a lot of things for you. I think that was very unkind

of you, unless you thought Hills would suit your taste better. If that was the reason, of course I can't complain, only I can't see why I shouldn't be able to buy just as pretty things as Hills can. I flatter myself I have done so, and I am certain I could have bought a prettier cabinet than he has for you if I had known you wanted a thing like that. Never mind, you had some good, though to me, unknown reason . . . [5]

A week later he again showed his jealousy:

KANAGAWA
October 29th (1859)
. . . Hills has been doing nothing but buying curios since we have been here. I only wish I had *his taste* and then, perhaps, I might have been trusted by some people to buy curios for them, but unfortunately, you see, I have not got a bit, at least some people think so . . . [6]

A month later he was still indignant:

SHANGHAI
Sunday, November 27th (1859)
. . . Dalziel is going to forward to you 3 little boxes of Japan ware I got for you. There is very little, Mams! But you must take the will for the deed, only it was a great shame of you asking Hills to get a cabinet for you and not me, just as if you couldn't trust me. I am in a great rage about that and have been ever since . . . [7]

Fifteen days later he returned to his original complaint:

HONG KONG
December 12th (1859)
. . . It's only a horrid, old, disagreeable, snappish female that I don't care a pin's head for. You have roused my evil passions again about that infernal cabinet. I should so much like to smash it. I see it is a thing you care a good deal about by your mentioning it several times, and you go and ask Hills. Well, never mind, it's no use my growling about it now; but I think you might have trusted me, Mams. There, I won't say anything more about the confounded thing . . . [8]

His confounded temper was to make him many unnecessary enemies, but as his talents equalled his pugnacity, he quickly rose in the service and shone during and after the bombardment of Alexandria in 1882.[9] Like Louis, thirteen years his junior, he found the Navy in the 1870s, 1880s and 1890s disorganised, without a notable leader except Admiral Sir Geoffrey Phipps-Hornby. Like the majority of intelligent officers in the last quarter of the nineteenth century, he deplored the time wasted painting boats, the equivalent of the Army's spit and polish, the neglect of firing practice, the lack of training manoeuvres, naval staff and war plans, and the retention of appalling quarters for the ordinary sailor. He also saw the Navy had to be modernised or British ships would be outclassed and outgunned by the efficient new German Navy. Mountbatten's desire to exaggerate his father's importance made him minimise the strength of Fisher's character, and his assertion that Louis was from 1900 for ten years 'Jacky Fisher's patron and guide, protector and corrector',[10] was inaccurate. Mountbatten contradicted himself by stating: 'At sea he [Fisher] had been an autocrat. He never divulged his plans to anyone. At the Admiralty he was equally dictatorial and secretive.'[11] This was nearer to the truth, Fisher would have died rather than allow Louis to patronise him. He could only get along with such pallid First Lords of the Admiralty as Lord Selborne and Reginald McKenna, who both lacked a spark of genius, and the nervous Lord Tweedmouth,[12] who went mad. He easily persuaded these pliable superiors to accept his ideas, despite opposition from serving admirals he had earlier praised.

Among them were the popular Admiral Lord Charles Beresford and Captain Lambton who had written to Lord Selborne in 1904 questioning Fisher's arrogance. In 1906 they made the mistake of lumping Fisher and Louis together on every issue, and, regarding Louis as a spoilt rival, did their best to do him down. Fisher wrote to the King:

I have never known more malignant rancour and jealousy as manifested by Lord Charles Beresford and Hedworth Lambton as against Prince Louis and I regret to say Lord Tweedmouth (1st Lord) is frightened of what these two can do in inciting the service against the avowed intention of making Prince Louis an acting vice-admiral.[13]

Louis ignored the vendetta, except in a dignified, puzzled letter to the King, in which he argued Lambton deserved the KCB as he had

199

won the CB in 'an exceptionally brilliant manner.'[14] But Mountbatten never forgave his father's enemy and had his revenge seventy years later in a few sentences of suppressed hate:

> Hedworth Lambton was as tireless and unremitting an opponent to Louis as was Beresford. Lambton was a spoilt, handsome, lazy patrician who had the ear of the Prince of Wales but like Beresford had lost the confidence of the King. From 1906 to 1911 he fought tooth and nail to hold Louis back and reduce his influence. He succeeded in delaying Louis's promotion, complained when he got it (to Vice-Admiral) and complained louder when he was appointed second-in-command of the Mediterranean Fleet in February 1907. With Beresford as his ally he succeeded in keeping Louis out of the Admiralty for some three years, lobbying ministers, spreading suspicion about his competency and loyalty.
>
> Lambton loathed Louis's vigour, the importance he attached to success, and his manifest delight in his success when he achieved it. 'How very German!' we can hear him saying in his slurred, fruity voice.[15]

Lambton's slurred voice was the result of a post-war stroke. He died in 1929; Hough tells me he never met him. This passage can only have been dictated by Mountbatten, whose hatred of this rival was the measure of his love for his father. He may have been accurate about Lambton's jealousy, but by 1907 Fisher had turned the Navy into a cockpit, the loyal Louis into his severest critic; hatred was rife, loyalties shifting. Lambton once said to Fisher, 'Seize Beresford by the scruff of the neck and he'll collapse like every Irishman who ever breathed – he is a blusterer.'[16] The King joined in the argument and supported Fisher whom the Prince of Wales loathed.[17]

An equally spiteful Beresford wrote to a friend:

> I saw the Prince of Wales yesterday at Newmarket. He was really quite violent against the Mulatto [Fisher] . . . He said . . . that he must go, or the Navy would be ruined. I told him that the Navy was nearly ruined now.[18]

That the unbalanced Fisher was the catalyst of 'the great schism' is illustrated by the tone of his letter to Lord Esher in 1911:

. . . Hedworth Lambton's appointment to Portsmouth renders him eligible to be First Sea Lord, *and he will be* when the Unionist Government come in – a post in which he would ruin the Navy, but what's the good of my squealing! NEITHER WOULD IT BE PATRIOTIC! The Providence of God may take both Milne and Lambton into another world any day! *I believe in Providence!* Nearly all my enemies have gone to Hell![19]

As Fisher daily scribbled off such notes it's easy to see how his violent, Messianic personality, unsoftened by patience or gentility, excited opposition and animosity in the Navy. His faults are perfectly illustrated in a conversation he had with the King's equerry shortly after he became First Sea Lord. Ponsonby remembered:

So I got onto the problems of national defence which I had been studying and stated my opinions with a view to drawing him out. This had the desired effect and away he went. He said that unless we kept up the Navy to a two-power standard we were done. London would starve in a week unless the seas were kept clear to bring in supplies. He sketched out what was later called 'the blue-water school'. I told him that I quite agreed with him but unless he had an Army at home large enough to prevent raids and make it necessary for a foreign enemy to land large numbers of men, the Navy would be useless. If 20,000 men could dodge the Fleet and land somewhere in England, they could march on London and create such a scare that we should be forced to capitulate without striking a blow. He was delighted with my arguments and got so excited talking that he had to stop and hold my arm to prevent my going on. He sketched out rather a wild scheme which was to reduce the Army and Navy to experts alone, and then keep a huge reserve of men who could become either soldiers or sailors. A beginning had been made in this direction by the nucleus crew system, but he wanted to carry the idea much further and make it apply to the Army. I told him that I very much doubted whether an Army composed of 90 per cent raw recruits would be any good, and I imagined that the highly trained German Army would soon make mince-meat of them, but he maintained that any idea of our fighting the Germans on land was absurd. By this scheme he would be able to reduce the income-tax by half, and that alone would be a blessing.[20]

It is frightening to read that the man in charge of the reform of the Navy from 1904–10 should have made his inter-service plans with the fixed idea that war with Germany was 'absurd'.

The strangest part about this conversation is that Ponsonby, no respecter of persons, continued to admire Fisher whose personality carried his listeners with him, even when he was talking nonsense. Traditionally his violent nature has been forgiven due to the wisdom of his reforms and policies. But were they wise? Or did Fisher, Battenberg, Churchill and the naval establishment back the wrong horse?

Mountbatten in old age forgot that by 1907 Louis had become a stern critic of the reconstitution of the fleets. Certain of the reforms were debatable. Should Fisher have scrapped 154 ships? (An action with which Louis agreed.) Certainly their disappearance saved money. Many of them were wasting assets and needed endless repairs, but on the other hand if some of them had been retained and replaced, they would have served a useful purpose in protecting the helpless merchant ships which the German submarines later sank like sitting ducks.

Neither Louis, Fisher, Churchill or any sea lord foresaw the ceaseless submarine attacks on merchant ships, or the necessity for guarding convoys. The money saved by this 'scrapping' enabled the naval estimates to be momentarily reduced, while the programme for building all-big-gun-type battleships and their attendant vessels continued. Their criticism of design infuriated Fisher, but was later justified by a change of Dreadnought design enabling them to carry 6-inch guns for use against submarines.

After Jutland the Home Fleet had nothing to do except watch and wait; the German Fleet only once ventured out into the North Sea. This left Fisher's collection of Dreadnoughts and Invincibles, under Lord Beatty's command, stagnating, purposeless in their North Sea hideaways, awaiting an enemy who never appeared. Meanwhile the Germans made no attempt to make up for their battleship losses and concentrated on the building of submarines which nearly succeeded in starving Britain.

Was the shortage of convoy guard ships a sign of a Navy unbalanced by Fisher's reforms?

From 1904 onwards anyone who looked ahead and questioned the First Sea Lord's devotion to an all-big-gun ships' policy was brutally savaged. Fisher's behaviour created a previously unknown bitterness in the Admiralty. His treatment of Rear Admiral Wemyss, a possible naval secretary, illustrated his brutality:

In an interview with Sir John Fisher, the latter, well aware how much Wemyss desired the post of Naval Secretary, offered it to him, adding that such an appointment would be a gross job, since there were many men senior to him who ought to be preferred, while plainly intimating that the price he would have to pay would be absolute subserviency to his views. Wemyss indignantly refused to accept the post under such conditions, though it was one he most coveted at the time, and from that day on there was no more communication of any sort between the two men, who were only to meet once again, and that by chance, during the war.[21]

The increasing number of critics who had suffered from his spleen, chose as their spokesman Mountbatten's *bête noire*, the charming, indiscreet Lord Charles Beresford.

The Irishman's career was unthinkable today. Every now and again, he would stand for Parliament, get elected, make execrable speeches in the House of Commons – he was essentially a man of action – and return to the Navy. Earlier I described the touching farewell which Louis's men gave him when he left HMS *Drake*. Beresford, on leaving the Mediterranean command, in Malta received an equally pleasing send off; every ship in Malta harbour sailed out to say farewell. By the time he was forced to haul down his flag in 1909 his personality had won him the ear of the nation. Naval chiefs in that patriotic era appealed to the public imagination to a degree inconceivable today. Unlike Fisher, he was a witty, aristocratic 'card'; in his youth he had been helped by an early, later chequered, friendship with King Edward VII. The country saw in him a reincarnation of Nelson.

Years later Mountbatten, out of loyalty to his father, tried to dismiss Beresford as a blimpish buffoon, opposed to every reform.

His flagship was like the palace of some mediaeval tyrant, and he liked to have on board his wife, his motor car and his fat pet bulldog, behind whom there followed at all times a sailor with a dustpan and brush.[22]

Mediaeval tyrants did not have motor cars!

Mountbatten's hatred of Beresford and distortion of his character was a loyal inexactitude which contradicted Fisher's own early opinions and those of Marder, who described Lord Charles's personality:

> Here was one of the most engaging personalities of the time – frank, open, dashing, impulsive, fluent. The officers and men under his command loved and admired 'Charlie B.' because of his charm, geniality, high spirits, humour, and his unvarying kindness and thoughtfulness. His professional attainments unfortunately did not match the attractiveness of his personality. He had a singular gift for handling men and getting the best out of them, he was indefatigable, and he excelled in the art of pure seamanship; but very definitely he was not a tactician or strategist of note. Nevertheless, it is only fair to point out that Beresford and his supporters honestly believed he would make a better First Sea Lord than Fisher. He had been Second-in-Command under Fisher in the Mediterranean and in those days they had seen eye to eye on many subjects. They had remained on friendly terms until the autumn of 1906 . . .
>
> The definite break began with the fleet redistribution scheme. Thereafter Beresford, egged on by the malcontents, found more and more to criticise in Fisher's reforms. The role of being agin those in power came naturally to Beresford, a real Irishman.[23]

Marder's belief that their break was caused by the Fleet redistribution scheme was correct; was Beresford's judgement underestimated? Stupid men are often right. They have the advantage of understanding essentials! The redistribution of the Fleets scheme was conceived when Louis was Assistant Director of Naval Intelligence at the Directorate, which planned how to meet the German threat. Unfortunately, when Fisher came to implement it in 1906–1907, he realised if he followed Louis's plans he would be putting Beresford, as Admiral of the Channel Fleet, in command of the greatest naval force in the world. The idea of promoting a hated adversary to a position of importance rivalling his own, was unacceptable. To frustrate his rival he implemented the scheme by ineffectual stages, which destroyed the balance of Louis's carefully laid plans. Beresford recorded his objections, which despite possible exaggerations, illustrate the chaos caused by Fisher's jealousy:

> During this period [1907], an extraordinary confusion prevailed at the Admiralty. Its character may be briefly indicated by a summary

of the various changes in the organisation and distribution of the Fleet, beginning in the previous year (1906):

In October, the sea-going Fleets were reduced in strength by about one-quarter, and a new Home Fleet was formed of nucleus crew ships. The Channel Fleet was reduced from sixty-two fighting vessels, the balance being transferred to the Home Fleet. An order was issued under which ships taken from the Channel, Atlantic and Mediterranean Fleets for purposes of refitting were to be replaced during their absence by ships from the Home Fleet.

In December, the Nore Division of the Home Fleet was given full crews instead of nucleus crews.

In April, 1907, an order was issued that no more than two battleships in each Fleet were to be refitted at one time.

In September, the Channel Fleet was increased from twenty-one vessels to sixty vessels.

In August, 1908, the orders substituting Home Fleet ships for ships from sea-going fleets under repair, and ordaining that no more than two battleships should be absent at one time, were cancelled; with the result that the Channel Fleet went to sea in the following December short of eight battleships, two armoured cruisers, one unarmoured cruiser, one scout, and 20 destroyers, 32 vessels in all.

When the Home Fleet was finally constituted, in March, 1907, there were no less than three commanders-in-chief in Home Waters; one commanding the Home Fleet, one the Nore Division, and one (myself) the Channel Fleet. In time of war the supreme command was to be exercised by me, over the whole number of fighting vessels, 244 in all. But in time of peace they could not be trained or exercised together,[24] nor had any one of the commanders-in-chief accurate information at any given moment of the state or disposition of the forces of any other commander-in-chief.[25]

Any admiral would have been bemused by such confusing and contrary changes of direction. Although often contradicted by Hough, Mountbatten, in *Louis and Alexander*, pretended Louis and Fisher brought in necessary reforms together in opposition to all advice, and stood united together against Beresford's stupid complaints. But Louis's opinion of Fisher's piecemeal implementation of his plan supports Beresford's view that the First Sea Lord, out of spite, implemented the scheme in a manner which destroyed its cohesion.

His criticism of Fisher's administration echoed Beresford's, and showed that he had matured into the clearest thinker in the Navy, overshadowing his contemporaries, including the First Sea Lord. His lucid letter of 23 January 1907 to James Thursfield[26] is the most devastating indictment of Fisher's failings ever published especially as it was written by a friend and admirer. The following excerpts clear Louis of complicity in Fisher's *spiteful* reorganisation plans and contradict Mountbatten's assertion that the two men worked closely together until 1910.

H.M.S. Drake,
SECOND CRUISER SQUADRON, PORTLAND
January 23rd, 1907

My dear Thursfield,

. . . Now the first and so far only scheme (and this is a big one in its effect) brought out by J.F. of which I had not a previous inkling, is this 'Home Fleet'. Since I have been within reach of the Admiralty this winter, and have discovered bit by bit the particulars of this grand scheme, I am more and more astounded. It is simply topsy-turvey and opposed to all our hitherto accepted principles . . .

. . . Another ridiculous point: Whenever a ship of one of the sea-going fleets requires periodical repairs, her place will be taken pro. tem. by a ship from the Home Fleet. And yet this Home Fleet is to be our first striking force, for which purpose it is to consist of our best ships. Fancy a *Dreadnought* swinging round the buoy off Sheerness, flying the flag of the occupant of Admiralty House! Why, it is criminal! I can use no other word.

I am very sorry to have to go against J.F. but can't help it. If J.F. were to put the scheme before me, he would have a reply like the one I have written above. After our July interview I can't volunteer it. The feeling amongst all thinking naval men is of consternation. May entirely agrees with me and means to tell Lord Tweedmouth. Towards the King, Prince of Wales, and others I keep silence, but I shall not rest until this whole monstrous scheme is knocked on the head, and the principles, which J.F. lectured to us about with iteration and emphasis, at Malta, and now tramples under foot, are once more firmly established.

Very sincerely yours,
(Sgd.) LOUIS BATTENBERG[27]

The only difference between Beresford's and Louis's criticisms of Fisher's 'reform' of the Home Fleet was that the latter argued his case with an ability denied to the Irishman.

In an extract of a letter to Admiral King-Hall in February 1909, Louis again showed his distrust of Fisher:

You know how much I admire J.F. He is a truly great man, and almost all his schemes have benefited the Navy. But he has started this pernicious partisanship in the Navy – there is no denying it. Anyone who in any way opposed J.F. went under. His hatred of C.B. has led him to maintain for the past two years an organization of our Home forces which was indefensible and not adapted to war. This is so patent that everyone must see it, and constitutes a serious indictment.[28]

Fisher had arranged his fleets in such a haphazard manner that if war had been declared in 1907, Beresford would have been proved right, and the Channel Fleet would have had only eight big-gun vessels to take on twice the number of German ships of equivalent gun power. This was indefensible and justified Louis's criticisms. (It is interesting to note Fisher's admiring biographer Marder did not quote Louis's logical letters.) Mountbatten's defective memory, perverted by hero worship, made him unintentionally damage his father's reputation by trying to prove he was a supporter of a policy he condemned.

Unfortunately Fisher's behaviour drove Beresford into such a rage that he could not see that Louis's original plan would have benefited him. Carried away by choler and anti-Germanism, the Irishman insisted on lumping his two opponents together as enemies of the state, stressing Louis was nothing but a 'bloody untrustworthy German'.

In 1908 Beresford deliberately cut Fisher at a levee in London, an act of insubordination. Such behaviour, and his inability to keep quiet, forced the Liberal government to see that, despite his national popularity, he had to go. A tactical solution was reached by reducing the period of commands from three years to two. He was retired on 24 March 1909, a 'heart of oak martyr'. Portsmouth and Waterloo thronged with admirers welcoming home their hero.

Encouraged both by his popularity and a legacy, he bought a large house in London, and began a press campaign against Fisher on 2

April by sending a circular to the newspapers, criticising the unreadiness of the Fleet for war. On the same day an orchestrated attack by Sir George Armstrong disclosed that in 1906 Fisher had printed and distributed letters from a junior officer called Bacon, on the workings of the Mediterranean Fleet, then under Beresford's command. Parliament and a section of the press deplored that a First Lord should undermine discipline by using a junior officer to spy on his Admiral and circulate unfavourable reports. Fisher could provide no adequate justification for his conduct except that Beresford had done the same thing. Nervously he wrote to Lord Esher on 13 April:

> Imagine what a state of affairs when a meeting of Naval Officers on the active list in a room in Grosvenor Street is able to coerce the Cabinet and force the strongest Board of Admiralty to totter to its fall! Why, the 'young Turks' are not in it! The Country must indeed be in a bad way if so governed![29]

The attacks caused such national unrest, that on 22 April the Prime Minister, Asquith, took the extraordinary step of setting up a sub-committee of Imperial Defence under his chairmanship, to investigate Beresford's charges. Its members included Sir Edward Grey, Lord Crewe, John Morley and Lord Haldane, the most esteemed names in the Liberal party. The public was astounded and enthralled. Not surprisingly Fisher was livid with rage, and on 6 May wrote to W. H. Steed a letter illustrating his unbalanced temperament.

Admiralty, Whitehall
May 6th, 1909

Private
My blessed Sheet Anchor!
   I was at it till midnight, so had no time to write last night to bless you for your letter. I fear you are not wise in your own interests to back me! HOWEVER, IT MAKES ONE FEEL THE DEEPER! SECRET. THE ATMOSPHERE OF THIS ENQUIRY IS PRO-BERESFORD! Think of the holy calm in that junk when they had pitched Jonah overboard! But isn't it really incredible that a serious enquiry by Cabinet Ministers should now be proceeding that the Country has been and still is in vital danger from Germany (this is Beresford's gunnery,) and requiring only a few hours for its mobiliz-

ation! The Admiralty being dislocated and the Navy in revolution because fearful of a windbag! The Press and the Public à la Beresford! 'The prophets prophesy falsely, the people love to have it so, and what shall we do in the end thereof?'

Anyhow, my dear Friend, although, Moses-like, your splendid fire is unabated, don't please injure yourself for my sake! (It's cunning to get rid of me on Beresford and not on 'two keels to one'!)

Yours till the Angels smile on us!

J.F.[30]

The Committee met fifteen times, and Admiral of the Fleet Sir Arthur Wilson, a member of the Committee of Imperial Defence, was cross-examined at the thirteenth meeting, an original idea as he was asked privately to express his opinion on the policies of the First Sea Lord to whom he was the obvious successor. Fisher considered the inquiry a serious affront to both himself and the Navy, but even his defender Marder admits his bellicose character was responsible for the row. The Committee's report was published as a parliamentary paper on 12 August, the evidence was kept secret but the Committee's general conclusion was:

In the opinion of the Committee, the investigation has shown that during the time in question no danger to the country resulted from the Admiralty's arrangements for war, whether considered from the standpoint of the organization and distribution of the fleets, the number of ships, or the preparation of War Plans.

They feel bound to add that arrangements quite defensible in themselves, though not ideally perfect, were in practice seriously hampered through the absence of cordial relations between the Board of Admiralty and the Commander-in-Chief of the Channel Fleet. The Board of Admiralty do not appear to have taken Lord Charles Beresford sufficiently into their confidence as to the reasons for dispositions to which he took exception; . . . and Lord Charles Beresford, on the other hand, appears to have failed to appreciate and carry out the spirit of the instructions of the Board, and to recognize their paramount authority.[31]

This was not the vindication Fisher had expected. In a letter to Reginald McKenna on 19 August he showed his dismay.

FISHER TO REGINALD MCKENNA

[South Tyrol]
August 19th, 1909

My dear First Lord,

I am not going to give you all my mind about the Beresford Report, which I have just assimilated, as I don't see you can do anything with advantage to the Admiralty, or without injury to yourself, BUT it's a cowardly document! It ignores Beresford's want of loyalty at the outset of the two years, and so how could the Admiralty give him its confidence, and the poisonous allusion to the Naval War Staff in the concluding passages is a covert onslaught on the Admiralty, utterly neglecting the big business the Admiralty did in starting the War College, and practically showing forth the great advance in strategicial thinking by the concentration of our forces instead of their previous dispersal.[32]

On 27 August he wrote, in curious English, to Esher: '. . . No – it has been a bitter disappointment – more bitter because each of the five members of the Committee so expressive to me and to two others of the complete victory of the Admiralty. Cowards all!'[33]

Beresford was delighted and circulated another letter to the press on 16 August saying his charges had been justified. He was marginally right; Fisher was not cleared and was forced to realise he had put himself into an impossible position by becoming a contentious figure forbidding peace. He resigned, and accepted a peerage, knowing if he stayed ways would be found to push him aside. His Achilles heel had been a blinkered belief in the rightness and righteousness of his narrow views. The man who, as a boy, would not stomach Hills sharing Mrs Warden's affection, would not share power with his friends or foes, and was prepared to destroy the unity and efficiency of the Navy to avoid doing so. His egoism marred his judgement and negated his abilities, and it should not be forgotten that at Jutland the British Navy suffered greater losses than the German due to inaccurate gunnery, unwise placing of the gunpowder magazine and thinness of deck armour on the Dreadnoughts' decks, due to Fisher's willingness to cut naval expenditure and refusal to build new docks.[34]

This long discourse on the schism is relevant due to its effect on Louis's career, which was damaged during the years of internal naval warfare as his plan for the redistribution of the Fleets would have benefited both the Navy and Beresford. What could he do? He could not ally himself publicly with the supporters of Beresford and Lambton, who continually insulted his nationality, impugned his loyalty and blocked his promotion. The result was he became a target of the anti-German movement, which grew year by year and was increased by the popular press from 1912 until his resignation in 1914. It is true he did not publicly express his own strong opinions of Fisher's maladministration and tell the First Lord what he wrote to Thursfield.[35] His discretion was unwise and allowed his enemies, out of jealousy, to convince themselves he was an outright Fisher man. Biding their time they waited and vindictively knifed him in the back at a moment when he was undermined by his Germanic associations.

NOTES

1. Captain the Hon. Hedworth Lambton, later Admiral of the Fleet Sir Hedworth Meux. He changed his name in 1909 to inherit a brewery fortune and was one of King George V's first choices to succeed Battenberg as First Sea Lord. Churchill dismissed him as a 'nonsense man'.
2. Second Earl of Selborne, First Lord of the Admiralty.
3. This reference is almost certainly to the Prince of Wales.
4. Lambton to Selborne, 28 January 1904, Lambton MS.
5. Marder (ed.), *Fear God and Dread Nought*, vol. 1, ch. 1, p. 34.
6. Ibid., p. 34.
7. Ibid., p. 40.
8. Ibid., p. 41.
9. See Marder, *Letters of Lord Fisher*, vol. 1, letters 34–40, pp. 105–111.
10. Hough, *Louis and Victoria*, ch. 8, p. 194.
11. Ibid., ch. 8, p. 244.
12. Three First Lords of the Admiralty between 1904–10, theoretically Fisher's overlords.
13. Hough, *Louis and Victoria*, ch. 8, p. 196.
14. Royal Archives W57/95.
15. Hough, *Louis and Victoria*, ch. 10, p. 238.
16. Marder (ed.), *Fear God and Dread Nought*, vol. 2, *Years of Power: 1904–1914*, Letter 90, p. 142, Fisher to King Edward.
17. Rose, *King George V*, ch. 3, p. 73.
18. Ibid.
19. Marder (ed.), *Fear God and Dread Nought*, vol. 2, Letter 366, pp. 458–9. Fisher to Esher.
20. Ponsonby, *Recollections of Three Reigns*, ch. 10, pp. 128–9.

21. Lady Wester Wemyss, *The Life and Letters of Lord Wester Wemyss*, pp. 99–100.
22. Hough, *Louis and Victoria*. I know of no mediaeval tyrant who had on his boat a pet bulldog followed by an attendant.
23. Marder (ed.), *Fear God and Dread Nought*, vol. 2, pp. 39–40.
24. The 'fleet cooperation' disrupted for years by Fisher's hatred of Beresford was illustrated by the disastrous lack of communication between Jellicoe's captains at Jutland. See Geoffrey Bennett, *Jutland*, David and Charles, 1972, pp. 127–53.
25. *The Memoirs of Admiral Lord Charles Beresford*, vol. 2, Methuen, Ltd. 1914, pp. 551–2.
26. Later Sir James Thursfield, *Times* correspondent and leader writer, 1881–1924.
27. Kerr, *Prince Louis of Battenberg*, pp. 216–21.
28. Ibid., p. 225.
29. Marder (ed.), *Fear God and Dread Nought*, vol. 2, Fisher to Esher, 13 April 1909, p. 211.
30. Ibid., pp. 248–9.
31. Ibid., pp. 212–13.
32. Ibid., p. 260.
33. Lord Fisher, *Memories*, Hodder and Stoughton, 1917, p. 192.
34. See Bennett, *Jutland*, ch. 6, p. 159.
35. See Louis's letter to Thursfield, p. 206.

18

Louis went on half-pay for three months in 1910 and then commanded with skill and humanity the Third and Fourth Divisions of the Home Fleet. In December 1911 he became Second Sea Lord. This caused a vulgar cry of protest from a new enemy, Horatio Bottomley, who published in *John Bull*:

SHOULD A GERMAN 'BOSS' OUR NAVY?
Bull-dog breed or Dachshund?
by M.H.

. . . I thought that there was some limit to our grovelling and kissing the toes of the German Emperor and German cadgers, waiters, musicians, and bands, but I never imagined that a British ruler of the King's Navy would appoint a German to be in the position to know every secret of Britain's protection, and an arbiter of Britain's defences against Germany in the war that threatens us. But such is the fact. Prince Louis of Battenberg is to-day one of the chiefs of the British Navy! . . .

. . . Britain is, as I have said, a happy hunting ground for starveling Germans who, for social and monetary reasons, renounce allegiance to their country. But consider the *vice versa* for a minute. Have we any measure for the contempt with which we regard a Britisher who renounces *his* country and becomes a naturalised German or Frenchman? What an impregnable fortress Britain is, with an imported patriot as its chief naval bulwark!

WAKE UP, BRITAIN!

I write strongly, not because the 'brain of our Navy,' as our egregious Press styles him, is a German and a Battenberg, but because I believe it is a crime against our Empire to trust our secrets of national defence to any alien. History has shown us how in times of supreme arbitrament the *condottieri* of old sold their hirers to the

213

highest bidder, and used all the knowledge they acquired for the advantage of their own, their native land . . .[1]

Bottomley told the public what the Kaiser's boastings made them wish to hear, and the anti-German feeling in the country against the King's German relations, and indirectly the King and Queen themselves, acutely worried the royal pair and their advisers.

In 1912 Louis commanded the Blue Fleet and was beaten for the first time in his career in the annual manoeuvres. Was this a sign that the tension of the last few years had told? He was now fifty-eight and suffered from gout. Nevertheless his mind remained clear. He was appointed First Sea Lord on 9 December 1912. His task was formidable; Fisher had left no feasible plan of action in the event of war breaking out, or created the naval staff he had called for before he was appointed First Sea Lord. Another notable failure of the pre-war naval programme was that in the ten years before 1914 Fisher, Battenberg, Churchill and numerous naval chiefs frequently praised the merits of submarines. However, Dreadnoughts and Invincibles were always preferred to them in building programmes, and only 27 underwater vessels were completed by 1914. Nobody misread the future more incorrectly than Winston Churchill. The result of this complacency was that no anti-submarine tactics were considered and it took enormous losses in the merchant fleet to cause the adoption of protected convoys.

Why were submarines neglected whose ability to sink and disappear had been proved, in order to build battleships vulnerable to torpedoes? Why by 1914 had no safe harbours been provided for our fleets? Was the so-called British victory at Jutland invaluable to Germany? The answer to these three questions is 'yes'. After Jellicoe's victory on 31 May 1916, German policy was to keep their battleships safe in harbour, and to keep the British Fleet to the North Sea while they concentrated on the building of submarines, which sank so many British merchantmen. At one period Britain was down to six weeks' supply of food and oil. But for America entering the war we could have been starved to defeat.[2]

Louis unfortunately never stopped giving his enemies ammunition. He spent his last two leaves in Germany. His sister remembered how they sat peacefully on the banks of the Rhine,[3] happily looking at holidaymakers who he must have known he would soon be fighting.

When war broke out the country was dismayed by a succession of naval disasters. In the Battle of Coronel Admiral Cradock behaved with incredible stupidity and lost himself and his squadron. Later a new battleship, the *Audacious*, was mined, and then came the sinking of the *Hogue*, *Cressy* and *Aboukir*. Lord Jellicoe described this costly tactical error for which Louis was ultimately responsible:

> This policy of cruiser sweeps has been adopted as the result of experience in the various Naval Manoeuvres carried out in previous years in the North Sea. These had demonstrated quite clearly that the alternative policy of stretching cruiser patrol lines across the Sea, is a very simple matter. Further, a line of cruisers occupying regular patrol positions is always in peril of successful submarine attack, the loss of the cruisers *Hogue*, *Cressy* and *Aboukir* showed this.[4]

To have allowed these ships, manned by many of his second son's contemporaries, to follow dangerous outdated tactics, showed the extent of Louis's decline; in 1913 he had submitted to the Council of Admirals a criticism of the fatal formation as being vulnerable to U-boat attack. Kerr believed that if he had not been undermined by personal attacks, he would have changed it. The next day he told a member of his staff: 'I should not have given in to them.'[5] This admission, to one of his admirers, must incline the reader to the belief that he was past his best. Churchill agreed, and Asquith wrote to Venetia Stanley on 14 October:

> He [Winston] has quite made up his mind that the time has come for a drastic change in his Board; our poor blue-eyed German will have to go . . .[6]

Two days earlier the Prime Minister told Miss Stanley of the King's embarrassment about Louis retaining his position.

> He [the King] is a good deal agitated about Louis of Battenberg's position: he & the Queen receive heaps of letters abusing them for their cousins (Albert of Sch. Holst. & the Duke of Coburg) who are actually fighting against us and for 'the damned German spy' whom their relationship keeps at the Admiralty.[7]

Fortunately this letter was not published until 1982 and Mountbatten remained all his life unaware of the nature of the King's feelings for his father in 1914. Fate on this occasion was kind. Bottomley returned to his pet hate on 24 October:

THE GREAT SPY PERIL

. . . Blood is said to be thicker than water; and we doubt whether all the water in the North Sea could obliterate the blood-ties between the Battenbergs and the Hohenzollerns when it comes to a question of a life and death struggle between Germany and ourselves. We shall further repeat our demand that Prince Louis of Battenberg be relieved of his position as First Sea Lord, and that some British sailor should take his place.[8]

On 26 October a measured, fair but for Louis damning, leader appeared in the *Globe*:

FIRST SEA LORD

At the Board of Admiralty the duties of the various members are very strictly defined and apportioned, and those of the First Sea Lord may roughly be summarised as organisation for war, distribution and movements of the Fleet. This great office which, it will be observed, carries with it the strategic control of our Navy, is at present held by Prince Louis of Battenberg, the eldest son of Prince Alexander of Hesse. He was naturalised as an Englishman and entered the British Service as a cadet in 1868, and his rise to the highest position open to any Naval officer is due entirely to the great professional ability he has shown throughout his career, and in no way to the accident of birth. He enjoys the full confidence of the King, of the Government, of his colleagues on the Board and of the Service, and we know that his eagerness to defeat and annihilate the German Fleet is as great as any born Briton among us. But in the position in which the country now finds itself, public opinion is of vital importance, and though every well-informed person knows that the character of Prince Louis of Battenberg is beyond challenge, it is imperative that the man in the street should be equally satisfied. At present he is not, and it is a plain though most disagreeable duty to say so.

Rumours, as injurious as they are baseless, are flying from mouth to mouth, and we can produce abundant proof that the uneasiness is increasing. Nor is it very much to be surprised at. This war has revealed such long-meditated treachery in high places, such astounding evidence that the rulers of Germany do not recognise the same code of national, or even private, honour as ourselves, that suspicion naturally fastens upon everyone of German origin. We receive day by day a constantly growing stream of correspondence, in which the wisdom of having an officer who is of German birth as the professional head of the Navy is assailed in varying terms. We would gladly dismiss all these letters from our mind, but we cannot. They are too numerous, too insistent, and too obviously the expression of a widespread feeling. There comes a time when no responsible organ of public opinion can keep silence without sacrificing the tacit obligation under which it lies to its readers, and in our judgement that time has now arrived . . .

. . . To the many correspondents who have addressed us on this subject we have as yet no reply to make. We can say, with all the emphasis of profound conviction, that we know them to be utterly mistaken, and that for the honour and loyalty of the First Sea Lord we would ourselves give any pledge that could be required. But to do so is to do no more than express a personal belief, which carries with it only the authority that may be supposed to attach to the statements of a journal which has, we hope, a well-deserved reputation for straight-forwardness and accuracy. It is hardly possible that the suspicions we have referred to are unknown to Prince Louis himself, and the uselessness of any personal repudiation on his part must give him the most poignant distress. No one is more entitled to sympathy than the man who knows himself to be the soul of honour, but who is the subject of malignant gossip or of unfounded suspicion, and who has no means of putting himself right with the world. For the sake of the First Sea Lord himself, no less than for that of a nation over whose destinies he now exercises such paramount influence, we ask that some authoritative statement of a nature so emphatic and so unqualified so as to remove at once and forever every cloud of doubt and to silence every breath of rumour.[9]

As Churchill had decided to get rid of Louis, this, in part, eloquent leader could not have appeared at a more convenient time. Occasional sentences suggest it was written or revised by more than one hand;

certain phrases have the faint echo of a familiar oratorical style. It would be interesting to know if the letter was edited or inspired by the First Lord.

On 28 October Louis resigned in a dignified letter, and received a farewell bite from the malevolent *John Bull*; a cartoon pictured him sadly leaving the Admiralty. In the foreground his successor, Lord Fisher, stands jaunty, smiling. Under the caption 'Jacky's the boy . . .' appeared the triumphant rhyme:

> Unanimously we accord
> A welcome to the First Sea Lord
> Beside his great intrinsic worth
> He is a man of British birth.[10]

Louis retired quietly to live at Kent House, in the Isle of Wight, refusing all invitations because he neither wished to hurt the King or embarrass his friends from whom he kept aloof. He cannot have been happy; he was not a man to thrive on inactivity, but he was pleased by his sons' naval appointments.

To estimate his worth as a sailor is difficult, his service coincided with the Pax Britannica, and he was never involved in action at sea. Esher described him as 'mediocre' but his character developed with age. Comparing him dispassionately with Fisher, it is possible to argue their positions had been reversed; he could have reorganised the Navy efficiently, without brutality. Power came to him too late and in unfortunate circumstances, partly created by his own behaviour. In maturity he inspired love and admiration, and was unequalled in his generation as a peacetime tactician, able to express himself clearly and concisely. But he had his limitations and cannot avoid responsibility for (1) failing to realise the full implications of underwater ships and our shortage of submarines, (2) the limitations of lightly armoured all-big-gun ships, (3) the unpreparedness of our naval bases in 1914, (4) the necessity for convoys in 1914, (5) the shortage of small anti-submarine vessels to guard the convoys. His contemporaries were equally to blame for these shortages and miscalculations, which nearly lost Britain the war.

NOTES
1. *John Bull*, 23 December 1911.
2. Bennet, *Jutland*, ch. 6, pp. 163–5.

3. Marie of Battenberg, *Reminiscences*.
4. Jellicoe's *The Grand Fleet*, cited Kerr, *Prince Louis of Battenberg*, ch. 11, p. 247.
5. Quoted Kerr, *Prince Louis of Battenberg*, ch. 11, p. 248.
6. Asquith, *Letters to Venetia Stanley*, p. 287, letter 191.
7. Ibid., p. 285, letter 189.
8. *John Bull*, 24 October 1914.
9. The *Globe*, 26 October 1914.
10. *John Bull*, 7 November 1914.

19

Louis's sufferings were not over. For many years anti-German feeling had upset and alarmed the King and Queen. Anti-German outbursts increased in 1914 when reports of German atrocities were encouraged by the Government to stimulate recruitment. It was not surprising that fingers were pointed at the Hanoverian King of England and his Teck wife: *John Bull* as usual was a bitter critic. The scurrilous 1911 article which described Louis as a *condottiere* had revived the eighteenth-century habit of savagely mocking the royal family and their Hanoverian hangers-on:

> It was our self-abasement that paved the way for the present arrogance of Germany. It began with that treacherous blackguard George I, and continued its pollution of the stream of English public life in the way Thackeray described in *The Four Georges*, for truly:

> > George the First was little good,
> > Little better was George the Second;
> > What mortal man e'er heard a word
> > Of any good of George the Third?
> > When George the Fourth to hell descended,
> > God be praised! the Georges ended.

> That tribe of Georges did 'peter out,' but their blighting influence, that saddled England with over seven-hundred million pounds of National debt *to pay the cowardly Hessians and Hanoverians 1s. per day* to fight for their own country, permeated the Army, the Navy, and every Government department in England. In the old days the populace expressed very freely, both in words and deeds, its opinion of the mob of foreign hangers-on who had flocked here from the petty German Court with the monarch who had been invited over 'for the good of the nation'. The tale – probably

founded on fact – goes that the carriage of some of these mercenaries was stopped in St. James's by a threatening crowd, whereupon a terrified old harridan poked her head out of the window and cried: 'Mine goot peoples, mine goot peoples, vy you do tis? Ve come over for all your goots!' To which a vulgar wit replied, 'Yes, damn you, and our chattels as well!'

TRUE AND FALSE PATRIOTISM

Every true Englishman, Irishman, Scotsman, and Welshman, and every colonist who had washed his mind of cant, felt ashamed and humiliated at the records of the Court of that period. The Court Circular proclaimed in every issue that 'No English need apply.' The 'pinch-your-pocket Bergs,' 'Morganatic marriage Bergs,' 'Schweinbergs,' and the rest of Germany had England as a 'happy hunting ground.' One starving princeling, who possessed a wife and three sweet pledges of affection, was 'battened' on the British taxpayer at £6,000 per year. Another received the same yearly amount for marrying one of our princesses, and the climax was reached when a 'wrong side of the blanket' royalty, whose worth in Germany was £80 a year, was given £6,000 per annum to marry another princess.[1]

After the outbreak of war, Bottomley's sentiments were frequently repeated. This was bad luck on King George V who had served eight, sea-sick years in the British Navy, and had never liked or cultivated his German relations. After his elder brother died he lived the life of an English sporting gentleman in a house many squires would have despised. Unfortunately he had a guttural accent although he could not speak German. Naturally he was aware of the strongly anti-German feeling in the country, although his private secretary Lord Stamfordham kept many abusive letters from him.

The public's protests were comprehensible. The daily list of casualties in the first three years of the war meant there was hardly a family in the country who had not lost a friend or relation. British propaganda about German atrocities may have made the nation throw its heart into the war, but at the same time it unintentionally drew attention to the fact the King and Queen were pure Germans, although they did their best to show they had no sympathies for their enemy-relations.

As early as 24 September 1914 Lord Stamfordham wrote to General

French's military secretary, asking him to contradict a rumour the King had visited German prisoners: 'HM has seen no German prisoners (and has no desire to see any of them!)'.[2] And on 9 April 1917 Sir Clive Wigram, an assistant secretary, complained to the same officer of an unfortunate visit to Windsor of two Greco-Germans,[3] the Grand Duchess George and Prince Andrew of Greece, adding: 'There is no doubt their Majesties lost ground over this.' He added the King had no desire to welcome his German cousins, the Tsar and Tsarina, to England. Later George V was responsible for the withdrawal of a destroyer which was to have brought the whole family out of Russia; regrettably he allowed Lloyd George to take the blame.[4] This long-hidden, uncharacteristic action showed how shaken he was by the personal attacks, which increased as the casualties mounted.

Something had to be done, and in June 1917 the King decided to change his family name to Windsor,[5] and to give new names to his and the Queen's German relations. Louis's letter to his daughter shows his grief at having to stop calling himself *Prince* and *Serene Highness* and to accept the Marquisate of Milford Haven. Despite nearly fifty years of service in the British Navy he still venerated his German title, and bitterly regretted the diminution of his status:

> 6 June 1917
> Kent House
> East Cowes
> Isle-of-Wight

My beloved Louise,

I have had very serious news of far-reaching effects on us all to tell you. George Rex telegraphed to me last week he wished to see me as soon as possible. I took the next steamer & was closeted with him for a long time. The upshot of a long statement about his being attacked as being Half-German & surrounding himself by relatives with German names, & C. was that he must ask us Holsteins, Tecks & Battenbergs to give up using in England our German titles & to assume English surnames . . . It has been suggested that we shd turn our name into English, viz: *Battenhill* or *Mountbatten*. We incline to the latter as a better sound . . . Of course we are at his mercy. We only are allowed to use our German title as the Sovereign has always recognized it, but he can refuse this recognition at any moment. If so we are plain Mister, which would be impossible . . . For you, my dear children we feel deeply . . . It is a terrible upheaval & break with one's past – another consequence of this awful war. Mama is splendid & is determined to give up her own title & rank, which is quite her own & not due to marriage with me, & to call herself by my name and title only . . .

Newspaper comment will be unpleasant, but unavoidable. Whether the republicans will be satisfied remains to be seen. I fear the throne here is beginning to shake also . . .

Goodbye my dear dear child. All this is very terrible. I shall miss my old & laboriously write a new fancy name

> Every yr old loving B
> father[6]

It is a sad letter revealing Louis's incomprehension of the nature of British antagonism to Germany.

So disappeared the family name of Battenberg after an existence of only sixty-five years, to be replaced by an anglicised version. The next generation of the family produced another Louis, his second son, whose career I will deal with in a second volume. During the First World War he missed Jutland due to a broken leg. He then joined the *Lion* where his most dangerous enemy was a sadistic sub-lieutenant who invented pretexts for beating midshipmen. Mountbatten apparently once took eighteen strokes without a murmur.[7] For a short time he was joined by his elder brother George, whose brilliance may have increased his younger brother's desire to succeed. To separate the pair Mountbatten was posted to the *Queen Elizabeth*, where he heard, with apparent amusement, his father had been forced to change his name. What he actually thought will never be known, but his lifelong reverence for his German ancestors may have made him simulate mirth to conceal pain.[8] If so, it was another pinprick, encouraging him to attempt by his own efforts the restoration of his family's lost glory.

Lord Milford Haven lived quietly in the war years, following his dismissal. In 1918 his feelings were hurt when, with Fisher, he was not invited to the surrender of the German Fleet. But the battle of the great schism was not yet over; the pair's old enemy Wester Wemyss had succeeded Jellicoe as First Sea Lord and was determined his two old chiefs should be punished. A last shot was fired at Louis on 9 December when he received a formal note saying he would not be employed again, and suggesting he might wish to resign to make room for a younger man.[9] He did as he was told, but bitterly hurt, wrote to King George V's private secretary:

10 December 1918

My dear Stamfordham,
Would you kindly inform the King that in response to a letter from Admiral Wemyss I have just sent in my papers. As he did not appear to be aware of the reasons why I am still on the active list I informed him in reply that I had the promise of H.M. Government, when I resigned office, that I should hoist my flag directly the war was over.

Please don't trouble to reply, &
believe me,
Yours very sincerely,
Milford Haven[10]

Fortunately, an admirer, Arthur Lee,[11] became First Lord of the Admiralty in 1921 and arranged for Lord Milford Haven to take the chair at a Navy Club dinner on 21 July. Louis's old friend Mark (now Admiral) Kerr described the event:

. . . as Prince Louis was going to take the chair hundreds came up for it from all over the country, and when he stood up to answer the toast for his health, the cheering was the greatest that I have ever heard, and continued for over five minutes, which so affected him that he had great difficulty in speaking.[12]

Lee later suggested to George V, who agreed, that Louis should be promoted to the rank of Admiral of the Fleet on the retired list. A delighted old man went for a week's cruise to Scotland aboard the battleship *Repulse* (on which his son Mountbatten was serving as a junior officer). His next plan was to join his elder son Georgie on his ship in the Mediterranean, but on returning to London he fell ill and died 11 September 1921. It was fortunate he had been re-instated and honoured one month earlier.

It is fitting to allow the loyal Kerr to have the last word on his hero:

It is difficult for anyone who has served under him to avoid superlatives in speaking of Prince Louis. I think what struck one most was the fact that he was one's beau-ideal of a gentleman, not

224

only in manners, but in thought. Meanness was unknown to him, and generosity was the essence of his character. It is seldom that these qualities are combined with a clear-thinking brain, a power of imagination, and thorough efficiency, as was the case with him. In addition to this he was a born leader, and officers and men followed him from love and not from fear, and the last virtue which he possessed, though not the least, was a great sense of justice. It was enough to know that he commanded a ship or a squadron, to be assured that that ship or squadron would be at the top of the Navy in happiness and efficiency. One quality of Nelson's was conspicuous in him. He trusted his officers, and they knew he would shoulder their responsibilities as well as his own, and in no case did he ever let them down.[13]

This is a touching epitaph to a man who, despite his limitations and insensitivity, was for the last twenty-five years of his life the soul of probity and honour.

NOTES

1. *John Bull*, 23 December 1911.
2. Stamfordham to Sir William Lambton, Lambton MS.
3. Wigram to Sir William Lambton, Lambton MS.
4. See Rose, *George V*, ch. 6, pp. 208–18.
5. See Appendix 3, Royal Nomenclature.
6. Hough, *Louis and Victoria*, ch. 14, p. 320.
7. Ziegler, *Mountbatten*, ch. 3, p. 4.
8. Ibid., ch. 14, p. 320.
9. Hough, *Louis and Victoria*, ch. 14, p. 330.
10. Ibid., quoting Royal Archives, KGV Q711/3.
11. Arthur Lee, later Viscount Lee of Fareham, 1868–1947.
12. Kerr, *Prince Louis of Battenberg*, ch. 12, p. 285.
13. Kerr, *Land, Sea, and Air*, ch. 8, pp. 150–51.

APPENDIX I: A FAMILY GAME

Mountbatten's obsession with his ancestors is illustrated by the methods by which he checked and rechecked his own and his nephew's grand relationships. He explained his system to E. H. Cookridge in his book *From Battenberg to Mountbatten*. I quote an abridgement:

The simplest example of the relationship between the Queen and her husband can be taken from their common descent from King Christian IX of Denmark, whose second child was Queen Alexandra, the wife of King Edward VII (and great-grandmother of our Queen) and whose third child William became the King of Greece under the name of George I (and was the grandfather of Prince Philip, the Duke of Edinburgh). The code table can be drawn thus:

D–2	(Queen Alexandra)
D–2–B	(King George V)
D–2–B–2	(King George VI)
D–2–B–2–A	(Queen Elizabeth II)
D–3	(King George I of Greece)
D–3–F	(Prince Andrew of Greece)
D–3–F–5	(the Duke of Edinburgh)

which shows that the Queen and her husband are second cousins once removed.

However, the system becomes more complex with descent from other Heads of Families. Both the Queen and Prince Philip are, of course, also descended from Queen Victoria, and thus they become third cousins:

V (Queen Victoria)

V–2 (King Edward VII)	= /brother and sister/ =	V–3 (Princess Alice, m. Gd. Duke Louis of Hesse)
V–2–B (King George V)	= /first cousins/ =	V–3–A (Princess Victoria of Hesse, m. Pr. *Louis of Battenberg*, Marquess of Milford Haven)
V–2–B–2 (King George VI)	= /second cousins/ =	V–3–A–1 (*Princess Alice of Battenberg*, married Prince Andrew of Greece)
V–2–B–2–A (Queen Elizabeth II)	= /third cousins/ =	V–3–A–1–E (Prince Philip, the Duke of Edinburgh)

One can use other permutations, particularly for Prince Philip, taking into account his descent from King George III of England, his relationship to the family of the Tsar of Russia, and his direct lineage from the grand-ducal family of Hesse-Darmstadt. His codes then become, alternatively: X–(for George III) –5–A–3–A–1–E, R– (for Tsar Nicholas I) –5–B–6–E, and H–(for Hesse) –2–A–1–A –5.[1]

A complicated but doubtless fascinating game!

NOTES
1. Cookridge, *From Battenberg to Mountbatten*, ch. 1, pp. 2–7.

227

APPENDIX 2: THE HESSE-HOMBURGS

Ziegler wrote in *Mountbatten* that only the houses of Hesse-Darmstadt and Hesse-Cassel survived into the nineteenth century. This was incorrect; during this period there were no less than five separate branches descending from the Margrave who divided his lands in 1567. Both the official biographer and the myth forgot the three families of Hesse-Philippsthal, Hesse-Philippsthal-Barchfeld and Hesse-Homburg. It is difficult to find a single interesting event relating to the Philippsthal branches, but the landgraves of Hesse-Homburg played a part in the social history of Europe completely ignored by Mountbatten. Their activities were recorded by Count Egon Corti in his book *The Wizard of Homburg and Monte Carlo*.[1] All quotations in this Appendix come from this little known work.

The strange 'casino' story began on 16 March 1837, when a court in Bordeaux found the twin brothers Louis and François Blanc guilty of corrupting telegraph officials for their own profit during the years 1834 to 1836. The two brothers, sons of a tax collector near Avignon, escaped imprisonment but had to leave Bordeaux and search for new opportunities. They went to Paris to start a casino but unfortunately gambling was outlawed in the following year. Eventually they settled on Homburg, one of the few pocket handkerchief old-fashioned states which had been allowed to retain their independence in 1816.

This Lilliput covered only 275 square kilometres of land! The capital from which it took its name had 3,000 inhabitants. Nevertheless the Landgrave Ludovic was a sovereign and a member of the German federation. Unfortunately both he and his state were bankrupt as the family trade of selling peasants for military service had ceased to be profitable.

The Landgravine followed a German custom and left her husband in 1837 for a cavalry lieutenant called von Bismarck, a kinsman of the future Chancellor. Her disappearance was not her husband's only sorrow, as despite the savings caused by her flight, he hadn't enough money to live in Homburg and became governor of the fortress of Luxembourg. Meanwhile in his homeland, 'Everywhere reigned poverty, and the little wooden houses of Homburg crowded round the castle as closely as possible, seeking protection and work from their lord; but the court itself was financially embarrassed, and could not help.'

The Landgrave and his burghers searched for a method of raising money and in desperation decided to turn the city into a spa. Unfortunately the Landgrave was too poor to build gaming rooms, and had to ask Meyer Amschel, Baron Rothschild of Frankfurt, for a loan.

However, the Rothschilds decided it was beneath their dignity to enter into a partnership with a semi-bankrupt landlord, and withdrew their offer, forcing the wretched Landgrave to mortgage his estates, castles and houses.

This enabled him to build a pump-room, which was a limited success. Understanding a more professional touch was needed, he got in touch with the Blanc twins, and died.

He was succeeded by his fifth brother Philip, who eventually came to an agreement with the French brothers that they would build magnificent rooms which would be leased back to him for the next twenty-nine years. The only restriction was Homburgians were not allowed to gamble.

The Landgrave's severest critic, the German author Karl August Varnhagen von Ense, described Homburg as a 'nest of vagabonds, adventurers, cut-purses and disreputable women', while he dismissed the Landgrave as an unrespected weakling gratified by those who wished to be received at his parody of a court. The writer was particularly hard on the Elector of Hesse-Cassel who, he wrote: '. . . played all day, stooping over the table, watching the cards and pushing his gold backwards and forwards; a revolting sight, this German prince scornfully squandering in the company of gamblers the blood of his subjects with his gold for a second time.'

Gradually gambling became more popular and made a profit of 270,000 gulden in 1848. Corti wrote:

Thus, from the Landgrave down to the least of his subjects, everybody in this little principality, which had been so wretched not long since, could live in perfect indifference to the rest of the world, with their eyes fixed upon the casino, the success of which was producing such a magical revival throughout these territories.

Unfortunately the Landgrave Ferdinand died aged eighty-three in 1866 and the line became extinct. The heir was A's eldest brother the Grand Duke of Hesse-Darmstadt. As he was poor (his heir's wife Princess Alice had to continually beg for money from her reluctant mother, Queen Victoria, to build herself a palace), the legacy was welcome. However, it did little good to the new owner, as he backed the losing side in the Prussian war and Homburg became an insignificant part of the new German Empire. Had this seizure been delayed for a few years, Queen Victoria would have been the mother-in-law of the owner of a state whose main source of income was a casino!

In 1867 the disapproving Prussian government announced all gambling would be phased out within seven years. Meanwhile Louis Blanc had taken over the gambling operations in Monte Carlo. In 1874 he lent the French government nearly five million francs to build the Paris Opera House, and from that moment became a member of the establishment.

In 1875 his daughter fell in love with a young Prince Constantine Radziwill, the seventh child of a junior branch of a Lithuanian family, whose younger branches had always married unattractive women for money. Blanc, aware of this dangerous characteristic, sent an investigator to look into the young man's affairs. The report of the Radziwills' French home was comic:

The family occupies the first storey, six of the windows overlooking the street. On the ground-floor there is a shop on each side of the entrance (a grocer and clothier); in a little show-case fastened to the doorpost are some false teeth; the courtyard is dirty and produces a bad impression . . . He added that, according to his informant, 'both brothers had several mistresses' . . .

Blanc, despite the false teeth, was reassured to find that while Radziwill's fortune was 'non-existent' his daughter's suitor's 'unhealthy lungs could not be too bad if he had several mistresses'.

It is a pity the myth ignores the consequences of the cooperation between a petty criminal and a bankrupt Hesse Landgrave which resulted in the return of prosperity to a small state and the creation of

Monte Carlo. It is a romantic story, a good deal more interesting than the dull lives of the fat, uninspiring princes and princesses of Hesse. But casinos have little in common with Charlemagne.

NOTES
1. Count Egon Corti, *The Wizard of Homburg and Monte Carlo*, English translation, Thornton Butterworth, 1954.

APPENDIX 3: MEMBERS OF THE HAUKE FAMILY

Friedrich Karl Emmanuel HAUCKE or HAUKE
   1737–1810 Married Salome Schweppenhauser
  |

 Maurycy 1775–1830
 m. Sophie de la Fontaine, daughter of a French doctor
  |

Maurycy Kazimierz Napoleon Capt. Polish
 Army 1808–1852
Leopold and Emilia twins 1810–12
Wladyslaw Leopold Maurycy 1812–41
 Lt. 5th Lancers Polish Army
Jozef 1814–31
 Lt. 2nd Lancers Polish Army
Zofia Salomea Teresa   Children
Wincenty Walery 1817–62
 Russian Major
Konstanty Karol 1819–91
 Russian Lt. of Hussars
Emilia Joanna Wiktoria 1821–90
Julia Teresa Salomea 1825–96 Wife of
 Prince Alexander of Hesse, made
 Princess of Battenberg 1858
Aleksander 1827–9

Ludwika Adalia
Teodor Ludwik
Aleksander Jan Jozef 1814–68 General
Salomea Maria 1830–94   First
Aleksander 1831–55   Cousins
 Russian Hussars
Jozef Ludwik 1834–71
Maria 1836–8

Is it remarkable considering the number of Hauke descendants who must throng Europe, that none appear to be on friendly terms with the Mountbatten family?

It is understandable that Mountbatten should have neglected his interesting ancestors and relations because they were descended from the 'lackey Haucke', not Charlemagne, and fought against Russia and Germany. But should he, considering his family's origins, have passionately schemed that his name, an anglicisation of 'Battenberg', was joined to the name of Windsor? Julia Hauke's children took their mother's name – as morganatics they were not allowed to call themselves 'Hesse' after she was created Countess and later Princess of Battenberg, although Mountbatten's grandfather declined to change his name from Hesse. Did Mountbatten persuade Prince Philip his romantic reconstruction of the origins of the family was the truth? Was the Queen aware of the true history of the Battenbergs and why the name and title was given to Prince Philip's maternal great-grandmother, when she appeared to publicly approve her daughter, Princess Anne's, decision to sign herself Mountbatten-Windsor, on her marriage certificate? These relevant questions can only be answered by an account of the nomenclature of the royal house of England.

ROYAL NOMENCLATURE

The naming of successive royal dynasties in England has followed a haphazard and sometimes opportunistic pattern. Few sovereigns or subjects worried about the correct names of their Royal House and family until King George V was upset by anti-German hysteria during the First World War. In July 1917, with an uncharacteristic flamboyance, he tried to silence patriotic criticism by renouncing his German ancestry and proclaiming the new House of Windsor.

Historians disagree on the ruling House's name before the change. Some maintain that it had continued to be the House of Hanover even after 1837, when Queen Victoria succeeded to the thrones of England, Scotland and Ireland, but as a woman she could not inherit the throne and titles of Hanover, which passed to her uncle the Duke of Cumberland. Others claimed her marriage to Prince Albert of Saxe-Coburg and Gotha changed the name of the Royal House to that of her husband, among them apparently her grandson King George V, who specifically required all members of his family in 1917 to abandon any title connected with Saxe-Coburg and Gotha, although no member of his family had used the names.

Queen Mary often referred to the pre-1837 Hanoverian line (from which she was descended through her mother, Princess Mary of Cambridge, a granddaughter of George III) as the 'old' royal family. This implied that she believed her husband's family belonged to the upstart dynasty of Saxe-Coburg and Gotha. She was probably reflecting the views of King Edward VII, who had been irritated before he came to the throne in 1901 that the Almanach de Gotha described the British royal family as members of the '*Maison des Guelfes ou Brunswick-Lunebourg*'. The last hyphenated names, strange as they may be to the British public, belong to the once royal house of Hanover.

In 1866 Bismarck incorporated that country into the Prussian Empire, and the head of the family became known as the Duke of Luneburg, Brunswick, Cumberland etc. etc. This enabled the young Kaiser to refer to our royal family as his subjects, a joke the Prince of Wales did not enjoy. In 1902, the 'Gotha' changed its mind and decided that England was ruled by the '*Maison de Saxe-Coburg et Gotha*'. Genealogists argue that if King Edward VII was a Hanoverian, his correct name was Guelf; if a Saxe-Coburg, Wettin. Not surprisingly neither name was ever used.

King George V's proclamation of 1917 did not only change the name of the Royal House, it also adopted a surname for his family, Windsor. Why did a conservative king make a revolutionary gesture, putting members of the royal family on the same level of nomenclature as his subjects?

The answer is that in December 1917, by Letters Patent under the Great Seal (i.e. on the advice of his ministers) he declared that the style of Royal Highness and the titles of Prince and Princess should cease to proliferate. This was sensible; he had four sons and saw modern medicine would produce a mass of royal descendants without the means to support their dignity.

His decision meant in future the Royal House would be confined to the grandchildren of the sovereign in the male line only and to the eldest living son of the son of the Prince of Wales. There the attributes of royalty were to stop. The following generation – his great-grandchildren – were to be either non-royal peers or commoners, who would require a surname. This, the King declared, was to be Windsor.

What George V did not foresee was that a generation before the severance period of royalty was reached, a Queen would ascend the throne, marry and wish her children to bear not only their princely style but also the adopted family name of her husband.

It may be asked how her husband, born Prince Philip of Greece and Denmark, acquired his family name; no other member of these Royal Houses had used one. The Prince's need for a designation was caused by his wish to remain in the Royal Navy, which he had joined as a Dartmouth cadet in 1939. By a temporary concession, he and others of foreign birth were allowed to serve in the war; but to receive a permanent commission he had in peace time to become a British subject. Wheeler-Bennett gave his version of events which led up to a constitutional imbroglio.

By the close of 1946, however, the matter of Prince Philip's naturalization was once more in train, but there remained the vexed question of the name by which he would be known. On the precedent of the two daughters of Prince Christian of Schleswig-Holstein and Princess Helena, who, at the time of the great shedding of German titles in 1917, merely dropped 'Schleswig-Holstein' from their names and retained the style of 'Highness', the King was prepared to grant the right and privilege of the title 'His Royal Highness Prince Philip', and this was agreed to by the Prime Minister and Lord Mountbatten. The matter, however, was unexpectedly disposed of by Prince Philip himself, who announced, with some determination, that, while he great appreciated His Majesty's offer, he preferred not to take advantage of it but to be known, after his naturalization as a British subject, simply as 'Lieutenant Philip . . . RN.' This decision both pleased and impressed King George, who at once assented to it.

The question of title being thus settled, there remained only the problem of finding a suitable surname. The Royal House of Greece and Denmark had given up their family name and the suggestion of 'Oldcastle' – an anglicized form of Oldenburg, whence the House of Schleswig-Holstein-Sonderburg-Glucksburg had originally sprung – was not popular. It remained for the Home Secretary, Mr. Chuter Ede, to suggest that the new British subject take his mother's name of Mountbatten. This was at once agreed to by all parties and the announcement was accordingly made in the *London Gazette* of March 18, 1947.[1]

Prince Philip's decision to refuse to become a simple British royal highness is the source of the present muddle. We have only Mountbatten's word that his suggested name came from Mr Chuter Ede, not usually remembered as having an imaginative mind or being an expert in genealogy. Whether or not Prince Philip knew it, taking his uncle's surname was the first move in a forty-year campaign to change the name of the royal family from Windsor to Mountbatten-Windsor.

Lord Mountbatten opened the previously secret campaign with unseemly haste a short time after the death of King George VI. On 8 February 1952 Queen Mary sent for the prime minister's private secretary, John Colville,[2] who felt so strongly about the way things have turned out that the summer before his death he wrote down his memories of the episode:

Shortly after King George VI died in February 1952, Prince Ernst August of Hanover asked Queen Mary if he might come and see her at Marlborough House. He told her that he had been staying at Broadlands with Lord Mountbatten and that Mountbatten had announced at a large dinner party that the house of Windsor no longer reigned but that the royal house was now the House of Mountbatten.

Queen Mary was greatly disturbed and asked me as Private Secretary to the Prime Minister to come and see her at once. I usually went to see her every Thursday at 6 p.m., by permission of the Prime Minister, to tell her what was going on in the world. This, however, was an urgent call to go in the morning and I duly went. When I arrived she told me what Prince Ernst August had said and begged me to inform the Prime Minister at once that when King George V had chosen the name of Windsor for the royal house he intended it to be in perpetuity. She hoped that the Prime Minister and the Cabinet would take the appropriate action.

I went back to 10 Downing Street and told Winston Churchill, who was indignant. When he informed the Cabinet of what Queen Mary had said they unanimously authorised him to advise the

Queen, with a capital A, that the name of the royal house was and should remain Windsor.

Churchill did so. It caused a considerable flurry, for Prince Philip felt that as his name, by deed poll, was Mountbatten, his children should also bear it. Queen Mary, however, indignantly pointed out that Prince Philip was not really a Mountbatten, but a Glucksburg.

As a result of Queen Mary's protest the Prime Minister advised the Queen to make a public declaration putting the continuation of the House of Windsor beyond doubt, even though Prince Philip himself sent the Prime Minister what Colville earlier called 'a strongly, but ably, worded memorandum' pleading for the change. According to Lady Longford, in her biography of the Queen, *Elizabeth R*, the Prince complained that the Government's failure to accept the name of Mountbatten would make him 'an amoeba, a bloody amoeba'.[3] The Government, however, declined to contradict King George V's Proclamation of 1917, or to affront public opinion so soon after the war against Germany, by hyphenating an anglicised German name with the simple, historic English name of Windsor. On 9 April 1952, on the advice of her ministers and in language which is unlikely to have reflected her true feelings, the Queen 'declared in Council her Will and Pleasure that She and Her children shall be styled and known as the House and Family of Windsor, and that Her descendants other than female descendants who marry and their descendants shall bear the name of Windsor'.

Some of Prince Philip's supporters argued that this imposed Declaration went too far, for while the name of the Royal House undoubtedly remained Windsor from reign to reign, it was an anomaly that the Queen's descendants, contrary to common law, could not bear her husband's assumed family name.

The impending birth of the Queen's third child eight years later gave her an opportunity to modify her unpalatable declaration of 1952. Having won the approval of the Prime Minister, Harold Macmillan, she made a second declaration in Council on 8 February 1960, eleven days before the birth of Prince Andrew:

THE DECLARATION

The following official announcement was issued yesterday at the Court at Buckingham Palace after a meeting of the Privy Council:-

Her Majesty was this day pleased to make the following declaration: 'My Lords,

Whereas on the 9th day of April 1952, I did declare in Council My Will and Pleasure that I and My children shall be styled and known as of the House and Family of Windsor, and that My descendants, other than female descendants who marry and their descendants, shall bear the name of Windsor:

And whereas I have given further consideration to the position of those of My descendants who will enjoy neither the style, title or attribute of Royal Highness, nor the titular dignity of Prince, and for whom therefore a surname will be necessary.

And whereas I have concluded that the Declaration made by Me on the 9th day of April 1952, should be varied in its application to such persons.

Now therefore I declare My Will and Pleasure that, while I and My children shall continue to be styled and known as the House and Family of Windsor, My descendants other than descendants enjoying the style, title or attribute of Royal Highness and the titular dignity of Prince or Princess and female descendants who marry and their descendants shall bear the name of Mountbatten-Windsor.'

The next day *The Times*, reporting the Declaration, stated what was understood to be the correct constitutional procedure when a British sovereign changes his or her family's name:

MINISTERS' ADVICE

Such a declaration is a matter of prerogative, but in a constitutional monarchy is considered to be one of those prerogatives exercised only on the advice of Ministers. The member countries of the Commonwealth were informed a few days ago, in time for their opinions to be communicated. The Queen's private secretary informed the Governors-General, and Prime Ministers of Republics within the Commonwealth were informed through the Commonwealth Relations Office.

The timing of the announcement is to be explained by the imminence of the birth of a child to the Queen. On the assumption that the new baby is a boy the name of Mountbatten-Windsor would come into use as the surname of his grandchildren; and the Cabinet have fully approved the Queen's wish that from the time of his birth he should have the right to transmit to his grandchildren a name which joins the name of his father to that of his mother.[4]

It was further announced from Buckingham Palace:

The Queen has always wanted, without changing the name of the Royal House established by her grandfather, to associate the name of her husband with her own and his descendants. The Queen has had this in mind for a long time and it is close to her heart.

While removing the supposed slur of the past eight years on Prince Philip's name, the declaration seemed to serve no immediate purpose as it only concerned the Queen's great-grandchildren.

The position appeared clear cut. However, in 1973 when Princess Anne married Captain Mark Phillips, she was referred to on her marriage certificate as 'Anne Elizabeth Alice Louise Mountbatten-Windsor'.

Behind the unexpected use of the surname in the first, instead of the third, generation lay a powerful influence. Philip Ziegler wrote that in the spring of 1973 Lord Mountbatten wrote to the Prince of Wales: 'When Anne marries in November her marriage certificate will be her first opportunity to settle the Mountbatten-Windsor name for good . . . If you can make quite sure that her surname is entered as Mountbatten-Windsor it will end all arguments. I hope you can fix this.'[5]

Whether or not the Prince of Wales did as he was asked, it was improper of Mountbatten to have asked his great-nephew behind the Queen's back to alter a decision taken in Council.

The result of this scheming was that Princess Anne signed herself Mountbatten-Windsor on her marriage certificate. Many believed she was merely paying a belated compliment to her beloved great-uncle before taking her husband's name. But this was contradicted after the wedding by an announcement from Buckingham Palace stating that 'the use of the surname had been at the Queen's express wish and without seeking the advice of her Ministers'.

Was the Queen exerting her royal prerogative in supporting her daughter? Had she forgotten the wording of her 1960 Declaration? Whatever the explanation, Princess Anne's description was not at the time thought to have established a precedent. But it did; for although no surname was attached to the Prince of Wales when he married Lady Diana Spencer in 1981, Prince Andrew was described on his marriage certificate in 1986 as Andrew Albert Christian Edward Mountbatten-Windsor, by whose permission it is not known. This time there was no mention of the Queen's approval or disapproval. Had she remembered the phrasing of her 1960 Declaration, 'I and my children shall continue to be styled and known as the House and family of Windsor . . .' and changed her mind since Princess Anne's wedding? The conscious or unconscious contradiction by the Queen's children of her Declaration of 1960 raises a number of questions.

If the Duke of York, the second son of the Queen, can call himself Mountbatten-Windsor, will his younger sons be styled by the same name instead of the customary York? If so, why has he called his daughter Princess Beatrice of York? Has the custom been broken which was followed by the late Dukes of Gloucester and Kent, all of whose children became Princes and Princesses of their father's title, e.g. Prince William of Gloucester, Prince Michael of Kent? Furthermore, if the Queen's second son has changed his family name in the first and not the third generation to Mountbatten-Windsor, why was the Prince of Wales's second son styled at his christening Henry Charles Albert David of Wales? And what will Prince Henry's sons be called? Confusion reigns! It will also be interesting to see whether the Queen's third son Prince Edward one day follows the example of Princess Anne and Prince Andrew in having the name Mountbatten-Windsor on his wedding certificate.

Ziegler appears to have been unaware of the meaning of the 1960 Declaration and over-simplified the problem by writing in *Mountbatten*: 'On February 8th the Queen [ref. 8612] announced in Council that with certain qualifications her descendants should bear the name Mountbatten-Windsor . . . It seemed the battle was won. Mountbatten's mind, however, was not entirely at ease.'[6] Ziegler was wrong in suggesting the battle was won. The Queen's statement meant that only those who did not receive the attributes of royalty could use the prefix Mountbatten. This was why Mountbatten was 'uneasy' and he immediately started persuading the young Princes and Princess to defy the unwritten constitution and the Declaration issued by their mother the Queen. Their subsequent actions suggest he succeeded and that they believe their royal name is their own business and has nothing to do with the elected representatives of the nation. The matter should be clarified. It may be that the Queen wishes to assert her royal prerogative. If so, will she be initiating a questionable unwritten constitutional precedent?

I would conclude by respectfully asking a question; is it wise of the Queen's children to contradict their mother's assurances in Council that the name of the royal family should remain Windsor, by hyphenating it with Mountbatten? The latter is an anglicised German name, only assumed by Prince Philip in 1947, and only invented in 1851 to save the face of a six-month pregnant, unmarried girl. It has no connection with England.

NOTES
1. Wheeler-Bennett, *King George VI*, pp. 850–51.
2. Sir John Colville died early in 1988. He was principal private secretary to the Queen as Princess Elizabeth and before and after to Sir Winston Churchill during his two periods of office.
3. Elizabeth Longford, *Elizabeth R*, Weidenfeld and Nicolson, 1983, ch. 10, p. 156.
4. *The Times*, of February 1960.
5. Ziegler, *Mountbatten*, ch. 51, pp. 681–2.
6. Ibid.

APPENDIX 4: SYPHILIS AND THE EMPEROR FREDERICK III OF GERMANY

Extracts from Michaela Reid's *Ask Sir James*, Appendix 2, pp. 261,

On 9 November 1887 Professor von Schrötter from Vienna, and Dr Krause from Berlin arrived in San Remo, and were joined a day later by Dr Moritz Schmidt who had been sent by the Emperor. They had been summoned to examine the throat of the Imperial Crown Prince Frederick. Schrötter affirmed that the disease was cancer and recommended excision of the whole larynx. Krause considered that the disease was 'a malignant neoplasm', but thought it wise to give potassium iodide first in order to make sure that it was not syphilis. Schmidt agreed with Krause and urged that large doses of potassium iodide should be given before embarking on the more serious course of an operation, on the ground that syphilitic infection might exist dating from many years back. In 1869, on the occasion of the opening of the Suez Canal by the Empress Eugénie, the Crown Prince had fallen prey to a beautiful Spaniard, Dolores (Cada).[1] Evidence of syphilis appeared a short time later and had been treated by the Khedive's physician. Mackenzie, as has been seen, thought it best to wait until the swelling of the larynx had subsided and then removed a small piece of new growth for microscopic inspection. At this stage there was still a tiny glimmer of hope that a past indiscretion of the Crown Prince might be the cause of his malady rather than the fatal disease which at heart all the medical men suspected.[2]

Sir Morell Mackenzie was harshly criticised by the German medical profession for not operating earlier. Lady Reid defends him:

Statistics show that an operation would almost certainly have been fatal, and had it by some extraordinary chance proved otherwise, the Crown Prince would have been left voiceless and in a miserable state from which death would have been a mercy. It is true that Mackenzie relied too implicitly on the result of microscopic examination, but his insistence on biopsy was well in advance of his time. All along he felt that there was a fair chance that the Crown Prince had syphilis of the larynx, and although he admitted the possibility of cancer, he claimed that it could not be proved. At the time, his perseverance in the use of palliative treatment was the kindest and wisest course open to him, and one in which the patient concurred.

Extracts from R. Scott Stevenson, *Morell Mackenzie*, Heinemann, 1946, ch. 8.

A SUMMING-UP

Looking back nearly sixty years, there seems no doubt that the Emperor Frederick III did die of cancer of the larynx; but the whole course of the disease was far from typical, and on careful examination of the available evidence there is more than a suspicion that the cancer supervened upon syphilis. The fact that at San Remo four of the most experienced laryngologists in Europe agreed to treat the German Crown Prince with a specific remedy for the delayed results of syphilis (tertiary syphilis) shows how speculative must have been the diagnosis of many tumours of the larynx at this period, before bacteriological examination of the lungs, and the Wasserman and Kahn blood tests for syphilis were known, and the microscopic examination of many pathological conditions was still far from precise.

There is no printed or written documentary evidence, other than the prolonged administration of potassium iodide, that Morell Mackenzie ever suggested that the disease from which the Crown Prince was suffering might have been tertiary syphilis, though it is well known that cancer of the larynx often follows syphilis; but it is within the knowledge of the present writer that, after the death of the Emperor, Morell Mackenzie told (as a secret) one of his most intimate friends, the late Dr. Richard King Pierce, that he felt sure the Emperor Frederick had had syphilis of the larynx before the cancer appeared.

With all these facts in mind there need be little wonder that Morell

Mackenzie appeared to be vacillating in his conduct of the case and so laid himself open to criticism. It is true that in May, 1887, Mackenzie considered the laryngeal condition was not cancer; in November, 1887, he told the Crown Prince that the disease 'looked very much like cancer, but that it was impossible to be certain'; a few days later he agreed with his colleagues that the disease was cancer – and yet assented to large doses of potassium iodide being given in case it was not; on 18th February, 1888, he described the disease as chronic interstitial inflammation of the larynx; at the beginning of March he accepted the microscopic evidence in favour of cancer produced by Waldeyer, and signed a joint statement with his colleagues to that effect; on 24th March he thought the disease might after all possibly be limited to perichondritis; in April he told Queen Victoria that the Emperor would not live above a few weeks; in May he was expressing hopes about 'permanent improvement'; and on 31st May he told the Empress Frederick that the Emperor "might recover, though it was not probable"; on 6th June, only nine days before the Emperor's death, he discontinued daily bulletins as no longer necessary; and then on 16th June he signed a report that the disease from which the Emperor had died was cancer.

Mackenzie kept changing his mind, however, only in accordance with the varying signs and symptoms presented by the patient, possibly because of an underlying but persistent suspicion of the presence of syphilis, and his various opinions were shared by distinguished colleagues of the highest medical standing in Germany. He rightly tried to emphasize the important and indeed decisive part played in regard to diagnosis by the pathological opinion of Professor Virchow.[2]

Mackenzie's opinions, although shared by German doctors, would explain the extraordinary animosity shown to him in Germany and the refusal to publish his report.

NOTES

1. Jean de Bonnefon, *Drame Impériale*, Paris 1888. Cited Reid.
2. R. Scott Stevenson, *Morell Mackenzie*, Heinemann, 1946, ch. 8.

SELECT BIBLIOGRAPHY

E. M. Almedingen, *The Emperor Alexander II*, Bodley Head, 1962.

Dorothy Anderson, *The Balkan Volunteers*, Hutchinson, 1968.

H. H. Asquith, *Letters to Venetia Stanley*, Oxford University Press, 1982.

J. F. Badderley, *Russia in the Eighties*, Longmans, 1921.

Valentine Baker, *Pasha's War in Bulgaria*, Sampson, Low Searle and Rivington, 2 vols, 1879.

Consuelo Vanderbilt Balsan, *The Glitter and the Gold*, Windmill Press, 1953.

Princess Marie of Battenberg, *Reminiscences*, George Allen Unwin, 1925.

Bemberger (ed.), *Diary of the Crown Princess Victoria*, German edition, 1928.

Daphne Bennett, *Vicky*, Constable, 1971.

Geoffrey Bennet, *Jutland*, David and Charles, 1972.

A. G. Benson, *Edwardian Excursions*, John Murray, 1981.

The Memoirs of Admiral Lord Charles Beresford, vol. 2, Methuen, 1914.

Bismarck, *Grosse Politik*, German edition.

Memoirs of Sergeant Bourgogne, *Retreat from Moscow*, tr. J. W. Fortescue, Folio Society, 1985.

Viscount Bryce, *The Holy Roman Empire*, Macmillan, 1919.

G. E. Buckle (ed.), *The Letters and Journals of Queen Victoria*, vol. 3, 1879–1885, John Murray, 1928.

Prince von Bülow, *Memoirs 1849–1897*, translated by Geoffrey Dunlop and F. A. Voight, Putnam, 1934.

Burke's Peerage entry for 'Geddes'.

Cassell's History of the Russo-Turkish War 1879, vol. 2, Cassell, 1880.

E. H. Cookridge, *From Battenberg to Mountbatten*, Arthur Barker, 1966.

Count Egon Corti, *The Downfall of Three Dynasties*, Methuen, 1934.

Count Egon Corti, *The English Empress*, Cassell, 1957.

Count Egon Corti, *The Wizard of Homburg and Monte Carlo*, unknown translator, Thornton Butterworth, 1954.

Count Egon Corti, *Alexander von Battenberg*, Cassell, 1954.

Edward Crankshaw, *Bismarck*, Macmillan, 1981.

Ghislain de Diesbach, *Secrets of the Gotha*, translated by Margaret Crosland, Chapman and Hall, 1964.

David Duff, *Hessian Tapestry*, David and Charles, 1979.

Lady Duff Gordon, *Last Letters from Egypt*, London, 1867.

Encyclopaedia Britannica, op. cit. 1926 edition, entry for 'Hesse-Cassel'.

Stanley G. Evans, *Short History of Bulgaria*, Laurence Wishart, 1960.

Lord Fisher, *Memories*, Hodder and Stoughton, 1917.

Roger Fulford (ed.), *Beloved Mama*, Evans Bros, 1981.

Roger Fulford (ed.), *Darling Child*, Evans Bros, 1976.

Roger Fulford (ed.), *Your Dear Letter*, Evans Bros, 1971.

William Ewart Gladstone, *Bulgarian Horrors and the Eastern Question*, 1876.

Maxim Gorki, *Fragments of my Diary*, Philip Allan, 1924.

A. Hertzen (ed.), *Memoirs of Catherine the Great*, Trubner and Co., 1859.

Richard Hough, *Louis and Victoria*, Weidenfeld and Nicolson, 2nd ed., 1984.

Richard Hough, *Mountbatten: Hero of our Time*, Weidenfeld and Nicolson, 1980.

Mark Kerr, *Prince Louis of Battenberg*, Longmans, 1934.

Mark Kerr, *Land, Sea, and Air*, 1934.

Elizabeth Longford, *Elizabeth R*, Weidenfeld and Nicolson, 1983.

Arthur J. Marder (ed.), *Fear God and Dread Nought: Letters of Lord Fisher*, Cape, 1952.

Marie Queen of Romania, *The Story of my Life*, 3 vols, Cassell, 1934–7.

Moneypenny and Buckle, *Disraeli*, numerous reprints.

John Morley, *The Life of W. E. Gladstone*, vol. 2, Macmillan, 1906.

W. E. Mosse, *Alexander II and the Modernisation of Russia*, English Universities Press, 1958.

Maurice Paléologue, *Tragic Romance of Alexander II*, translated by Arthur Chambers, Hutchinson, 1920s (undated).

Sir Frederick Ponsonby, *Letters of the Empress Frederick*, Macmillan, 1928.

Sir Frederick Ponsonby, *Recollections of Three Reigns*, Eyre and Spottiswoode, 1951.

Michaela Reid, *Ask Sir James*, Hodder and Stoughton, 1987.

Kenneth Rose, *King George V*, Weidenfeld and Nicolson, 1983.

Kenneth Rose, *Kings, Queens, Courtiers*, Weidenfeld and Nicolson, 1985.

General von Schwienitz, *Denwürdigkeiten des Botschafters*, vol. 2, Berlin, 1927 (translation).

R. Scott Stevenson, *Morell Mackenzie*, Heinemann, 1946.

Anthony Summers and Tom Mangold, *File on the Tsar*, Fontana Books, 1981.

B. A. Sumner, *Russia and the Balkans*, Oxford University Press, 1937.

Christopher Sykes, *Four Studies in Loyalty*, Collins, 1946.

A. J. P. Taylor, *The Course of German History*, Hamish Hamilton, revised impression, 1945.

Thackeray, *Four Georges*, Smith Elder, 1871, ch. 3, p. 92.

Queen Victoria to Earl Granville, Letters, second series.

Lady Wester Wemyss (ed.), *Life and Letters of Lord Wester Wemyss*, Eyre and Spottiswoode, 1935.

Bismarck und die Europäischen Gross Mächte 1879–1885, Windelband German Edition (translated).

Letters of Emperor William to Bismarck, Windelband German edition (translated).

Philip Ziegler, *Mountbatten*, Collins, 1985.

Wheeler-Bennett, *King George VI*, Macmillan, 1958.

Count Adam Zamoyski's notes on Hauke family (unpublished).

Globe   Hansard   John Bull   Vanity Fair

Royal Archives

Vienna Archives

Lambton MSS

INDEX